Haining, Peter, ed.
    Magic Valley travellers. Welsh stories of
fantasy and horror. Foreword by Richard
Hughes. N.Y., Taplinger ₍c1974₎

    1.Horror tales. I.t.

THE MAGIC VALLEY TRAVELLERS

In series with this volume:

THE WILD NIGHT COMPANY
Irish stories of fantasy and horror

THE CLANS OF DARKNESS
Scottish stories of fantasy and horror

both edited by Peter Haining

THE MAGIC VALLEY TRAVELLERS

Welsh stories of fantasy and horror

Edited by

Peter Haining

Foreword by

Richard Hughes

TAPLINGER PUBLISHING CO., INC
NEW YORK
1974

First published in the United States in 1974 by
TAPLINGER PUBLISHING CO., INC.
New York, New York

Library of Congress Catalog Card Number: 73-14368

ISBN 0-8008-5047-5

This book is dedicated to the memory of
RICHARD TAPLINGER
—publisher and friend
'*Myself, I favour a dark, funereal tale*'

CONTENTS

ACKNOWLEDGEMENTS

The editor is grateful to the following authors, agents and publishers for permission to reproduce copyright material in this collection.

"The Coffin" by Caradoc Evans. Copyright 1932 by Odhams Press Ltd., London. Copyright renewed by the Executors of Caradoc Evans 1958 and reprinted with their permission.

"A Stray from Cathay" by John Wyndham. Copyright 1953 by Future Publications Inc for "Fantasy Fiction". Reproduced by permission of the Author's Estate and Messrs David Higham Associates.

"The Stranger" by Richard Hughes. Copyright 1931 by Harper & Brothers. Reprinted by permission of William Morris Agency.

"The School for Witches" by Dylan Thomas. Copyright 1971 by the Trustees of the Estate of Dylan Thomas and reproduced with their permission.

"Week-end at Cwm Tatws" by Robert Graves. Copyright 1965 by International Authors N.V. and reproduced with their permission.

"Jordan" by Glyn Jones. Copyright 1971 by J. M. Dent & Sons Ltd. for "Selected Short Stories" and reproduced with their permission.

"The Dark Isle" by Robert Bloch. Copyright 1939 by "Weird Tales". Copyright renewed 1965 by Robert Bloch and reproduced by permission of the Scott Meredith Literary Agency.

"The Dark World" by Rhys Davies. Copyright 1955 by Dodd, Mead. Reproduced from "The Collected Stories of Rhys Davies" by permission of Dodd, Mead Inc.

I should also like to record my particular thanks to Richard Hughes both for his outstanding Foreword to this collection and his advice and suggestions so generously given.

'There is in Wales something so peculiarly fascinating in that old belief that "once upon a time" the world was less practical in its facts than now, less commonplace and humdrum, less subject to the inexorable laws of gravitation, optics and the like. What dramas it has yielded! What fantasy, what legends, what delights!'

WIRT SIKES

FOREWORD

by Richard Hughes

THE FIRST LINE of the first story here mentions 'Beli Mawr' (Plutarch does too), a king reputed to have reigned over Britain long before Caesar landed. Welsh genealogies preserved at the College of Heralds entitle my family, by direct descent, to quarter Beli Mawr's arms: likewise I claim descent from Aeneas the Trojan, whose mother was the Goddess Venus: so am surely fit sponsor for *any* compendium of Welsh fantasy.

Not that all Welsh traditions can be dismissed as fanciful. Few Londoners know or care that they tread on the bones of the hero of that same story, King Lludd, each time they walk up *Lud*gate Hill; but Welsh folk-memories are longer. We still use the pre-Saxon names of many towns in Britain, calling Bath 'Caerfaddon' for instance and Cambridge 'Caer Grawnt'. The Norman conquest must be too recent an event to have sunk in yet, for we still seem much bitterer about the Roman one. When she heard I had actually visited Rome, an old woman asked me anxiously: 'Did you find them still as unkind to the Welsh there as they used to?' (Did she think I'd have been paraded through the streets in chains, like Caractacus?) Then she waxed indignant over a so-called 'Roman' road in the hills above: 'What, *they* work on that road? No, never! They made *us* build the road—and have not yet paid us our wages!'

I once heard a mother threaten a naughty child with 'Be good, you —— or the Romans shall have you!' But certain recorded memories purport to go back further still, right into geological time. One ancient Welsh manuscript says of an expedition to Ireland: 'In those days the deep water was not wide. There were but two rivers, the Lli' (presumably an extension of the Clyde) 'and the

Archan (the Mersey-cum-Dee?). 'But thereafter the deep water grew wider as the sea overflowed the kingdoms.'

When Augustine first landed in Kent to convert the heathen Saxon, Christianity (more on the Eastern than Western model) was already long established in Wales. But Augustine claimed that the Pope's commission included 'reform' of the Celtic Church and his own jurisdiction over it. This outraged our British bishops; what right had any mere 'Bishop of Rome' to claim supremacy over the whole of Christendom? Must they submit to the Roman yoke all over again?—Nevertheless it was all but a thousand years before a Welsh dynasty on the English throne cast off that yoke again; and only in the present century were we given independence of Canterbury too.

In my own boyhood Wales was in effect a theocracy: the goings-on at Westminster were of little moment, the only authority which really counted in daily life was the iron rule of the Chapel Deacons and the 'Seiat Fawr'. Yet in spite of the Chapels' displeasure the countryside still teemed with most ancient supernatural presences. I don't just mean human ghosts, though these also abounded ... A farmer I knew, going out after dark to tend a sick cow, spent the whole night in the byre: 'I couldn't go back to the house,' he told me, 'the yard was so full of people' (Ifan not being the sort rudely to jostle his way through such a gathering of his own ancestors). Nor do I mean mere fairies—though who else could have baked that wonderful cake which another Ardudwy farmer found on his kitchen table, one morning in 1917, just a few hours before his son turned up unexpectedly on leave from the Front? No: more typically these apparitions took the form of hell-hounds and other spectral dogs. There was one such which haunted the Pass of Aberglaslyn, and scared the life out of a party of Beddgelert youths returning one night from an illicit game of whist in a lonely barn (you could be turned out of your chapel for card-playing, those days—it was as wicked as carting hay on a Sunday, or drinking a glass of beer, or dancing): 'Big as a calf he was, with flames coming out of his mouth and eyes like lamps-motorbicycle!'

There is a certain ruin which *may* mark the site of a sixth-century church: no one recalls any such sacred connection, but it is known that if you strike iron into the ground, at the east end of it, after midnight, either a black dog or a white dog will appear. If it is the white dog he will guide you to hidden treasure; but if it is the black dog you are compelled to follow him up the mountain where, after hours of wandering in the dark, he finally loses you (as likely as not with a broken leg). After a string of such disasters the farmer offered £5 to anyone else who would try; but since hitherto it had never once been the white dog who appeared it is hardly surprising that he found no takers.

There are many other such 'numinous' places, haunted by presences even more awful. I shall never forget my own experience one night when I ventured, alone, under a waning moon, after midnight, with a sack of stolen peat on my back, near a prehistoric altar-stone on the hillside. How my hair stood up on end even *before* fear struck me . . .

But I won't bore you with that story, there are so many better ones in the pages which follow.

INTRODUCTION

Here wandering shades the spell-bound valleys tread,
And midnight magic wakes the restless dead.
                              Matthew Lewis
                              "The House Upon the Heath:
                              A Welsh Tale", 1799

WHERE ELSE BUT Wales could such words be written?
Wales, since time immemorial, the chosen land of strange creatures,
phantoms and dragons; the place where, Chaucer tells us, 'In olde
dayes of the King Arthur/ All was this land fulfilled of fayrie.'
Wales, home of the druid and the wizard, of Merlin, Madoc, Glen-
dower and Gwydion son of Don, the 'best teller of tales in the
world'.

Lewis, author of the famous horror novel, *The Monk*, was, indeed, only re-stating what those who live there have always known,
and those who visit soon find out. Inspired by the dark valleys,
the misty plains, and the legend-enshrouded countryside, he saw a
'wonder world' of myth and fantasy. A world another, much later
and native-born weaver of words, Dylan Thomas, encapsulated in
a ringing phrase as 'a legendary lazy little black-magical bedlam'.
Thomas did not mean Wales in general, of course (though he
could have done), rather the small village of Laugharne. But in that
sentence are the two words which for me most accurately sum-
marise Wales and the Welsh—'legendary' and 'magical'.

For here so much is magic and legend. It is a country in which,
the great chronicler George Borrow tells us, 'Nature displays herself in her wildest, boldest and occasionally most magical forms.' It
has a tradition steeped in legend, of Kings and Princes from the
mists of time, of druids and magicians working their timeless spells.

And it has a literature of folklore and fantasy which is the envy of the world.

Who, for instance, has not heard of the immortal *Mabinogion* with its great legends of early Wales, or that most marvellous of epic romances, Malory's *Le Morte d'Arthur*, run through with the drama of the nation?

Alongside these is the unending oral tradition of folk-tales, still told around many a fireside despite the endeavours of Methodism to drive such things away.

Many are those who have contributed to this rich trove of tales, both those native born and those who have come to visit and then come again and again. For, make no mistake, the Welsh know how to tell a story and theirs is a skill which proves infectious to any who will learn.

Words, words, words, how peculiarly they enchant you when you are writing of Wales. How they beguile the unwary as he struggles to capture the magic and mystery of the country. How they run away with you like sun on slippery glass, like thoughts in a drunkard's dream or mists on the dark mountains of evening. Perhaps, though, one should not try to trap them, for is this not a country that has many fine story-tellers to do the job so much better?

Indeed it is; and one needs only to visit this rich storehouse to find a world of enchantment and delight.

The Magic Valley Travellers is an excursion into one particular area of this storehouse—that of fantasy and horror. It is a compilation of those stories, in both fact and fiction, which seem to me to bring alive the many facets of the strange and the mysterious which is Wales. It ranges from those earliest of tales, their origins lost in the mists of antiquity, to the stories of today, still vividly tinged with the fear of the unknown. It is a strong tradition, as Professor Gwyn Jones has noted only recently, constantly enduring, if still 'as precise and actual as Celtic fantasy of a thousand years ago'.

The short story has a particular and important place in Wales, whether it be written by the Welshman in Welsh, or the Welshman in English. So, let it be stated right away, that as this is a collection for international consumption it has drawn only on the work of the Anglo-Welsh writer and the English-speaking visitor—but this is not to say that there is not a vast amount of native material which could have been included. Indeed it is my regret that it is not possible to include work by perhaps the two foremost writers of short stories in Welsh today, Kate Roberts and D. J. Williams.

Nonetheless, I do believe this to be a representative selection of Welsh fantasy even if I have had to leave out for various reasons such revered names as Geraint Goodwin, Gwyn Jones, Alun Lewis, Gwyn Thomas, Jack Jones, Idris Davies, Richard Llewellyn and that marvellous triumverate of brothers, John Cowper, Llewelyn and Theodore Francis Powys. Then, too, there should be space for Jack London, born of a Welsh mother and full of the gift of the *Cymry*, Howard Spring, the Cardiff gardener's son, and, truly, Richard Burton, 'the world's most famous living Welshman' who has now added the title of story-teller to his many other talents.

But, still, enough of limitations—I think we have the scope and the extent of Welsh fantasy literature here. We travel from the lowlands to the hills and mountains, we have the old superstitions and the myths, the bizarre side of life and the predilection with death, the modern prejudices and the not-so-long-past Depression (though only a little of that, for therein lies too much real horror and this collection is, after all, intended as an entertainment).

That Welsh literature is alive and flourishing, I think there can be no doubt: books of Welsh interest find publishers around the world, the Eisteddfod still provides its annual quota of splendid stories and poems, and local publishing is a developing, if still somewhat restricted, industry.

Finally, let me add that though the controversy over the Welsh language has become such a heated and politically-explosive topic, I do not believe it should be allowed to obscure the importance of the *Welsh* story, whichever tongue it might be in. I hope you agree —for here, old and new, come some of the best, all brimming with magic and legend.

PETER HAINING

LLUDD AND LLEVELYS

(Traditional)

TRADITIONAL. *Despite extensive research over many centuries it has proved impossible to identify the author or even the approximate date when this very early tale of fantasy was written. Certainly it can be traced into the mists of Welsh antiquity and has probably been told in oral form for a great many years. It is to be found first in manuscript in the legendary Welsh volume,* Llyfr Coch O Hergest, The Red Book of Hergest, *which was written in the fourteenth century. This drew extensively on material of a much earlier date, but clearly demonstrated the rich vein of fabulous tales to be found in the country. Lady Charlotte Guest (1812–1895) the Welsh scholar and historian, who translated certain of the poems and prose romances from this work and published them as* The Mabinogion *in 1839–1849, noted with some authority that, 'Welsh literature has strong claims to be considered the cradle of European romance'. Tales like 'Lludd and Llevelys' certainly underline this, and in it we encounter the* Yddraig Coch, *the Red Dragon of Wales, the country's national symbol. The dragon has been the emblem of Wales since time immemorial and it is interesting to note that the reference to it which occurs in this story is the first to be found in Welsh literature. It makes the tale a doubly appropriate item with which to begin an excursion into Welsh fantasy literature.*

Beli the Great, the son of Manogan, had three sons, Lludd and Caswallawn and Nynyaw, and according to the story he had a fourth son called Llevelys. And after the death of Beli, the kingdom of the Island of Britain fell into the hands of Lludd, his eldest son; and Lludd ruled prosperously, and rebuilt the walls of London, and encompassed it about with numberless towers. And after that he bade the citizens build houses therein, such as no houses in the kingdom could equal. And moreover he was a mighty warrior, and generous and liberal in giving meat and drink to all that sought them. And though he had many castles and cities, this one loved he more than any. And he dwelt therein most part of the year, and therefore was it called Caer Lludd, and at last Caer London. And after the stranger-race came there, it was called London, or Lwndrys.

Lludd loved Llevelys best of all his brothers, because he was a wise and discreet man. Having heard that the King of France had died, leaving no heir except a daughter, and that he had left all his possessions in her hands, he came to Lludd his brother to beseech his counsel and aid; and that not so much for his own welfare as to seek to add to the glory and honour and dignity of his kindred, if he might go to France to woo the maiden for his wife. And forthwith his brother conferred with him, and this counsel was pleasing unto him.

So he prepared ships, and filled them with armed knights, and set forth towards France. And as soon as they had landed, they sent messengers to show the nobles of France the cause of the embassy. And by the joint counsel of the nobles of France and of the princes, the maiden was given to Llevelys, and the crown of the kingdom with her. And thenceforth he ruled the land discreetly and wisely and happily as long as his life lasted.

After a space of time had passed, three plagues fell on the Island of Britain, such as none in the islands had ever seen the like of. The first was a certain race that came, and was called the Coranians; and so great was their knowledge, that there was no discourse upon the face of the island, however low it might be spoken, but what, if the wind met it, it was known to them. And through this they could not be injured.

The second plague was a shriek which came on every May-eve over every hearth in the Island of Britain. And this went through people's hearts, and so scared them, that the men lost their hue and their strength, and the young men and the maidens lost their senses, and all the animals and trees, and the earth and the waters, were left barren.

The third plague was, that, however much of provisions and food might be prepared in the king's courts, were there even so much as a year's provision of meat and drink, none of it could ever be found, except what was consumed in the first night. And two of these plagues no one ever knew their cause, therefore was there better hope of being freed from the first than from the second and third.

And thereupon King Lludd felt greater sorrow and care, because that he knew not how he might be freed from these plagues. And he called to him all the nobles of his kingdom, and asked counsel of them what they should do against these afflictions. And by the common counsel of the nobles, Lludd the son of Beli went to Llevelys his brother, King of France, for he was a man great of counsel and wisdom, to seek his advice.

And they made ready a fleet, and that in secret and in silence, lest that race should know the cause of their errand, or any besides the king and his counsellors. And when they were made ready, they went into their ships, Lludd and those he chose with him. And they began to cleave the seas towards France.

And when these tidings came to Llevelys, seeing that he knew not the cause of his brother's ships he came on the other side to meet him, and with him was a fleet vast of size. And when Lludd saw this, he left all the ships out upon the sea except one only; and in that one he came to meet his brother, and he likewise with a single ship came to meet him. And when they were come together, each put his arms about the other's neck, and they welcomed each other with brotherly love.

After that Lludd had shown his brother the cause of his errand, Llevelys said that he himself knew the cause of the coming to those lands. And they took counsel together to discourse on the matter otherwise than thus, in order that the wind might not catch their words, nor the Coranians know what they might say. Then Llevelys caused a long horn to be made of brass, and through this horn they discoursed. But whatsoever words they spoke through this horn, one to the other, neither of them could hear any other but harsh and hostile words. And when Llevelys saw this, and that there was a demon thwarting them, and disturbing through this horn, he caused wine to be put therein to wash it. And through the virtue of the wine the demon was driven out of the horn. And when their discourse was unobstructed, Llevelys told his brother that he would give him some insects, whereof he should keep some to breed, lest by chance the like affliction might come a second time. And other of these insects he should take and bruise in water. And he assured him that it would have power to destroy the race of the Coranians. That is to say, that when he came home to his kingdom, he should call together all the people, both of his own race and of the race of the Coranians, for a conference, as though with the intent of making peace between them, and that when they were all together he should take his charmed water, and cast it over all alike. And he assured him that the water would poison the race of the Coranians, but that it would not slay or harm those of his own race.

'And the second plague,' said he, 'that is in thy dominion, be-hold it is a dragon. And another dragon of a foreign race is fight-ing with it, and striving to overcome it. And therefore does your dragon make a fearful outcry. And on this wise mayest thou come to know this. After thou hast returned home, cause the island to be measured in its length and breadth; and in the place where thou dost find the exact central point, there cause a pit to be dug, and cause a cauldron full of the best mead that can be made to be put in the pit, with a covering of satin over the face of the cauldron. And then in thine own person do thou remain there watching, and thou wilt see the dragons fighting in the form of terrific animals. And at length they will take the form of dragons in the air. And last of all, after wearying themselves with fierce and furious fight-ing, they will fall, in the form of two pigs, upon the covering, and they will sink in, and the covering with them, and they will draw it down to the very bottom of the cauldron. And they will drink up the whole of the mead; and after that they will sleep. Thereupon do thou immediately fold the covering around them, and bury them in a *kistvaen* in the strongest place thou hast in thy dominions, and hide them in the earth. And as long as they shall bide in that strong place, no plague shall come to the Island of Britain from elsewhere.

'The cause of the third plague,' said he, 'is a mighty man of magic, who takes thy meat and thy drink and thy store. And he, through illusions and charms, causes every one to sleep. Therefore it is needful for thee in thy own person to watch thy food and thy provisions. And lest he should overcome thee with sleep, be there a cauldron of cold water by thy side, and when thou art oppressed with sleep, plunge into the cauldron.'

Then Lludd returned back unto his land. And immediately he summoned to him the whole of his own race and of the Coranians. And, as Llevelys had taught him, he bruised the insects in water, the which he cast over them all together, and forthwith it destroyed the whole tribe of the Coranians, without hurt to any of the Britons.

And some time after this Lludd caused the island to be measured in its length and in its breadth. And in Oxford he found the central point, and in that place he caused the earth to be dug, and in that pit a cauldron to be set full of the best mead that could be made, and a covering of satin over the face of it. And he himself watched that night. And while he was there, he beheld the dragons fighting. And when they were weary they fell, and came down upon the top of the satin, and drew it with them to the bottom of the cauldron. And when they had drunk the mead they slept. And in their sleep Lludd folded the covering around them, and in the securest place he had in Snowdon he hid them in a *kistvaen*. Now after that, this spot was called Dinas Emrys, but before that, Dinas Ffaraon. And thus the fierce outcry ceased in his dominions.

And when this was ended, King Lludd caused an exceeding great banquet to be prepared. And when it was ready, he placed a vessel of cold water by his side, and he in his own proper person watched it. And as he abode thus clad with arms, about the third watch of the night, lo, he heard many surpassing fascinations and various songs. And drowsiness urged him to sleep. Upon this, lest he should be hindered from his purpose, and be overcome by sleep, he went often into the water. And at last, behold a man of vast size, clad in strong, heavy armour came in, bearing a hamper. And as he was wont, he put all the food and provisions of meat and drink into the hamper, and proceeded to go with it forth. And nothing was ever more wonderful to Lludd than that the hamper should hold so much.

And thereupon King Lludd went after him, and spoke unto him thus: 'Stop, stop,' said he, 'though thou hast done many insults and much spoil erewhile, thou shalt not do so any more, unless thy skill in arms and thy prowess be greater than mine.'

Then he instantly put down the hamper on the floor, and awaited him. And a fierce encounter was between them, so that the glittering fire flew out from their arms. And at the last Lludd grappled with him, and fate bestowed the victory on Lludd. And he threw the plague to the earth. And after he had overcome him by strength and might he besought his mercy.

'How can I grant thee mercy,' said the king, 'after all the many injuries and wrongs that thou hast done me?'

'All the losses that ever I have caused thee,' said he, 'I will make thee atonement for, equal to what I have taken. And I will never do the like from this time forth. But thy faithful vassal will I be.'

And the king accepted this from him.

MERLIN AND THE MAGICIANS

by Geoffrey of Monmouth

GEOFFREY OF MONMOUTH (c. *1100–1154*)
*was perhaps the most famous of all the early Welsh
chroniclers and his work was unquestionably the source
material for many later writers including Shakespeare, Milton,
Tennyson and Swinburne. A man of the church, Geoffrey
was first Archdeacon of Llandaff and then consecrated Bishop
of St Asaph in 1152. His masterwork was the* Historia
Regum Britanniae *which he wrote in Latin but which did not
appear in an English translation until as late as 1718. Although
presented as a History of Britain, the book makes little pre-
tence at accuracy. Geoffrey certainly drew inspiration from
existing legends and the work of chroniclers such as Gildas,
but much is sheer imagination and invention. (A contemporary
of Geoffrey, a Yorkshire monk, said the book 'lied saucily
and shamelessly'!) To whatever degree the book was original
or copied, however, there can be no denying that it proved a
great influence on English literature. Geoffrey first chronicled
the legends of King Arthur and the prophecies of Merlin
which were to be so successfully utilised in many succeeding
works, including the famous* Le Morte d'Arthur *of Sir
Thomas Malory (1485). King Arthur we shall meet in the
next story, but while still in the mists of medieval history
let us read the story on which the legend of Merlin is founded.
It is a tale which well deserves the praise given by the first
translator, Aaron Thompson: 'Truly, it contains much that is
fabulous.' Following the description of Merlin and his background, the original goes on to list at some length the various*

prophecies of the great magician, but these, I feel, have no
place in a general collection of stories such as this.

It then came about that King Vortigern, not knowing what to do
against the barbarians who were causing such desolation throughout his land, retired into Cambria to consider his future and what
he should do.

At last he had recourse to magicians for their advice, and commanded them to tell him what course to take. They advised him
to build a very strong tower for his own safety, since he had lost
all his other fortified places. Accordingly he made a progress about
the country, to find out a convenient situation, and came at last
to Mount Erir [Snowdon], where he assembled workmen from
several countries, and ordered them to build the tower.

The builders, therefore, began to lay the foundation; but whatever they did one day, the earth swallowed up the next, so as to
leave no appearance of their work. Vortigern, being informed of
this, again consulted with his magicians concerning the cause of it,
who told him that he must find out a youth that never had a
father, and kill him, and then sprinkle the stones and cement
with his blood; for by those means, they said, he would have a
firm foundation.

Hereupon messengers were forthwith dispatched away over all
the provinces, to inquire out such a man. In their travels they came
to a city, called afterwards Kaermerdin [Carmarthen], where
they saw some young men, playing before the gate, and went up to
them. But being weary with their journey, they sat down in the
ring, to see if they could meet with what they were in quest of.

Towards evening, there happened on a sudden a quarrel between
two of the young men, whose names were Merlin and Dabutius. In
the dispute, Dabutius said to Merlin: 'You fool, do you presume
to quarrel with me? Is there any equality in our birth? I am
descended of royal race, both by my father and mother's side. As
for you, nobody knows what you are, for you never had a
father.'

At that word the messengers looked earnestly on Merlin, and
asked the by-standers who he was. They told him, it was not

known who was his father; but that his mother was daughter to the king of Demetia, and that she lived in St Peter's Church among the nuns of that city.

Upon this the messengers hastened to the governor of the city, and ordered him, in the king's name, to send Merlin and his mother to the king. As soon as the governor understood the occasion of their message, he readily obeyed the order and sent them to Vortigern to complete his design.

When they were introduced into the king's presence, he received the mother in a very respectful manner, on account of her noble birth; and began to inquire of her by what man she had conceived.

'My sovereign lord,' said she, 'by the life of your soul and mine, I know nobody that begot him of me. Only this I know, that as I was once with my companions in our chambers, there appeared to me a person in the shape of a most beautiful young man, who often embraced me eagerly in his arms, and kissed me; and when he had stayed a little time, he suddenly vanished out of my sight. But many times after this he would talk with me when I sat alone, without making any visible appearance.

'When he had a long time haunted me in this manner, he at last lay with me several times in the shape of a man, and left me with child. And I do affirm to you, my sovereign lord, that excepting that young man, I know no body begot him of me.'

The king, full of admiration at this account, ordered Maugantius to be called, that he might satisfy him as to the possibility of what the woman had related. Maugantius being introduced, and having the whole matter repeated to him, said to Vortigern:

'In the books of our philosophers, and in a great many histories, I have found that several men have had the like original. For, as Apuleius informs us in his book concerning the Demon of Socrates, between the moon and the earth inhabit those spirits, which we call incubuses. These are of the nature partly of men, and partly of angels, and whenever they please assume human shapes, and lie with women. Perhaps one of them appeared to this woman, and begot that young man of her.'

Merlin, in the mean time was attentive to all that had passed, and then approached the king, and said to him, 'For what reason am I and my mother introduced into your presence?'

'My magicians,' answered Vortigern, 'advised me to seek out a man that had no father, with whose blood my building is to be sprinkled, in order to make it stand.'

'Order your magicians,' said Merlin, 'to come before me, and I will convict them of a lie.'

The king was surprised at his words, and presently ordered the magicians to come, and sit down before Merlin, who spoke to them after this manner: 'Because you are ignorant what it is that hinders the foundation of the tower, you have recommended the shedding of my blood for cement to it, as if that would presently make it stand. But tell me now, what is there under the foundation? For something there is that will not suffer it to stand.'

The magicians at this began to be afraid, and made him no answer. Then said Merlin. 'I entreat your majesty would command your workmen to dig into the ground, and you will find a pond deep under ground which had made it give way.'

Merlin after this went again to the magicians, and said, 'Tell me, ye false sycophants, what is there under the pond?' But they were silent.

Then said he again to the king, 'Command the pond to be drained, and at the bottom you will see two hollow stones, and in them two dragons asleep.'

The king made no scruple of believing him, since he had found true what he said of the pond and therefore ordered it to be drained: which done, he found as Merlin had said; and now was possessed with the greatest admiration of him. Nor were the rest that were present less amazed at his wisdom, thinking it to be no less than divine inspiration.

And thereafter his wisdom was much sought by all of high and low estate; and many and amazing were his predictions.

ARTHUR AND GORLAGON

(Anonymous)

ANONYMOUS. *Few characters figure larger in British folk history than King Arthur, the legendary defender of chivalry and man of valiant deeds, who allegedly still lies sleeping in a cave in Wales awaiting the call to save his beloved Isle. His exploits, and those of his Knights of the Round Table, have a place in the affection of people of all ages, and for students of history his saga bridges the gap between pagan and Christian Britain, and the end of the Roman Empire and the beginning of the British nation. Countless books, and in particular the famous* Le Morte D'Arthur, *have kept Arthur's memory ever fresh and to find a rare story about him is of importance. Yet 'Arthur and Gorlagon' is just that—a story of the famous King and his encounter with a werewolf which has never found a place in the canon of tales about Arthur. The tale was discovered at the turn of the century among the voluminous Rawlinson manuscripts in the Bodleian Library. It is believed to date from the late fourteenth century and was written in Latin. Translated by a British student of the Arthurian legends, it was read at a meeting of classical scholars in 1903 and subsequently published in their society's journal. Until this date it has never appeared in a collection of stories available to the general public. The word Gorlagon is a Welsh derivative of the Anglo-Saxon* werwolf *and by the very date of this tale it must be regarded as one of the earliest werewolf stories. For this collection I have edited the story slightly, but nothing can change what one scholar called 'the remarkable and valuable stature of this unique Arthurian legend'.*

At the City of the Legions, King Arthur was keeping the renowned festival of Pentecost, to which he invited the great men and nobles of the whole of his kingdom, and when the solemn rites had been duly performed he bade them to a banquet, furnished with everything thereto pertaining. And as they were joyfully partaking of the feast of rich abundance, Arthur, in his excessive joy, threw his arms around the Queen, who was sitting beside him, and embracing her, kissed her very affectionately in the sight of all. But she was dumbfounded at his conduct, and blushing deeply, looked up at him and asked why he had kissed her thus at such an unusual place and hour.

Arthur. Because amidst all my riches I have nothing so pleasing and amidst all my delights nothing so sweet, as thou art.

The Queen. Well, if, as you say, you love me so much, you evidently think that you know my heart and my affection.

Arthur. I doubt not that your heart is well disposed towards me, and I certainly think that your affection is absolutely known to me.

The Queen. Well, if, as you say, you love me so much, you acknowledge that you have never yet fathomed either the nature or the heart of a woman.

Arthur. I call heaven to witness that if up to now they have lain hid from me, I will exert myself, and sparing no pains, I will never taste food until by good hap I fathom them.

So when the banquet was ended Arthur called to him Caius, his server, and said, 'Caius, do you and Walwain my nephew mount your horses and accompany me on the business to which I am hastening. But let the rest remain and entertain my guests in my stead until I return.' Caius and Walwain at once mounted their horses as they were bidden and hastened with Arthur to a certain king famed for his wisdom, named Gargol, who reigned over the neighbouring country; and on the third day they reached a certain valley, quite worn out, for since leaving home they had not tasted food nor slept, but had ever ridden on uninterruptedly night and day. Now immediately on the further side of that valley there was a lofty mountain, surrounded by a pleasant wood, in

* *

whose recesses was visible a very strong fortress built of polished stone. And Arthur, when he saw it at a distance, commanded Caius to hasten on before him with all speed, and bring back word to him to whom the town belonged. So Caius, urging on his steed, hastened forward and entered the fortress, and on his return met Arthur just as he was entering the outer trench, and told him that the town belonged to King Gargol, to whom they were making their way.

Now it so happened that King Gargol had just sat down at table to dine; and Arthur, entering his presence on horseback, courteously saluted him and those who were feasting with him. And King Gargol said to him, 'Who art thou? and from whence? And wherefore hast thou entered into our presence with such haste?'

Arthur. 'I am Arthur,' he replied, 'the King of Britain: and I wish to learn from you what are the *heart, the nature, and the ways of women,* for I have very often heard that you are well skilled in matters of this kind.'

Gargol. Yours is a weighty question, Arthur, and there are very few who know how to answer it. But take my advice now, dismount and eat with me, and rest today, for I see that you are over-wrought with your toilsome journey; and tomorrow I will tell you what I know of the matter.

Arthur denied that he was overwrought, pledging himself withal that he would never eat until he had learnt what he was in search of. At last, however, pressed by the King and by the company who were feasting with him, he assented, and, having dismounted, he sat at table on the seat which had been placed for him opposite the King. But as soon as it was dawn, Arthur, remembering the promise which had been made to him, went to King Gargol and said, 'O my dear King, make known to me, I beg, that which you promised yesterday you would tell me today.'

Gargol. You are displaying your folly, Arthur. Until now I thought you were a wise man: as to the heart, the nature, and the ways of woman, no one ever had a conception of what they are, and I do not know that I can give you any information on the subject. But I have a brother, King Torleil by name, whose kingdom borders on my own. He is older and wiser than I am:

and indeed, if there is any one skilled in this matter, about which you are so anxious to know, I do not think it has escaped him. Seek him out, and desire him on my account to tell you what he knows of it.

So, having bidden Gargol farewell, Arthur departed, and instantly continuing his journey arrived after a four days' march at King Torleil's, and as it chanced found the King at dinner. And when the King had exchanged greetings with him and asked him who he was, Arthur replied that he was King of Britain, and had been sent to the King by his brother King Gargol, in order that the King might explain to him a matter, his ignorance of which had obliged him to approach the royal presence.

Torleil. What is it?

Arthur. I have applied my mind to investigate the heart, the nature, and the ways of women, and have been unable to find anyone to tell me what they are. Do you therefore, to whom I have been sent, instruct me in these matters, and if they are known to you, do not keep them back from me.

Torleil. Yours is a weighty question, Arthur, and there are few who know how to answer it. Wherefore, as this is not the time to discuss such matters, dismount and eat, and rest today, and tomorrow I will tell you what I know about them.

Arthur replied, 'I shall be able to eat enough by-and-by. By my faith, I will never eat until I have learned that which I am in search of.' Pressed, however, by the King and by those who were sitting at table with him, he at length reluctantly consented to dismount, and sat down at the table opposite the King. But in the morning he came to King Torleil and began to ask him to tell what he had promised. Torleil confessed that he knew absolutely nothing about the matter, and directed Arthur to his third brother, King Gorlagon, who was older than himself, telling him that he had no doubt that Gorlagon was mighty in the knowledge of the things he was inquiring into, if indeed it was certain that anyone had any knowledge of them.

So Arthur hastened without delay to his destined goal, and after two days reached the city where King Gorlagon dwelt, and, as it chanced, found him at dinner, as he had found the others.

After greetings had been exchanged Arthur made known who he was and why he had come, and as he kept on asking for information on the matters about which he had come, King Gorlagon answered, 'Yours is a weighty question. Dismount and eat: and tomorrow I will tell you what you wish to know.'

But Arthur said he would by no means do that, and when again requested to dismount, he swore by an oath that he would yield to no entreaties until he had learned what he was in search of. So when King Gorlagon saw that he could not by any means prevail upon him to dismount, he said, 'Arthur, since you persist in your resolve to take no food until you know what you ask of me, although the labour of telling you the tale be great, and there is little use in telling it, yet I will relate to you what happened to a certain king, and thereby you will be able to test the heart, the nature, and the ways of women. Yet, Arthur, I beg you, dismount and eat, for yours is a weighty question and few there are who know how to answer it, and when I have told you my tale you will be but little the wiser.

Arthur. Tell on as you have proposed, and speak no more of my eating.

Gorlagon. Well, let your companions dismount and eat.

Arthur. Very well, let them do so.

So when they had seated themselves at table, King Gorlagon said, 'Arthur, since you are so eager to hear this business, give ear, and keep in mind what I am about to tell you.'

There was a king well known to me, noble, accomplished, rich, and far-famed for justice and for truth. He had provided for himself a delightful garden which had no equal, and in it he had caused to be sown and planted all kinds of trees and fruits, and spices of different sorts: and among the other shrubs which grew in the garden there was a beautiful slender sapling of exactly the same height as the King himself, which broke forth from the ground and began to grow on the same night and at the same hour as the King was born. Now concerning this sapling, it had been decreed by fate that whoever should cut it down, and striking his head with the slenderer part of it, should say, 'Be a wolf and have the understanding of a wolf,' he would at once become a wolf, and have the understanding of a wolf. And for this reason the King watched the sapling with great care and with great diligence, for he had no doubt that his safety depended upon it. So he surrounded the garden with a strong and steep wall, and allowed no one but the guardian, who was a trusted friend of his own, to be admitted into it; and it was his custom to visit that sapling three or four times a day, and to partake of no food until he had visited it, even though he should fast until the evening. So it was that he alone understood this matter thoroughly.

Now this king had a very beautiful wife, but though fair to look upon, she did not prove chaste, and her beauty was the cause of her undoing. For she loved a youth, the son of a certain pagan king; and preferring his love to that of her lord, she had taken great pains to involve her husband in some danger so that the youth might be able lawfully to enjoy the embraces for which he longed. And observing that the King entered the garden so many times a day, and desiring to know the reason, she often purposed to question him on the subject, but never dared to do so. But at last one day, when the King had returned from hunting later than usual, and according to his wont had entered the plantation alone, the Queen, in her thirst for information, and unable to endure that the thing should be concealed from her any longer (as it is customary for a woman to wish to know everything), when her husband had returned and was seated at table, asked him with a treacherous smile why he went to the garden so many times a day, and had been there even then late in the evening before taking food. The King answered that that was a matter which did not concern her, and that he was under no obligation to divulge it to her; whereupon she became furious, and improperly suspecting that he was in the habit of consorting with an adulteress in the garden, cried out, 'I call all the gods of heaven to witness that I will never eat with you henceforth until you tell me the reason.' And rising suddenly from the table she went to her bedchamber, cunningly feigning sickness, and lay in bed for three days without taking any food.

On the third day, the King, perceiving her obstinacy and fearing that her life might be endangered in consequence, began to beg and exhort her with gentle words to rise and eat, telling her that the thing she wished to know was a secret which he would never dare to tell anyone. To which she replied, 'You ought to have no secrets from your wife, and you must know for certain that I would rather die than live, so long as I feel that I am so little loved by you,' and he could not by any means persuade her to take refreshment. Then the King, in too changeable and irresolute a mood and too devoted in his affection for his wife, explained to her how the matter stood, having first exacted an oath from her that she would never betray the secret to anyone, and would keep the sapling as sacred as her own life.

The Queen, however, having got from him that which she had so dearly wished and prayed for, began to promise him greater devotion and love, although she had already conceived in her mind a device by which she might bring about the crime she had been so long deliberating. So on the following day, when the King had gone to the woods to hunt, she seized an axe, and secretly entering the garden, cut down the sapling to the ground, and carried it away with her. When, however, she found that the King was returning, she concealed the sapling under her sleeve, which hung down long and loose, and went to the threshold of the door to meet him, and throwing her arms around him she embraced him as though she would have kissed him, and then suddenly thrust the sapling out from her sleeve and struck him on the head with it once and again, crying, 'Be a wolf, be a wolf', meaning to add 'and have the understanding of a wolf', but she added instead the words 'have the understanding of a man'. Nor was there any delay, but it came about as she had said; and he fled quickly to the woods with the hounds she set on him in pursuit, but his human understanding remained unimpaired.

Arthur, see, you have now learned in part the heart, the nature, and the ways of woman. Dismount now and eat, and afterwards I will relate at greater length what remains. For yours is a weighty question, and there are few who know how to answer it, and when I have told you all you will be but little the wiser.

Arthur. The matter goes very well and pleases me much. Follow up, follow up what you have begun.

Gorlagon. You are pleased then to hear what follows. Be attentive and I will proceed.

Then the Queen, having put to flight her lawful husband, at once summoned the young man of whom I have spoken, and having handed over to him the reins of government, became his wife. But the wolf, after roaming for a space of two years in the recesses of the woods to which he had fled, allied himself with a wild she-wolf, and begot two cubs by her. And remembering the wrong done him by his wife (as he was still possessed of his human understanding), he anxiously considered if he could in any way take his revenge upon her. Now near that wood there was a fortress at which the Queen was very often wont to sojourn with the King. And so this human wolf, looking out for his opportunity, took his she-wolf with her cubs one evening, and rushed unexpectedly into the town, and finding the two little boys of whom the aforesaid youth had become the father by his wife, playing by chance under the tower without anyone to guard them, he attacked and slew them, tearing them cruelly limb from limb. When the bystanders saw too late what had happened they pursued the wolves with shouts. The wolves, when what they had done was made known, fled swiftly away and escaped in safety. The Queen, however, overwhelmed with sorrow at the calamity, gave orders to her retainers to keep a careful watch for the return of the wolves. No long time had elapsed when the wolf, thinking that he was not yet satisfied, again visited the town with his companions, and meeting with two noble counts, brothers of the Queen, playing at the very gates of the palace, he attacked them, and tearing out their bowels gave them over to a frightful death. Hearing the noise, the servants assembled, and shutting the doors caught the cubs and hanged them. But the wolf, more cunning than the rest, slipped out of the hands of those who were holding him and escaped unhurt.

The wolf, overwhelmed with very great grief for the loss of his cubs and maddened by the greatness of his sorrow, made nightly forays against the flocks and herds of that province, and attacked them with such great slaughter that all the inhabitants, placing in ambush a large pack of hounds, met together to hunt and catch him; and the wolf, unable to endure these daily vexations, made for a neighbouring country and there began to carry on his usual ravages. However, he was at once chased from thence by the inhabitants, and compelled to go to a third country: and now he began to vent his rage with implacable fury, not only against the beasts but also against human beings. Now it chanced that a king was reigning over that country, young in years, of a mild disposition, and far-famed for his wisdom and industry: and when the countless destruction both of men and beasts wrought by the wolf was reported to him, he appointed a day on which he would set about to track and hunt the brute with a strong force of huntsmen and hounds. For so greatly was the wolf held in dread that no one dared to go to rest anywhere around, but everyone kept watch the whole night long against his inroads.

So one night when the wolf had gone to a neighbouring village, greedy for bloodshed, and was standing under the eaves of a certain house listening intently to a conversation that was going on within, it happened that he heard the man nearest him tell how the King had proposed to seek and track him down on the following day, much being added as to the clemency and kindness of the King. When the wolf heard this he returned trembling to the recesses of the woods, deliberating what would be the best course for him to pursue.

In the morning the huntsmen and the King's retinue with an immense pack of hounds entered the woods, making the trees ring with the blast of horns and with shouting; and the King, accompanied by two of his intimate friends, followed at a more moderate pace. The wolf concealed himself near the road where the King was to pass, and when all had gone by and he saw the King approaching (for he judged from his countenance that it was the King) he dropped his head and ran close after him, and encircling the King's right foot with his paws he would have licked him affectionately like a suppliant asking for pardon, with such groanings as he was capable of. Then two noblemen who were guarding the King's person, seeing this enormous wolf (for they had never seen any of so vast a size), cried out, 'Master, see, here is the wolf we seek! see, here is the wolf we seek! strike him, slay him, do not let the hateful beast attack us!' The wolf, utterly fearless of their cries, followed close after the King, and kept licking him gently. The King was wonderfully moved, and after looking at the wolf for some time and perceiving that there was no fierceness in him, but that he was rather like one who craved for pardon, was much astonished, and commanded that none of his men should dare to inflict any harm on him, declaring that he had detected some signs of human understanding in him; so putting down his right hand to caress the wolf he gently stroked his head and scratched his ears. Then the King seized the wolf and endeavoured to lift him up to him. But the wolf, perceiving that the King was desirous of lifting him up, leapt up, and joyfully sat upon the neck of the charger in front of the King.

The King recalled his followers, and returned home. He had not gone far when lo! a stag of vast size met him in the forest pasture with antlers erect. Then the King said, 'I will try if there is any worth or strength in my wolf, and whether he can accustom himself to obey my commands.' And crying out he set the wolf upon the stag and thrust him from him with his hand. The wolf, well knowing how to capture this kind of prey, sprang up and pursued the stag, and getting in front of it attacked it, and catching it by the throat laid it dead in sight of the King. Then the King called him back and said, 'Of a truth you must be kept alive and not killed, seeing that you know how to show such service to us.' And taking the wolf with him he returned home.

So the wolf remained with the King, and was held in very great affection by him. Whatever the King commanded him he performed, and he never showed any fierceness towards or inflicted any hurt upon anyone. He daily stood at table before the King at dinner time with his forepaws erect, eating of his bread and drinking from the same cup. Wherever the King went he accompanied him, so that even at night he would not go to rest anywhere save beside his master's couch.

Now it happened that the King had to go on a long journey outside his kingdom to confer with another king, and to go at once, as it would be impossible for him to return in less than ten days. So he called his Queen, and said, 'As I must go on this journey at once, I commend this wolf to your protection, and I command you to keep him in my stead, if he will stay, and to minister to his wants.' But the Queen already hated the wolf because of the great sagacity which she had detected in him (and as it so often happens that the wife hates whom the husband loves), and she said, 'My lord, I am afraid that when you are gone he will attack me in the night if he lies in his accustomed place and will leave me mangled.' The King replied, 'Have no fear of that, for I have detected no such symptom in him all the long time he has been with me. However, if you have any doubt of it, I will have a chain made and will have him fastened up to my bed-ladder.' So the King gave orders that a chain of gold should be made, and when the wolf had been fastened up by it to the steps, he hastened away to the business he had on hand.

So the King set out, and the wolf remained with the Queen. But she did not show the care for him which she ought to have done. For he always lay chained up, though the King had commanded that he should be chained up at night only. Now the Queen loved the King's sewer with an unlawful love, and went to visit him whenever the King was absent. So on the eighth day after the King had started, they met in the bedchamber at midday and mounted the bed together, little heeding the presence of the wolf. And when the wolf saw them rushing into each other's impious embraces he blazed forth with fury, his eyes reddening, and the hair on his neck standing up, and he began to make as though he would attack them, but was held back by the chain by which he was fastened. And when he saw they had no intention of desisting from the iniquity on which they had embarked, he gnashed his teeth, and dug up the ground with his paws, and venting his rage over all his body, with awful howls he stretched the chain with such violence that it snapped in two. When loose he rushed with fury upon the sewer and threw him from the bed, and tore him so savagely that he left him half-dead. But to the Queen he did no harm at all, but only gazed upon her with venom in his eye. Hearing the mournful groans of the sewer, the servants tore the door from its hinges and rushed in. When asked the cause of all the tumult, that cunning Queen concocted a lying story, and told the servants that the wolf had devoured her son, and had torn the sewer as they saw while he was attempting to rescue the little one from death, and that he would have treated her in the same way had they not arrived in time to succour her. So the sewer was brought half dead to the guest-chamber. But the Queen fearing that the King might somehow discover the truth of the matter, and considering how she might take her revenge on the wolf, shut up the child, whom she had represented as having been devoured by the wolf, along with his nurse in an underground room far removed from any access; every one being under the impression that he had in fact been devoured.

After these events news was brought to the Queen that the King was returning sooner than had been expected. So the deceitful woman, full of cunning, went forth to meet him with her hair cut close, and cheeks torn, and garments splashed with blood, and when she met him cried, 'Alas! Alas! Alas! my lord, wretched that I am, what a loss have I sustained during your absence!' At this the King was dumbfounded, and asked what was the matter, and she replied, 'That wretched beast of yours, of yours I say, which I have but too truly suspected all this time, has devoured your son in my lap; and when your sewer was struggling to come to the rescue the beast mangled and almost killed him, and would have treated me in the same way had not the servants broken in; see here the blood of the little one splashed upon my garments is witness of the thing.' Hardly had she finished speaking, when lo! the wolf hearing the King approach, sprang forth from the bedchamber, and rushed into the King's embraces as though he well deserved them, jumping about joyfully, and gambolling with greater delight than he had ever done before. At this the King, distracted by contending emotions, was in doubt what he should do, on the one hand reflecting that his wife would not tell him an untruth, on the other that if the wolf had been guilty of so great a crime against him he would undoubtedly not have dared to meet him with such joyful bounds.

So while his mind was driven hither and thither on these matters and he refused food, the wolf sitting close by him touched his foot gently with his paw, and took the border of his cloak into his mouth, and by a movement of the head invited him to follow him. The King, who understood the wolf's customary signals, got up and followed him through the different bedchambers to the underground room where the boy was hidden away. And finding the door bolted the wolf knocked three or four times with his paw, as much as to ask that it might be opened to him. But as there was some delay in searching for the key—for the Queen had hidden it away—the wolf, unable to endure the delay, drew back a little, and spreading out the claws of his four paws he rushed headlong at the door, and driving it in, threw it down upon the middle of the floor broken and shattered. Then running forward he took the infant from its cradle in his shaggy arms, and gently held it up to the King's face for a kiss.

The King marvelled and said, 'There is something beyond this which is not clear to my comprehension.' Then he went out after the wolf, who led the way, and was conducted by him to the dying sewer; and when the wolf saw the sewer, the King could scarcely restrain him from rushing upon him. Then the King sitting down in front of the sewer's couch, questioned him as to the cause of his sickness, and as to the accident which had occasioned his wounds. The only confession, however, he would make was that in rescuing the boy from the wolf, the wolf had attacked him; and he called the Queen to witness to the truth of what he said. The King in answer said, 'You are evidently lying: my son lives: he was not dead at all, and now that I have found him and have convicted both you and the Queen of treachery to me, and of forging lying tales, I am afraid that something else may be false also. I know the reason why the wolf, unable to bear his master's disgrace, attacked you so savagely, contrary to his wont. Therefore confess to me at once the truth of the matter, else I swear by the Majesty of highest Heaven that I will deliver thee to the flames to burn.' Then the wolf making an attack upon him pressed him close, and would have mangled him again had he not been held back by the bystanders.

What need of many words? When the King insisted, sometimes with threats, sometimes with coaxing, the sewer confessed the crime of which he had been guilty, and humbly prayed to be forgiven. But the King, blazing out in an excess of fury, delivered the sewer up to be kept in prison, and immediately summoned the chief men from the whole of his kingdom to meet, and through them he held an investigation into the circumstances of this great crime. Sentence was given. The sewer was flayed alive and hanged. The Queen was torn limb from limb by horses and thrown into balls of flame.

After these events the King pondered over the extraordinary sagacity and industry of the wolf with close attention and great persistence, and afterwards discussed the subject more fully with his wise men, asserting that a being who was clearly endued with such great intelligence must have the understanding of a man, 'for no beast,' he argued, 'was ever found to possess such great wisdom, or to show such great devotion to any one as this wolf has shown to me. For he understands perfectly whatever we say to him: he does what he is ordered: he always stands by me, wherever I may be: he rejoices when I rejoice, and when I am in sorrow, he sorrows too. And you must know that one who has avenged with such severity the wrong which has been done me must undoubtedly have been a man of great sagacity and ability, and must have assumed the form of a wolf under some spell or incantation.'

At these words the wolf, who was standing by the King, showed great joy, and licking his hands and feet and pressing close to his knees, showed by the expression of his countenance and the gesture of his whole body that the King had spoken the truth.

Then the King said, 'See with what gladness he agrees with what I say, and shows by unmistakable signs that I have spoken the truth. There can now be no further doubt about the matter, and would that power might be granted me to discover whether by some act or device I might be able to restore him to his former state, even at the cost of my worldly substance; nay, even at the risk of my life.' So, after long deliberation, the King at length determined that the wolf should be sent off to go before him, and to take whatever direction he pleased whether by land or by sea. 'For perhaps,' said he, 'if we could reach his country we might get to know what has happened and find some remedy for him.'

So the wolf was allowed to go where he would, and they all followed after him. And he at once made for the sea, and impetuously dashed into the waves as though he wished to cross. Now his own country adjoined that region, being, however, separated from it on one side by the sea, though in another direction it was accessible by land, but by a longer route. The King, seeing that he wished to cross over, at once gave orders that the fleet should be launched and that the army should assemble.

So the King, having ordered his ship, and duly equipped his army, approached the sea with a great force of soldiers, and on the third day he landed safely at the wolf's country; and when they reached the shore the wolf was the first to leap from the ship, and clearly signified to them by his customary nod and gesture that this was his country. Then the King, taking some of his men with him, hastened secretly to a certain neighbouring city, commanding his army to remain on ship until he had looked into the affair and returned to them. However, he had scarcely entered the city when the whole course of events became clear to him. For all the men of that province, both of high and low degree, were groaning under the intolerable tyranny of the king who had succeeded to the wolf, and were with one voice lamenting their master, who by the craft and subtlety of his wife had been changed into a wolf, remembering what a kind and gentle master he was.

So having discovered what he wanted to know, and having ascertained where the king of that province was then living, the King returned with all speed to his ships, marched out his troops, and attacking his adversary suddenly and unexpectedly, slew or put to flight all his defenders, and captured both him and his Queen and made them subject to his dominion.

So the King, relying on his victory, assembled a council of the chief men of the kingdom, and setting the Queen in the sight of them all, said, 'O most perfidious and wicked of women, what madness induced you to plot such great treachery against your lord! But I will not any longer bandy words with one who has been judged unworthy of intercourse with anyone; so answer the question I put to you at once, for I will certainly cause you to die of hunger and thirst and exquisite tortures, unless you show me where the sapling lies hidden with which you transformed your husband into a wolf. Perhaps the human shape which he has lost may thereby be recovered.' Whereupon she swore that she did not know where the sapling was, saying that it was well known that it had been broken up and burnt in the fire. However, as she would not confess, the King handed her over to the tormentors, to be daily tortured and daily exhausted with punishments, and allowed neither food nor drink. So at last, compelled by the severity of her punishment, she produced the sapling and handed it to the King.

And the King took it from her, and with glad heart brought the wolf forward into the midst, and striking his head with the thicker part of the sapling, added these words, 'Be a man and have the understanding of a man.' And no sooner were the words spoken than the effect followed. The wolf became a man as he had been before, though far more beautiful and comely, being now possessed of such grace that one could at once detect that he was a man of great nobility. The King seeing a man of such great beauty metamorphosed from a wolf standing before him, and pitying the wrongs the man had suffered, ran forward with great joy and embraced him, kissing and lamenting him and shedding tears. And as they embraced each other they drew such long protracted sighs and shed so many tears that all the multitude standing around were constrained to weep. The one returned thanks for all the many kindnesses which had been shown him: the other lamented that he had behaved with less consideration than he ought. What more? Extraordinary joy is shown by all, and the King, having received the submission of the principal men, according to ancient custom, retook possession of his sovereignty. Then the adulterer and adulteress were brought into his presence, and he was consulted as to what he judged ought to be done with them. And he condemned the pagan king to death. The Queen he only divorced, but of his inborn clemency spared her life, though she well deserved to lose it. The other King, having been honoured and enriched with costly presents, as was befitting, returned to his own kingdom.

Now, Arthur, you have learned what the heart, the nature, and the ways of women are. Have a care for yourself and see if you are any the wiser for it. Dismount now and eat, for we have both well deserved our meal I, for the tale I have told, and you for listening to it.

Arthur. I will by no means dismount until you have answered the question I am about to ask you.

Gorlagon. What is that?

Arthur. Who is that woman sitting opposite you of a sad countenance, and holding before her in a dish a human head bespattered with blood, who has wept whenever you have smiled, and who has kissed the bloodstained head whenever you have kissed your wife during the telling of your tale?

Gorlagon. If this thing were known to me alone, Arthur (he replied), I would by no means tell it you; but as it is well known to all who are sitting at table with me, I am not ashamed that you also should be made acquainted with it. That woman who is sitting opposite me, she it was who, as I have just told you, wrought so great a crime against her lord, that is to say against myself. In me you may recognise that wolf who, as you have heard, was transformed first from a man into a wolf, and then from a wolf into a man again. When I became a wolf it is evident that the kingdom to which I first went was that of my middle brother, King Torleil. And the King who took such great pains to care for me you can have no doubt was my youngest brother, King Gargol, to whom you came in the first instance. And the bloodstained head which that woman sitting opposite me embraces in the dish she has in front of her is the head of that youth for love of whom she wrought so great a crime against me. For when I returned to my proper shape again, in sparing her life, I subjected her to this penalty only, namely, that she should always have the head of her paramour before her, and that when I kissed the wife I had married in her stead she should imprint kisses on him for whose sake she had committed that crime. And I had the head embalmed to keep it free from putrefaction. For I knew that no punishment could be more grievous to her than a perpetual exhibition of her great wickedness in the sight of all the world.

Arthur, dismount now, if you so desire, for now that I have invited you, you will, so far as I am concerned, from henceforth remain where you are.

So Arthur dismounted and ate, and on the following day returned home a nine days' journey, marvelling greatly at what he had heard.

THE LIVING DEAD MAN

by Walter Map

WALTER MAP OR MAPES *(c. 1137–1209) is the man credited with having reduced many of the Arthurian legends to their present shape and is therefore a most appropriate writer to follow the story of 'Arthur and Gorlagon'. Born of Welsh parents in Herefordshire, he studied in Paris and later became a clerk to the Royal household. He travelled extensively throughout Europe and developed a reputation as a poet and chronicler. His major work was the* De Nugis Curialium *which recorded the important events of the period with particular emphasis on court gossip, to which Map lent an ever-aware ear. In his later years he became strongly drawn to the Church and was successively Canon of St Paul's and Archdeacon of Oxford. His writing indicates that he was deeply interested in the legends and folk-tales of his native Wales, and of all such items, 'The Living Dead Man' seems to me the best and most interesting from the point of view of this book. Like 'Arthur and Gorlagon' its very early date makes it one of the oldest known vampire stories and it contains all the elements which subsequently gave such fascination to tales of the undead. (Students of macabre literature may be interested to know that the famous scholar and modern master of the ghost story, M. R. James, edited a version of Map's* De Nugis Curialium *published in 1915.)*

I know of a strange portent that occurred in Wales, and concerns a dead man who walked by night and caused those he summoned to die of a dreadful sickness.

William Laudun or Landun, an English knight, strong of body

and of proven valour, came to Gilbert Foliot, then Bishop of Hereford, now of London, and said,

'My Lord, I come to you for advice. A Welshman of evil life died of late unchristianly enough in my village, and straightway after four nights took to coming back every night to the village, and will not desist from summoning singly and by name his fellow villagers, who upon being called at once fall sick and die within three days, so that now there are very few of them left.'

The Bishop, marvelling, said: 'Peradventure the Lord has given power to the evil angel of that lost soul to move about in the dead corpse. However, let the body be exhumed, cut the neck through with a spade, and sprinkle the body and the grave well with holy water and replace it.'

When this was done, the survivors were none the less plagued by the former illusion.

So one night when the summoner had now left but few alive, he called William himself, citing him thrice. He, however, bold and quick as he was, and awake to the situation, darted out with his sword drawn, and chased the demon, who fled, up to the grave and there, as he fell into it, clave his head to the neck.

From that hour the ravage of that wandering pestilence ceased, and did no more hurt either to William himself or to any one else.

THE FAIRY PEOPLE

by Giraldus Cambrensis

GIRALDUS CAMBRENSIS (c. *1147–1223*) *has been described as 'one of the most learned men of a learned age' and certainly in his writing set a standard of literature which makes his words still live vividly today. Born about 1147 at Manorbier Castle, Pembrokeshire, he was, by his own admission, reared on adventure and romance and learned all the great tales of legend in his youth. His education was placed in the hands of his uncle, the Bishop of St David's, and not surprisingly he took Holy Orders in 1172. After a somewhat chequered career in the Church, in which he was refused a Bishopric by Henry II, he became preceptor to Prince John and toured with him in Ireland. From this journey resulted his first major work,* Topographia Hibernica *(1185) which described the natural history and inhabitants of the country. In 1188 he went with the Archbishop of Canterbury around Wales preaching on behalf of the Third Crusade, and produced his most distinguished and heartfelt book, the* Itinerarium Cambriae *(Itinerary through Wales). Despite repeated later attempts to become leader of the Church in Wales, Giraldus found his endeavours constantly frustrated on political grounds and he eventually devoted the rest of his life to study. He died in 1223 and only in comparatively recent times has his memory again become revered. Of his several interesting tales about the folklore of Wales, I believe 'The Fairy People' to be the most outstanding; it also has the distinction of being the oldest written fairy story we possess. According to biographers of Giraldus it was written while he was staying in the Vale of Neath—and it is here, says a legend, that one can find 'the passage which leads to Fairy Land'.*

A short time before our days, a circumstance worthy of note occurred in these parts, which Elidorus, a priest, most strenuously affirmed had befallen himself. When a youth of twelve years, and learning his letters, since, as Solomon says, 'The root of learning is bitter, although the fruit is sweet,' in order to avoid the discipline and frequent stripes inflicted on him by his preceptor, he ran away, and concealed himself under the hollow bank of a river.

After fasting in that situation for two days, two little men of pigmy stature appeared to him, saying, 'If you will come with us, we will lead you into a country full of delights and sports.' Assenting and rising up, he followed his guides through a path, at first subterraneous and dark, into a most beautiful country, adorned with rivers and meadows, woods and plains, but obscure, and not illuminated with the full light of the sun. All the days were cloudy, and the nights extremely dark, on account of the absence of the moon and stars.

The boy was brought before the king, and introduced to him in the presence of the court; who, having examined him for a long time, delivered him to his son, who was then a boy. These men were of the smallest stature, but very well proportioned in their make; they were all of a fair complexion, with luxuriant hair falling over their shoulders like that of a woman. They had horses and greyhounds adapted to their size. They neither ate flesh nor fish, but lived on milk diet, made up into messes with saffron. They never took an oath, for they detested nothing so much as lies. As often as they returned from our upper hemisphere, they reprobated our ambition, infidelities, and inconstancies; they had no form of public worship, being strict lovers and reverers, as it seemed, of truth.

The boy frequently returned to our hemisphere, sometimes by the way he had first gone, sometimes by another: at first in company with other persons, and afterwards alone, and made himself known only to his mother, declaring to her the manners, nature, and state of that people. Being desired by her to bring a present of gold, with which that region abounded, he stole, while at play with the king's son, the golden ball with which he used to divert himself, and brought it to his mother in great haste; and when he reached the door of his father's house, but not unpursued, and was entering it in a great hurry, his foot stumbled on the threshold, and falling down into the room where his mother was sitting, the two pigmies seized the ball which had dropped from his hand, and departed, shewing the boy every mark of contempt and derision.

On recovering from his fall, confounded with shame, and execrating the evil counsel of his mother, he returned by the usual track to the subterraneous road, but found no appearance of any passage, though he searched for it on the banks of the river for nearly the space of a year. But since those calamities are often alleviated by time, which reason cannot mitigate, and length of time alone blunts the edge of our afflictions, and puts an end to many evils, the youth having been brought back by his friends and mother, and restored to his right way of thinking, and to his learning, in process of time attained the rank of priesthood.

Whenever David II, bishop of St David's, talked to him in his advanced state of life concerning this event, he could never relate the particulars without shedding tears. He had made himself acquainted with the language of that nation, the words of which, in his younger days, he used to recite, which, as the bishop often had informed me, were very conformable to the Greek idiom.

If a scrupulous inquirer should ask my opinion of the relation here inserted, I answer with Augustine, 'that the divine miracles are to be admired, not discussed'. Nor do I, by denial, place bounds to the divine power, nor, by assent, insolently extend what cannot be extended. But I always call to mind the saying of St Jerome; 'You will find,' says he, 'many things incredible and improbable, which nevertheless are true; for nature cannot in any respect prevail against the lord of nature.' These things, therefore, and similar contingencies, I should place, according to the opinion of Augustine, among those particulars which are neither to be affirmed, nor too positively denied.

THE SIN-EATER

by John Aubrey

JOHN AUBREY *(1626–1697) is the first of the con-*
tributors to this collection who was not born in Wales, although
he did own a large estate in the country and recorded aspects
of its folklore in his voluminous writings. Born near Chippen-
ham and educated at Trinity College, Oxford, Aubrey at first
took up the law, but failed to be called to the bar. In 1652
he succeeded to estates in Wiltshire, Herefordshire and Wales,
but protracted lawsuits deprived him of them one by one. In
his later years he became involved with a group of agitators,
and, by his own admission, 'ran the danger of arrests'. Through-
out his life he was a prolific writer and apart from his study
of famous men, Brief Lives, *which still preserves his repu-*
tation, he undertook wide-ranging antiquarian studies of Surrey
and Wiltshire. Strangely, only his Miscellanies *(1696) was*
published during his lifetime and to this day much of his
writing remains in manuscript form. Of his study of Wales,
quite the most fascinating item refers to the extraordinary and
uniquely Welsh figure, the Sin-Eater. Indeed Aubrey may
well have been the first writer to have committed details of
this phenomenon to paper. According to folklore, the Sin
Eater was an impoverished peasant who was paid by the rela-
tives of a deceased person to 'take unto himself the sins of
the dead man or woman'. Despite emphatic statements by
local people that such practices were unheard of, Aubrey re-
corded the following account in 1686. Other visiting writers to
Wales have also subsequently made mention of it, but the
denials of its existence have persisted to this day. For what
reason, one can only conject . . .

The custom of the Sin-Eater has, I believe, been much observed heretofore all over Wales and is still used to this day in North Wales. It is an old custom, perhaps one of the strangest to be found anywhere, and in my understanding observed as follows.

In Wales it was the custom at funerals to hire poor people who were to take upon them the sins of the party deceased.

One of these people (he was a long, lean, ugly, lamentable poor rascal), I remember, lived in a cottage at Llangors in Brecon.

The manner of the custom was that when the corpse was brought out of the house, and laid on the bier, a loaf of bread was brought out, and delivered to the Sin-Eater, over the corpse. Also a mazard bowl made of maple wood, full of beer (which he was to drink up) and sixpence in money.

In consideration of these gifts he took upon himself, *ipso facto*, all the sins of the defunct, and freed him or her from walking after they were dead.

The minister at this place, e.g. at Llangors, a Mr Gwin, did try to hinder this custom about 1640 but found it of no avail, so strong was the belief among the people.

Though rarely seen in our days, it was observed by some people in the strictest time of the Presbyterian Government; as at Dynder (*nolens volens* the parson of the parish), the kindred of a woman, deceased there, had this ceremony punctually performed, according to her will.

There was also a woman in those times who kept for many years beside her bed a mazard bowl for the Sin-Eater. It happened that as she lay dying the bowl mysteriously disappeared and her kindred were afraid to tell her.

Seeking it at her bedside as she began to draw her last breath, she found it was not there and commenced to wail that she could not, would not, die until it was in her hand. All about her began to search but not a trace could be found.

During that night, when all believed she must die, the woman prayed most earnestly that the Lord could not take her until the gift for the Sin-Eater was ready. And, in the morning, when her kindred went up to her room, they found her lying with the missing bowl upon her breast and she quite dead.

THE FATAL PREDICTION

by Ann of Swansea

ANN OF SWANSEA, *Mrs Julia Ann Curtis (1764–1838) was one of the leading writers in the prolific Gothic Horror and Romance period of literature which so enraptured readers in Britain, Europe and America from 1765 to 1840.*[1] *She was a woman as lively, spirited and prone to notoriety as her books, which, though impossibly rare today, are of considerable merit. After two unsuccessful marriages and a hasty departure from America during a yellow fever scare, she settled in Swansea and devoted the rest of her life, as one biographer has noted, 'to scandal, outrage and writing'. Mrs Curtis was a woman of undoubted beauty and apart from being the mistress of Edmund Kean during his extensive touring of Wales, also opened an ill-fated 'school of dancing and deportment for young ladies' which encouraged wealthy male patrons to 'adopt' young girls. Perhaps her greatest act of notoriety, however, was an unsuccessful attempt to poison herself in Westminster Abbey. She also forced the famous Mrs Siddons to pay her an annual retainer to stop calling herself the actress's younger sister. (There is reason to believe, however, that this was a genuine claim—but doubtless Mrs Siddons was exasperated at continually having to pay the bills run up in her name by her 'sister'.) Mrs Curtis began her literary career with poems contributed to the Swansea news-*

[1] Readers interested in this period of macabre fiction may care to study Peter Haining's two-volume survey of the genre which contains many of the finest short stories written at that time: *Great British Tales of Terror* and *Great Tales of Terror from Europe and America* (Gollancz, 1972). The two volumes have also appeared in America as one book, *Gothic Tales of Terror* (Taplinger, 1972).

paper, The Cambrian *and then scored an immediate success in 1810 with her Gothic novel,* Cambrian Pictures; Or, Every One has Errors, *which appeared under the name 'Ann of Swansea'. Over a dozen more works followed, including* Deeds of the Olden Time *in 1826, which re-told a number of famous Welsh legends. 'The Fatal Prediction', taken from that book, is perhaps best fitted to this collection and while a little laboured in style, is nonetheless a fine example of the Gothic horror story.*

On the south-west coast of the principality of Wales stands a romantic little village, inhabited chiefly by the poorer class of people, consisting of small farmers and oyster dredgers, whose estates are the wide ocean, and whose ploughs are the small craft, in which they glide over its interminable fields in search of the treasures which they wring from its bosom; it is built on the very top of a hill, commanding on one side, a view of an immense bay, and on the other, of the peaceful green fields and valleys, cultivated by the greater number of its quiet inhabitants. Distinctions were unknown in the village, every man was the equal of his neighbour.

But, though rank and its unpolished distinctions were strange in the village, the superiority of talent was felt and acknowleged almost without a pause or a murmur. There was one who was as a king amongst them, by the mere force of a mightier spirit than those with whom he sojourned had been accustomed to feel among them: he was a dark and moody man, a stranger, evidently of a higher order than those around him, who had but a few months before, without any apparent object, settled among them: he was poor, but had no occupation—he lived frugally, but quite alone—and his sole employments were to read during the day, and wander out unaccompanied into the fields or by the beach during the night. Sometimes indeed he would relieve a suffering child or rheumatic old man by medicinal herbs, reprove idleness and drunkenness in the youth, and predict to all the good and evil consequences of their conduct: and his success in some cases, his foresight in others, and his wisdom in all, won for him a high reputation among the cottagers to which his taciturn habits contributed not a little, for, with the vulgar as with the educated, no talker was ever seriously taken for a conjuror, though a silent man is often decided to be a wise one.

There was but one person at all disposed to rebel against the despotic sovereignty which Rhys Meredith was silently establishing over the quiet village, and that was precisely the person most likely to effect a revolution; she was a beautiful maiden, the glory and boast of the village, who had been the favourite of, and to a certain degree educated by, the late lady of the manor; but she had died, and her pupil, with a full consciousness of her intellectual superiority, had returned to her native village, where she determined to have an empire of her own, which no rival should dispute: she laughed at the maidens who listened to the predictions of Rhys, and she refused her smiles to the youths who consulted him upon their affairs and their prospects; and as the beautiful Ruth was generally beloved, the silent Rhys was soon in danger of being abandoned by all, save doting men and paralytic women, and feeling himself an outcast in the village.

But to be such was not the object of Meredith; he was an idle man, and the gifts of the villagers contributed to spare him from exertion; he knew too, that in another point of view this ascendancy was necessary to his purposes; and as he had failed to establish it by wisdom and benevolence, he determined to try the effect of fear. The character of the people with whom he sojourned was admirably calculated to assist his projects; his predictions were now uttered more clearly, and his threats denounced in sterner and stronger and plainer words; and when he predicted that old Morgan Williams, who had been stricken with the palsy, would die at the turn of tide, three days from that on which he spoke, and that the light little boat of gay Griffy Morris, which sailed from the bay in a bright winter's morning, should never again make the shore; and the man died, and the storm arose, even as he said; men's hearts died within them, and they bowed down before his words, as if he had been their general fate and the individual destiny of each.

Ruth's rosy lip grew pale for a moment as she heard of these things; in the next her spirit returned, and 'I will make him tell my fortune', she said, as she went with a party of laughers to search out and deride the conjuror. He was alone when they broke in upon him, and their mockeries goaded his spirit; but his anger was deep, not loud; and while burning with wrath, he yet could calmly consider the means of vengeance: he knew the master spirit with which he had to contend; it was no ordinary mind, and would have smiled at ordinary terrors. To have threatened her with sickness, misfortune, or death, would have been to call forth the energies of that lofty spirit, and prepare it to endure, and it would have gloried in manifesting its powers of endurance; he must humble it therefore by debasement; he must ruin its confidence in itself; and to this end he resolved to threaten her with crime. His resolution was taken and effected; his credit was at stake; he must daunt his enemy, or surrender to her power: he foretold sorrows and joys to the listening throng, not according to his passion, but his judgment, and he drew a blush upon the cheek of one, by revealing a secret which Ruth herself, and another, alone knew, and which prepared the former to doubt of her own judgment, as it related to this extraordinary man.

Ruth was the last who approached to hear the secret of her destiny. The wizard paused as he looked upon her—opened his book—shut it—paused—and again looked sadly and fearfully upon her; she tried to smile, but felt startled, she knew not why; the bright inquiring glance of her dark eye could not change the purpose of her enemy. Her smile could not melt, nor even temper the hardness of his deep-seated malice: he again looked sternly upon her brow, and then coldly wrung out the slow soul-withering words, 'Maiden, thou art doomed to be a murderer!'

From that hour Rhys Meredith became the destiny of Ruth Tudor. At first she spurned at his prediction, and alternately cursed and laughed at him for the malice of his falsehood: but when she found that none laughed with her, the men looked upon her with suspicious eyes, women shrunk from her society, and children shrieked at her presence, she felt that these were signs of truth, and her high spirit no longer struggled against the conviction; a change came over her mind when she had known how horrid it was to be alone. Abhorring the prophet, she yet clung to his footsteps, and while she sat by his side, felt as if he alone could avert the evil destiny which he alone had foreseen. With him only was she seen to smile; elsewhere, sad, silent, stern; it seemed as if she were ever occupied in nerving her mind for that which she had to do, and her beauty, already of the majestic cast, grew absolutely awful.

But there were moments when her naturally strong spirit, not yet wholly subdued, struggled against her conviction, and endeavoured to find modes of averting her fate: it was in one of these, perhaps, that she gave her hand to a wooer, from a distant part of the country, a mariner, who either had not heard, or did not regard the prediction of Rhys, upon condition that he should remove her far from her native village to the home of his family and friends, for she sometimes felt as if the decree which had gone forth against her, could not be fulfilled except upon the spot where she had heard it, and that her heart would be lighter if men's eyes would again look upon her in kindliness, and she no longer sat beneath the glare of these that knew so well the secret of her soul. Thus thinking, she quitted the village with her husband; and the tormentor, who had poisoned her repose, soon after her departure, left the village as secretly and as suddenly as he had entered it.

But, though Ruth could not depart from his corporeal presence, and look upon his cruel visage no more, yet the eye of her soul was fixed upon his shadow, and his airy form, the creation of her sorrow, still sat by her side; the blight that he had breathed upon her peace had withered her heart, and it was in vain that she sought to forget or banish the recollection from her brain. Men and women smiled upon her as before in the days of her joy, the friends of her husband welcomed her to their bosoms, but they could give no peace to her heart: she shrunk from their friendship, she shivered equally at their neglect, she dreaded any cause that might lead to that which, it had been said, she must do; nightly she sat alone and thought, she dwelt upon the characters of those around her and shuddered that in some she saw violence and selfishness enough to cause injury, which she might be supposed to resent to blood. Against the use of actual violence she had disabled herself; she had never struck a blow, her small hand would have suffered injury in the attempt; she understood not the usage of fire-arms, she was ignorant of what were poisons, and a knife she never allowed herself, even for the most necessary purposes: how then could she slay? At times she took comforts from thoughts like these, and at others, she was plunged in the darkness of despair.

Her husband went forth and returned upon the voyages which made up the avocation and felicity of his life, without noticing the deep-rooted sorrow of his wife; he was a common man, and of a common mind: his eye had not seen the awful beauty of her whom he had chosen; his spirit had not felt her power; and, if he had marked, he would not have understood her grief; so she ministered to him as a duty. She was a silent and obedient wife, but she saw him come home without joy, and witnessed his departure without regret; he neither added to nor diminished her sorrow: but destiny had one solitary blessing in store for the victim of its decrees—a child was born to the hapless Ruth, a lovely little girl soon slept upon her bosom, and, coming as it did, the one lone and lovely rosebud in her desolate garden, she welcomed it with a kindlier hope.

A few years went by unsoiled by the wretchedness which had marked the preceding: the joy of the mother softened the anguish of the condemned, and sometimes when she looked upon her daughter, she ceased to despair: but destiny had not forgotten her claim, and soon her hand pressed heavily upon her victim; the giant ocean rolled over the body of her husband, poverty visited the cottage of the widow, and famine's gaunt figure was visible in the distance. Oppression came with these, for arrears of rent demanded, and he who asked was brutal in his anger and harsh in his language to the sufferers.

Thus goaded, she saw but one thing that could save her, she fled from her persecutors to the home of her youth, and, leading her little Rachel by the hand, threw herself into the arms of her kin: they received her with distant kindness, and assured her that she should not want; in this they kept their promise, but it was all they did for Ruth and her daughter; a miserable subsistence was given to them, and that was embittered by distrust, and the knowledge that it was yielded unwillingly.

Among the villagers, although she was no longer shunned as formerly, her story was not forgotten; if it had been, her terrific beauty, the awful flashing of her eyes, her majestic stature, and solemn movements, would have recalled it to their recollections. She was a marked being, and all believed (though each would have pitied her, had they not been afraid) that evil destiny was not to be averted; she looked like one fated to some wonderful deed. They saw she was not one of them, and though they did not directly avoid her, yet they never threw themselves in her way, and thus the hapless Ruth had ample leisure to contemplate and grieve over her fate. One night she sat alone in her little hovel, and, with many bitter ruminations, was watching the happy sleep of her child, who slumbered tranquilly on their only bed: midnight had long passed, yet Ruth was not disposed to rest; she trimmed her dull light, and said mentally, 'Were I not poor, such a temptation might not assail me, riches would procure me deference; but poverty, or the wrongs it brings, may drive me to this evil; were I above want it would be less likely to be. O, my child, for thy sake would I avoid this doom more than for mine own, for if it should bring death to me, what will it not hurl on thee?—infamy, agony, scorn.'

She wept aloud as she spoke, and scarcely seemed to notice the singularity (at that late hour) of some one without, attempting to open the door; she heard, but the circumstance made little impression; she knew that as yet her doom was unfulfilled, and that, therefore, no danger could reach her; she was no coward at any time, but now despair had made her brave; the door opened, and a stranger entered, without either alarming or disturbing her, and it was not till he had stood face to face with Ruth, and discovered his features to be those of Rhys Meredith, that she sprung up from her seat, and gazed wildly and earnestly upon him.

Meredith gave her no time to question; 'Ruth Tudor,' said he, 'behold the cruellest of thy foes comes suing to thy pity and mercy; I have embittered thy existence, and doomed thee to a terrible lot; what first was dictated by vengeance and malice became truth as I uttered it, for what I spoke I believed. Yet, take comfort, some of my predictions have failed, and why may not this be false? In my own fate I have ever been deceived, perhaps I may be equally so in thine; in the mean time have pity upon him who was thy enemy, but who, when his vengeance was uttered, instantly became thy friend. I was poor, and thy scorn might have robbed me of subsistence in danger, and thy contempt might have given me up. Beggared by some disastrous events, hunted by creditors, I fled from my wife and son because I could no longer bear to contemplate their suffering; I have sought fortune all ways since we parted, and always has she eluded my grasp till last night, when she rather tempted than smiled upon me. At an idle fair I met the steward of this estate drunk and stupid, but loaded with gold; he travelled towards home alone; I could not, did not wrestle with the fiend that possessed me, but hastened to overtake him in his lonely ride. Start not! no hair of his head was harmed by me; of his gold I robbed him, but not of his life, though I had been the greater villain, I should now be in less danger, since he saw and marked my person: three hundred pounds is the meed of my daring, but I must keep it now or die. Ruth, thou too art poor and forsaken, but thou art faithful and kind, and wilt not betray me to justice; save me, and I will not enjoy my riches alone; thou knowest all the caves in the rocks, those hideous hiding places, where no foot, save thine, has dared to tread; conceal me in these till the pursuit be past, and I will give thee one half my wealth, and return with the other to gladden my wife and son.'

The hand of Ruth was already opened, and in imagination she grasped the wealth he promised; oppression and poverty had somewhat clouded the nobleness, but not the fierceness of her spirit. She saw that riches would save her from wrath, perhaps from blood, and, as the means to escape from so mighty an evil, she was not scrupulous respecting a lesser: independently of this, she felt a great interest in the safety of Rhys; her own fate seemed to hang upon his; she hid the ruffian in the caves and supplied him with light and food.

There was a happiness now in the heart of Ruth—a joy in her thoughts as she sat all the long day upon the deserted settle of her wretched fire-side, to which they had, for many years, been strangers. Many times during the past years of her sorrow she had thought of Rhys, and longed to look upon his face and sit under his shadow, as one whose presence could preserve her from the evil fate which he himself had predicted. She had long since forgiven him his prophecy; she believed he had spoken truth, and this gave a wild confidence in his power; a confidence that sometimes thought, 'if he can foreknow, can he not also avert?'

And she thought she would deserve his confidence, and support him in his suffering; she had concealed him in a deep dark cave, hewn far in the rock, to which she alone knew the entrance from the beach; there was another (if a huge aperture in the top of the rock might be so called), which, far from attempting to descend, the peasants and seekers for the culprit had scarcely dared to look into, so perpendicular, dark, and uncertain was the hideous descent into what justly appeared to them a bottomless abyss; they passed over his head in their search through the fields above, and before the mouth of his den upon the beach below, yet they left him in safety, though a little uncertain and afraid.

It was less wonderful, the suspicionless conduct of the villagers towards Ruth, than the calm prudence with which she conducted all the details relating to her secret; her poverty was well known, yet she daily procured a double portion of food, which was won by double labour; she toiled in the fields for the meed of oaten cake and potatoes, or she dashed out in a crazy boat on the wide ocean to win with the dredgers the spoils of the oyster beds that lie on its bosom; the daintier fare was for the unhappy guest, and daily did she wander among the rocks, when the tides were retiring, for the shellfish which they had flung among the fissures in their retreat, which she bore, exhausted with fatigue, to her home—and which her lovely child, now rising into womanhood, prepared for the luxurious meal; it was wonderful too, the settled prudence of the little maiden, who spoke nothing of the food which was borne from their frugal board; if she suspected the secret of her mother, she respected it too much to allow others to discover that she did so.

Many sad hours did Ruth pass in the robber's cave; and many times, by conversing with him upon the subject of her destiny, did she seek to alleviate the pangs its recollection gave her; but the result of such discussions were by no means favourable to her hopes; Rhys had acknowledged that his threat had originated in malice, and that he intended to alarm and subdue, but not to the extent that he had effected: —'I know well,' said he, 'that disgrace alone would operate upon you as I wished, for I foresaw you would glory in the thought of nobly sustaining misfortune; I meant to degrade you with the lowest; I meant to attribute to you what I now painfully experience to be the vilest of the vices; I intended to tell you, you were destined to be a thief, but I could not utter the words I had arranged, and I was struck with horror at those I heard involuntarily proceeding from my lips; I would have re-called them but I could not; I would have said, "Maiden, I did but jest," but there was something that seemed to withold my speech and press upon my soul, "so as thou hast said shall this thing be"—yet take comfort, my own fortunes have ever deceived me, and doubtlessly ever will, for I feel as if I should one day return to this cave and make it my final home.'

He spoke solemnly and wept—but the awful eye of his com-panion was unmoved as she looked on in wonder and contempt at his grief. 'Thou knowest not how to endure,' said she to him, 'and as soon as night shall again fall upon our mountains, I will lead thee forth on thy escape; the danger of pursuit is now past; at midnight be ready for thy journey, leave the cave, and ascend the rocks by the path I shewed thee, to the field in which its mouth is situated; wait me there a few moments, and I will bring thee a fleet horse, ready saddled for the journey, for which thy gold must pay, since I must declare to the owner that I have sold it at a distance, and for more than its rated value.'

That midnight came, and Meredith waited with trembling anxiety for the haughty step of Ruth; at length he saw her, and hastily speaking as she descended the rock:

'You must be speedy in your movements,' said she, 'when you leave me; your horse waits on the other side of this field, and I would have you hasten, lest his neighings should betray your purpose. But, before you depart, Rhys Meredith, there is an ac-count to be settled between us: I have dared danger and privation for you; that the temptations of the poor may not assail me, give me my reward, and go.'

Rhys pressed his leathern bag to his bosom, but answered nothing to the speech of Ruth: he seemed to be studying some evasion, for he looked upon the ground, and there was trouble in the working of his lip. At length he said cautiously, 'I have it not with me; I buried it, lest it should betray me, in a field some miles distant; when I go thither I will dig it up, and send it to thee from the place of my destination.'

Ruth gave him one glance of her awful eye when he had spoken; she had detected his meanness, and smiled at his capacity to deceive. 'What dost thou press to thy bosom so earnestly?' she demanded; 'surely thou art not the wise man I deemed thee, thus to defraud my claim: thy friend alone thou mightest cheat, and safely: but I have been made wretched by thee, guilty by thee, and thy life is in my power; I could, as thou knowest, easily raise the village, and win half thy wealth by giving thee up to justice; but I prefer reward from thy wisdom and gratitude; give, therefore, and be gone.'

But Rhys knew too well the value of the metal of sin to yield one half of it to Ruth; he tried many miserable shifts and lies, and at last, baffled by the calm penetration of his antagonist, boldly avowed his intention of keeping all the spoil he had won with so much hazard. Ruth looked at him with scorn, 'Keep thy gold,' she said; 'if it can thus harden hearts, I covet not its possession; but there is one thing thou must do, and that ere thou movest thy foot. I have supported thee with hard earned industry—that I give thee; more proud, it should seem, in bestowing I could be, from such as thee, in receiving: but the horse that is to bear thee hence tonight I borrowed for a distant journey; I must return with it, or its value; open thy bag, pay me for that, and go.'

But Rhys seemed afraid to open his bag in the presence of her he had wronged. Ruth understood his fears; but, scorning vindication of her principles, contented herself with entreating him to be honest, 'Be more just to thyself and me,' she persisted: 'the debt of gratitude I pardon thee; but, I beseech thee, leave me not to encounter the consequence of having stolen from my friend the animal which is his only means of subsistence; I pray thee, Rhys, not to condemn me to scorn.'

It was to no avail that Ruth humbled herself to entreaties; Meredith answered not, and while she was yet speaking, cast sidelong looks towards the spot where the horse was waiting for his service, and seemed meditating whether he should not dart from Ruth, and escape her entreaties and demands by dint of speed. Her stern eye detected his purpose; and, indignant at his baseness, and ashamed of her own degradation, she sprung suddenly towards him, made a desperate clutch at the leathern bag, and tore it from the grasp of the deceiver. Meredith made an attempt to recover it, and a fierce struggle ensued, which drove them both back towards the yawning mouth of the cave from which he had just ascended to the world. On its very verge, on its very extreme edge, the demon who had so long ruled his spirit now instigated him to mischief, and abandoned him to his natural brutality: he struck the unhappy Ruth a revengeful and tremendous blow. At that moment a horrible thought glanced like lightning through her soul; he was to her no longer what he had been; he was a robber, ruffian, liar; one whom to destroy was justice, and perhaps it was he—
'Villain!' she cried, 'thou—thou didst predict that I was doomed to be a murderer! art thou—art thou destined to be the victim?' She flung him from her with terrific force, as he stood close to the abyss, and the next instant heard him dash against its sides, as he was whirled headlong into the darkness.

It was an awful feeling, the next that passed over the soul of Ruth Tudor, as she stood alone in the pale sorrowful-moonlight, endeavouring to remember what had chanced. She gazed on the purse, on the chasm, wiped the drops of agony from her heated brow, and then, with a sudden pang of recollection, rushed down to the cavern. The light was still burning, as Rhys had left it, and served to shew her the wretch extended helplessly beneath the chasm. Though his body was crushed, the bones splintered, and his blood was on the cavern's sides, he was yet living, and raised his head to look upon her, as she darkened the narrow entrance in her passage: he glared upon her with the visage of a demon, and spoke like a fiend in pain. 'Me hast thou murdered!' he said, 'but I shall be avenged in all the life to come. Deem not that thy doom is fulfilled, that the deed to which thou art fated is done: in my dying hour I know, I feel what is to come of thee; thou art yet again to do a deed of blood!' 'Liar!' shrieked the infuriated victim. 'Thou art yet doomed to be a murderer!' 'Liar!' 'Thou art—and of—thine only child!' She rushed to him, but he was dead.

Ruth Tudor stood for a moment by the corpse, blind, stupefied, deaf, and dumb; in the next she laughed aloud, till the cavern rung with her ghastly mirth, and many voices mingled with and answered it; but the voices scared and displeased her, and in an instant she became stupidly grave; she threw back her dark locks with an air of offended dignity, and walked forth majestically from the cave. She took the horse by his rein, and led him back to the stable: with the same unvarying calmness she entered her cottage, and listened to the quiet breathings of her sleeping child; she longed to approach her nearer, but some new and horrid fear restrained her, and held back her anxious step: suddenly remembrance and reason returned, and she uttered a shriek, so loud and shrill, that her daughter sprung from her bed, and threw herself into her arms.

It was in vain that the gentle Rachel supplicated her mother to find rest in sleep. 'Not here,' she muttered, 'it must not be here; the deep cave and the hard rock, these shall be my resting place; and the bed-fellow, lo! now, he waits my coming.' Then she would cry aloud, clasp her Rachel to her beating heart, and as suddenly, in horror thrust her from it.

The next midnight beheld Ruth Tudor in the cave, seated upon a point of rock, at the head of the corpse, her chin resting upon her hands, gazing earnestly upon the distorted face. Decay had already begun its work; and Ruth sat there watching the progress of mortality, as if she intended that her stern eye should quicken and facilitate its operation. The next night also beheld her there, but the current of her thoughts had changed, and the dismal interval which had passed appeared to be forgotten. She stood with her basket of food: 'Wilt thou not eat!' she demanded; 'arise, strengthen thee for thy journey; eat, eat, thou sleeper; wilt thou never awaken? Look, here is the meat thou lovest'; and as she raised his head, and put the food to his lips, the frail remnant of mortality shattered at her touch, and again she knew that he was dead.

It was evident to all that a shadow and a change was over the senses of Ruth; till this period she had been only wretched, but now madness was mingled with her grief. It was in no instance more apparent than in her conduct towards her beloved child: indulgent to all her wishes, ministering to all her wants with a liberal hand, till men wondered from whence she derived the means of indulgence, she yet seized every opportunity to send her from her presence. The gentle-hearted Rachel wept at her conduct, yet did not complain, for she believed it the effect of the disease, that had for so many years been preying upon her soul. Her nights were passed in roaming abroad, her days in the solitude of her hut; and even this became painful, when the step of her child broke upon it. At length she signified that a relative of her husband had died and left her wealth, and that it would enable her to dispose of herself as she had long wished; so leaving Rachel with her relatives, she retired to a hut upon a lonely heath, where she was less wretched, because abandoned to her wretchedness.

In many of her ravings she had frequently spoken darkly of her crime, and her nightly visits to the cave; and more frequently still she addressed some unseen thing, which she asserted was for ever at her side. But few heard these horrors, and those who did, called to mind the early prophecy, and deemed them the workings of insanity in a fierce and imaginative mind. So thought also the beloved Rachel, who hastened daily to embrace her mother, but not now alone as formerly; a youth of the village was her companion and protector, one who had offered her worth and love, and whose gentle offers were not rejected. Ruth, with a hurried gladness, gave her consent, and a blessing to her child; and it was remarked that she received her daughter more kindly, and detained her longer at the cottage, when Evan was by her side, than when she went to the gloomy heath alone. Rachel herself soon made this observation, and as she could depend upon the honesty and prudence of him she loved, she felt less fear at his being a frequent witness of her mother's terrific ravings. Thus all that human consolation was capable to afford was offered to the sufferer by her sympathising children.

But the delirium of Ruth Tudor appeared to increase with every nightly visit to the secret cave of blood; some hideous shadow seemed to follow her steps in the darkness, and sit by her side in the light. Sometimes she held strange parley with this creation of her frenzy, and at others smiled upon it in scornful silence; now, her language was in the tones of entreaty, pity, and forgiveness; anon, it was the burst of execration, curses, and scorn. To the gentle listeners her words were blasphemy; and, shuddering at her boldness, they deemed, in the simple holiness of their own hearts, that the evil one was besetting her, and that religion alone could banish him. Possessed by this idea, Evan one day suddenly interrupted her tremendous denunciations upon her fate, and him who, she said, stood over her to fulfil it, with imploring her to open the book which he held in his hand, and seek consolation from its words and its promises. She listened, and grew calm in a moment; with an awful smile she bade him open, and read at the first place which should meet his eye: 'From that, the word of truth, as thou sayest, I shall know my fate; what is there written I will believe.' He opened the book, and read:

'Whither shall I go from thy spirit, or whither shall I flee from thy presence? If I go up into heaven, thou art there: if I make my bed in hell, thou art there; if I take the wings of the morning, and dwell in the uttermost parts of the sea, even there shall thy hand lead me, and thy right hand shall hold me.'

Ruth laid her hand upon the book: 'It is enough; its words are truth; it hath said there is no hope, and I find comfort in my despair: I have already spoken thus in the secrecy of my heart, and I know that he will be obeyed; the unnamed sin must be—.' Evan knew not how to comfort, so he shut up his book and retired; and Rachel kissed the cheek of her mother, as she bade her a tender goodnight. Another month and she was to be the bride of Evan, and she passed over the heath with a light step, for the thought of her bridal seemed to give joy to her mother. 'We shall all be happy then,' said the smiling girl, as the youth of her heart parted from her hand for the night; 'and heaven kindly grant that happiness may last.'

The time appointed for the marriage of Rachel Tudor and Evan Edwards had long passed away, and winter had set in with unusual sternness even on that stormy coast; when, during a land tempest, on a dark November afternoon, a stranger to the country, journeying on foot, lost his way in endeavouring to find a short route in his destination, over stubble fields and meadow lands, by following the footmarks of those who had preceded him. The stranger was a young man, of a bright eye and a hardy look, and he went on buffeting the elements, and buffeted by them, without a thought of weariness, or a single expression of impatience. Night descended upon him as he walked, and the snow-storm came down with unusual violence, as if to try the temper of his mind, a mind cultivated and enlightened, though cased in a frame accustomed to hardships, and veiled by a plain, nay, almost rustic exterior. The thunder roared loudly above him, and the wind blowing tremendously, raised the new-fallen snow from the earth, which, mingling with the showers as they fell, raised a clatter about his head which bewildered and blinded the traveller, who, finding himself near some leafless brambles and a few clustered bushes of the mountain broom, took shelter under them to recover his senses, and reconnoitre his position. 'Of all these ingredients for a storm,' said he, smilingly to himself, 'the lightning is the most endurable after all; for if it does not kill, it may at least cure, by lighting the way out of a labyrinth, and by its bright flashes, I hope to discover where I am.' In this hope he was not mistaken: the brilliant and beautiful gleam shewed him, when the snow shower had somewhat abated, every stunted bush and blade of grass for some miles, and something, about the distance of one, that looked like a white-washed cottage of some poor encloser of the miserable heath upon which he was now standing. Full of hope of a shelter from the storm, and, lit onwards by the magnificent torch of heaven, the stranger trod cheerily forwards, and in less than half an hour, making full allowance for his retrograding between the flashes, arrived at his beacon the white cottage, which, from the low wall of loose limestones by which it was surrounded, he judged to be, as he had already imagined, the humble residence of some poor tenant of the manor. He opened the little gate, and was proceeding to knock at the door, when his steps were arrested by a singular and unexpected sound; it was a choral burst of many voices, singing slowly and solemnly that magnificent dirge of the church of England, the 104th psalm. The stranger loved music, and the sombrous melody of that fine air had an instant effect upon his feelings; he lingered in solemn and silent admiration till the majestic strain had ceased; he then knocked gently at the door, which was instantly and courteously opened to his enquiry.

On entering, he found himself in a cottage of a more respectable interior than from its outward appearance he had been led to expect: but he had little leisure or inclination for the survey of its effects, for his senses and imagination were immediately and entirely occupied by the scene which presented itself on his entrance. In the centre of the room into which he had been so readily admitted, stood, on its tressels, an open coffin; lights were at its head and foot, and on each side sat many persons of both sexes, who appeared to be engaged in the customary ceremony of watching the corpse previous to its interment in the morning. There were many who appeared to the stranger to be watchers, but there were but two who, in his eye, bore the appearance of mourners, and they had faces of grief which spoke too plainly of the anguish that was reigning within: one at the foot of the coffin, was a pale youth just blooming into manhood, who covered his dewy eyes with trembling fingers that ill concealed the tears which trickled down his wan cheek, beneath: the other—; but why should we again describe that still unbowed and lofty form? The awful marble brow upon which the stranger gazed, was that of Ruth Tudor.

There was much whispering and quiet talk among the people while refreshments were handed amongst them; and so little curiosity was excited by the appearance of the traveller, that he naturally concluded that it must be no common loss that could deaden a feeling usually so intense in the bosoms of Welsh peasants: he was even checked for an attempt to question; but one man—he who had given him admittance, and seemed to possess authority in the circle—informed the traveller that he would answer his questions when the guests should depart, but till then he must keep silence. The traveller endeavoured to obey, and sat down in quiet contemplation of the figure who most interested his attention, and who sat at the coffin's head. Ruth Tudor spoke nothing, nor did she appear to heed aught of the business that was passing around her. Absorbed by reflection, her eyes were generally cast to the ground; but when they were raised the traveller looked in vain for that expression of grief which had struck him so forcibly on his entrance; there was something wonderfully strange in the character of her perfect features: could he have found words for his thought, and might have been permitted the expression, he would have called it triumphant despair; so deeply agonised, so proudly stern, looked the mourner who sat by the dead.

The interest which the traveller took in the scene became more intense the longer he gazed upon its action; unable to resist the anxiety which had begun to prey upon his spirit, he arose and walked towards the coffin, with the purpose of contemplating its inhabitant: a sad explanation was given, by its appearance, of the grief and the anguish he had witnessed; a beautiful girl was reposing in the narrow house, with a face as calm and lovely as if she but slept a deep and refreshing sleep, and the morning sun would again smile upon her awakening: salt, the emblem of immortal soul, was placed upon her breast; and, in her pale and perishing fingers, a branch of living flowers were struggling for life in the grasp of death, and diffusing their sweet and gracious fragrance over the cold odour of mortality. These images, so opposite, yet so alike, affected the spirit of the gazer, and he almost wept as he continued looking upon them, till he was aroused from his trance by the strange conduct of Ruth Tudor, who had caught a glimpse of his face as he bent in sorrow over the coffin. She sprung up from her seat, and darting at him a terrible glance of recognition, pointed down to the corpse, and then, with a hollow burst of frantic laughter, shouted—'Behold thou liar!'

The startled stranger was relieved from the necessity of speaking by some one taking his arm and gently leading him to the farther end of the cottage: the eyes of Ruth followed him, and it was not till he had done violence to himself in turning from her to his conductor, that he could escape their singular fascination. When he did so, he beheld a venerable man, the pastor of a distant village, who had come that night to speak comfort to the mourners, and perform the last sad duty to the dead on the morrow. 'Be not alarmed at what you have witnessed, my young friend,' said he; 'these ravings are not uncommon: this unhappy woman, at an early period of her life, gave ear to the miserable superstitions of her country, and a wretched pretender to wisdom predicted that she should become a shedder of blood: madness has been the inevitable consequence in an ardent spirit, and in its ravings she dreams she has committed one sin, and is still tempted to add to another.'

'You may say what you please, parson,' said the old man who had given admittance to the stranger, and who now, after dismissing all the guests save the youth, joined the talkers, and seated himself on the settle by their side, 'You may say what you please about madness and superstition; but I know Ruth Tudor was a fated woman, and the deed that was to be I believe she has done: aye, aye, her madness is conscience; and if the deep sea and the jagged rocks could speak, they might tell us a tale of other things than that: but she is judged now; her only child is gone—her pretty Rachel. Poor Evan! he was her suitor: ah! he little thought two months ago, when he was preparing for a gay bridal, that her slight sickness would end thus: he does not deserve it; but for her —God forgive me if I do her wrong, but I think it is the hand of God, and it lies heavy, as it should.' And the grey-haired old man hobbled away, satisfied that in thus thinking he was shewing his zeal for virtue.

'Alas! that so white a head should acknowledge so hard a heart!' said the pastor; 'Ruth is condemned, according to his system, for committing that which a mightier hand compelled her to do; how harsh and misjudging is age! But we must not speak so loud,' continued he; 'for see, the youth Evan is retiring for the night, and the miserable mother has thrown herself on the floor to sleep; the sole domestic is rocking on her stool, and therefore I will do the honours of this poor cottage to you. There is a chamber above this, containing the only bed in the hut; thither you may go and rest, for otherwise it will certainly be vacant tonight: I shall find a bed in the village; and Evan sleeps near you with some of the guests in the barn. But, before I go, if my question be not unwelcome and intrusive, tell me who you are, and whither you are bound.'

'I was ever somewhat of a subscriber to the old man's creed of fatalism,' said the stranger, smiling, 'and I believe I am more confirmed in it by the singular events of this day, My father was a man of a certain rank in society, but of selfish and disorderly habits. A course of extravagance and idleness was succeeded by difficulties and distress. Harassed by creditors, he was pained by their demands, and his selfishness was unable to endure the sufferings of his wife and children. Instead of exertion, he had recourse to flight, and left us to face the difficulties from which he shrunk. He was absent for years, while his family toiled and struggled with success. Suddenly we heard that he was concealed in this part of the coast; the cause which made that concealment necessary I forbear to mention; but as he suddenly disappeared from the eyes of men, though we never could trace him beyond this part of the country. I have always believed that I should one day find my father, and have lately, though with difficulty, prevailed upon my mother to allow me to make my residence in this neighbourhood; but my search is at an end today—I believe that I have found my father. Roaming along the beach, I penetrated into several of those dark caverns of the rocks, which might well, by their rugged aspects, deter the idle and the timid from entering. Through the fissures of one I discovered, in the interior, a light. Surprised, I penetrated to its concealment, and discovered a man sleeping on the ground. I advanced to awake him, and found but a fleshless skeleton, cased in tattered and decaying garments. He had probably met his death by accident, for exactly over the corpse I observed, at a terrific distance, the day-light, as if streaming down from an aperture above. Thus the wretched man must have fallen, but how long since, or who had discovered his body, and left the light which I beheld, I knew not, though I cannot help cherishing a strong conviction that it was the body of Rhys Meredith that I saw.'

'Who talks of Rhys Meredith,' said a stern voice near the coffin, 'and of the cave where the outcast rots?' They turned quickly at the sound, and beheld Ruth Tudor standing up, as if she had been intently listening to the story. 'It was I who spoke, dame,' said the stranger gently, 'and my speech was of my father, of Rhys Meredith; I am Owen his son.'

'Son! Owen Rhys!' said the bewildered Ruth, passing her hand over her forehead, as if to enable her to recover the combinations of these names; 'and who art thou, that thus givest human ties to him who is no more of humanity? Why speakest thou of living things as pertaining to the dead? Father! he is father to nought save sin, and murder is his only begotten!'

She advanced to the traveller as she spoke, and again caught a view of his face; again he saw the wild look of recognition, and an unearthly shriek followed the convulsive horror of her face. 'There! there!' she said, 'I knew it must be thyself; once before tonight have I beheld thee, yet what can thy coming bode? Back with thee, ruffian! for is not thy dark work done?'

'Let us leave her,' said the good pastor, 'to the care of her attendant; do not continue to meet her gaze; your presence may increase, but cannot allay her malady: go up to your bed and rest.'

He retired as he spoke; and Owen, in compliance with his wish, ascended the ruinous stair which led to his chamber, after he had beheld Ruth Tudor quietly place herself in her seat at the open coffin's head. The room to which he mounted was not of the most cheering aspect, yet he felt that he had often slept soundly in a worse. It was a gloomy unfinished chamber, and the wind was whistling coldly and drearily through the uncovered rafters above his head. Like many of the cottages in that part of the country, it appeared to have grown old and ruinous before it had been finished; for the flooring was so crazy as scarcely to support the huge wooden bedstead, and in many instances the boards were entirely separated from each other, and in the centre, time, or the rot, had so completely devoured the larger half of one, that through the gaping aperture Owen had entire command of the room and the party below, looking down immediately above the coffin. Ruth was in the same attitude as when he left her, and the servant girl was dozing by her side. Everything being perfectly tranquil, Owen threw himself upon his hard couch, and endeavoured to compose himself to rest for the night, but this had become a task, and one of no easy nature to surmount; his thoughts still wandered to the events of the day, and he felt there was some strange connexion between the scene he had just witnessed, and the darker one of the secret cave. He was an imaginative man, and of a quick and feverish temperament, and he thought of Ruth Tudor's ravings, and the wretched skeleton of the rock, till he had worked out in his brain the chain of events that linked one consequence with the other: he grew restless and wretched, and amidst the tossings of impatient anxiety fatigue overpowered him, and he sunk into a perturbed and heated sleep. His slumber was broken by dreams that might well be the shadows of his waking reveries. He was alone (as in reality) upon his humble bed, when imagination brought to his ear the sound of many voices again singing the slow and monotonous psalm; it was interrupted by the outcries of some unseen things who attempted to enter his chamber, and, amid yells of fear and execrations of anger, bade him 'Arise, and come forth, and aid': then the coffined form which slept so quietly below, stood by his side, and in beseeching accents, bade him 'Arise and save her.' In his sleep he attempted to spring up, but a horrid fear restrained him, a fear that he should be too late; then he crouched like a coward beneath his coverings, to hide from the reproaches of the spectre, while shouts of laughter and shrieks of agony were poured like a tempest around him: he sprung from his bed and awoke.

It was some moments ere he could recover recollection, or shake off the horror which had seized upon his soul. He listened, and with infinite satisfaction observed an unbroken silence throughout the house. He smiled at his own terrors, attributed them to the events of the day, or the presence of a corpse, and determined not to look down into the lower room till he should be summoned thither in the morning. He walked to the casement, and looked abroad to the night; the clouds were many, black, and lowering, and the face of the sky looked angrily at the wind, and glared portentously upon the earth; the sleet was still falling; distant thunder announced the approach or departure of a storm, and Owen marked the clouds coming from afar towards him, laden with the rapid and destructive lightning: he shut the casement and returned towards his bed; but the light from below attracted his eye, and he could not pass the aperture without taking one glance at the party.

They were in the same attitude in which he had left them; the servant was sleeping, but Ruth was earnestly gazing on the lower end of the room upon something, without the sight of Owen; his attention was next fixed upon the corpse, and he thought he had never seen any living thing so lovely; and so calm was the aspect of her repose, that it more resembled a temporary suspension of the faculties, than the eternal stupor of death, her features were pale, but not distorted, and there was none of the livid hue of death in her beautiful mouth and lips; but the flowers in her hand gave stronger demonstration of the presence of the power, before whose potency their little strength was fading; drooping with a mortal sickness, they bowed down their heads in submission, as one by one they dropped from her pale and perishing fingers. Owen gazed, till he thought he saw the grasp of her hand relax, and a convulsive smile pass over her cold and rigid features; he looked again; the eye-lids shook and vibrated like the string of some fine strung instrument; the hair rose, and the head cloth moved; he started up ashamed: 'Does the madness of this woman affect all who would sleep beneath her roof?' said he; 'what is this that disturbs me—or am I yet in a dream? Hark! what is that?' It was the voice of Ruth; she had risen from her seat, and was standing near the coffin, apparently addressing someone who stood at the lower end of the room: 'To what purpose is thy coming now?' said she, in a low and melancholy voice, 'and at what cost thou laugh and gibe? Lo! you; she is here, and the sin you know of, cannot be; how can I take the life which another hath already withdrawn? Go, go, hence to thy cave of night, for this is no place of safety for thee.' Her thoughts now took another turn; she seemed to hide one from the pursuit of others; 'Lie still! lie still!' she whispered; 'put out thy light! so so, they pass by and mark thee not; thou art safe; good night, good night! now will I home to sleep'; and she seated herself in her chair, as if composing her senses to rest.

Owen was again bewildered in the chaos of thought, but for this time he determined to subdue his imagination, and, throwing himself upon his bed, again gave himself up to sleep; but the images of his former dreams still haunted him, and their hideous phantasms were more powerfully renewed; again he heard the solemn psalm of death, but unsung by mortals—it was pealed through earth up to the high heaven, by myriads of the viewless and the mighty: again heard the execrations of millions for some un-remembered sin, and the wrath and the hatred of a world was rushing upon him: 'Come forth! come forth!' was the cry; and amid yells and howls they were darting upon him, when the pale form of the beautiful dead arose between them, and shielded him from their malice; but he heard her say aloud, 'It is for this, that thou wilt not save me; arise, arise, and help!'

He sprung up as he was commanded: sleeping or waking he never knew; but he started from his bed to look down into the chamber, as he heard the voice of Ruth loud in terrific denuncia-tion: he looked: she was standing, uttering yells of madness and rage, and close to her was a well-known form of appalling recollec-tion—his father, as he had seen him last; he arose and darted to the door: 'I am mad,' said he; 'I am surely mad, or this is still a continuation of my dream': he looked again; Ruth was still there, but alone.

But, though no visible form stood by the maniac, some fiend had entered her soul, and mastered her mighty spirit; she had armed herself with an axe, and shouting, 'Liar, liar, hence!' was pursuing some imaginary foe to the darker side of the cottage: Owen strove hard to trace her motions, but as she had retreated under the space occupied by his bed, he could no longer see her, and his eyes involuntarily fastened themselves upon the coffin; there a new horror met them; the dead corpse had risen, and with wild and glaring eyes was watching the scene before her. Owen distrusted his senses till he heard the terrific voice of Ruth, as she marked the miracle he had witnessed; 'The fiend, the robber!' she yelled, 'it is he who hath entered the pure body of my child. Back to thy cave of blood, thou lost one! back to thine own dark hell!' Owen flew to the door; it was too late, he heard the shriek—the blow: he fell into the room, but only in time to hear the second blow, and see the cleft hand of the hapless Rachel fall back upon its bloody pillow; his terrible cries brought in the sleepers from the barn, headed by the wretched Evan, and, for a time, the thunders of heaven were drowned in the clamorous grief of man. No one dared to approach the miserable Ruth, who now, in utter frenzy, strode around the room, brandishing, with diabolical grandeur, the bloody axe, and singing a wild song of triumph and joy. All fell back as she approached, and shrunk from the infernal majesty of her terrific form; and the thunders of heaven rolling above their heads, and the flashings of the fires of eternity in their eyes, were less terrible than the savage glare and desperate wrath of the maniac: suddenly, the house rocked to its foundation; its inmates were blinded for a moment, and sunk, felled by a stunning blow, to the earth; slowly each man recovered and arose, wondering he was yet alive; all were unhurt, save one. Ruth Tudor was on the earth, her blackened limbs prostrate beneath the coffin of her child, and her dead cheek resting on the rent and bloody axe; it had been the destroyer of both.

THE INVISIBLE GIRL

by Mary Shelley

MARY WOLLSTONECRAFT SHELLEY
*(1797–1851) wrote the most famous and enduring horror
novel to emerge during the Gothic period,* Frankenstein, *in
1818. Like Mrs Curtis, the author of the previous story, Mary
Shelley lived a flamboyant and spirited life. She was born
the daughter of the social and political reformer, William
Godwin, and his wife, the pioneer feminist Mary Wollstonecraft. As a young girl she became the mistress and eventual
wife of the poet, Percy Shelley, and obviously influenced his
life greatly. She was an enthusiastic traveller, and apart from
many and varied wanderings on the Continent with Shelley,
also journeyed throughout England. Their lengthy sojourn
in Wales deeply affected both of them; Shelley wrote several
poems praising 'thy matchless vales' while Mary found the
source material for several short stories—including the remarkable tale which follows here. (Another friend and confidante
of the Shelleys, Matthew Lewis, was also a great lover of
Wales and set perhaps his most famous play,* The Castle
Spectre, *in Conway Castle.) 'The Invisible Girl' was written
by Mary Shelley after her husband's death in 1822, but the
notes on which it is based undoubtedly date from the period
when the couple 'journeyed with much delight through the
great fastness of Wales'.*

This slender narrative has no pretensions to the regularity of a
story, or the development of situations and feelings; it is but a
slight sketch, delivered nearly as it was narrated to me by one
of the humblest of the actors concerned: nor will I spin out a

circumstance interesting principally from its singularity and truth, but narrate, as concisely as I can, how I was surprised on visiting what seemed a ruined tower, crowning a bleak promontory over-hanging the sea, that flows between Wales and Ireland, to find that though the exterior preserved all the savage rudeness that be-tokened many a war with the elements, the interior was fitted up somewhat in the guise of a summer-house, for it was too small to deserve any other name. It consisted but of the ground-floor, which served as an entrance, and one room above, which was reached by a staircase made out of the thickness of the wall. This chamber was floored and carpeted, decorated with elegant furniture; and, above all, to attract the attention and excite curiosity, there hung over the chimney-piece—for to preserve the apartment from damp a fireplace had been built evidently since it had assumed a guise so dissimilar to the object of its construction—a picture simply painted in water-colours, which seemed more than any part of the adornments of the room to be at war with the rudeness of the building, the solitude in which it was placed, and the desolation of the surrounding scenery. This drawing represented a lovely girl in the very pride and bloom of youth; her dress was simple, in the fashion of the beginning of the eighteenth century; her countenance was embellished by a look of mingled innocence and intelligence, to which was added the imprint of serenity of soul and natural cheerfulness. She was reading one of those folio romances which have so long been the delight of the enthusiastic and young; her mandoline was at her feet—her parroquet perched on a huge mirror near her; the arrangement of furniture and hangings gave token of a luxurious dwelling, and her attire also evidently that of home and privacy, yet bore with it an appearance of ease and girlish ornament, as if she wished to please. Beneath this picture was inscribed in golden letters, 'The Invisible Girl'.

Rambling about a country nearly uninhabited, having lost my way, and being overtaken by a shower, I had lighted on this dreary looking tenement, which seemed to rock in the blast, and to be hung up there as the very symbol of desolation. I was gazing wist-fully and cursing inwardly my stars which led me to a ruin that could afford no shelter, though the storm began to pelt more seriously than before, when I saw an old woman's head popped out from a kind of loophole, and as suddenly withdrawn; a minute after a feminine voice called to me from within, and penetrating a little brambly maze that screened a door, which I had not before observed, so skilfully had the planter succeeded in concealing art with nature, I found the good dame standing on the threshold and inviting me to take refuge within. 'I had just come up from our cot hard by,' she said, 'to look after the things, as I do every day, when the rain came on—will ye walk up till it is over?' I was about to observe that the cot hard by, at the venture of a few rain drops, was better than a ruined tower, and to ask my kind hostess whether 'the things' were pigeons or crows that she was come to look after, when the matting of the floor and the carpeting of the staircase struck my eye. I was still more surprised when I saw the room above; and beyond all, the picture and its singular inscription, naming her invisible, whom the painter had coloured forth into very agreeable visibility, awakened my most lively curiosity; the result of this, of my exceeding politeness towards the old woman, and her own natural garrulity, was a kind of garbled narrative which my imagination eked out, and future inquiries rectified, till it assumed the following form.

Some years before, in the afternoon of a September day, which, though tolerably fair, gave many tokens of a tempestuous night, a gentleman arrived at a little coast town about ten miles from this place; he expressed his desire to hire a boat to carry him to the town of —— about fifteen miles farther on the coast. The menaces which the sky held forth made the fishermen loathe to venture, till at length two, one the father of a numerous family, bribed by the bountiful reward the stranger promised, the other, the son of my hostess, induced by youthful daring, agreed to undertake the voyage. The wind was fair, and they hoped to make good way before nightfall, and to get into port ere the rising of the storm. They pushed off with good cheer, at least the fishermen did; as for the stranger, the deep mourning which he wore was not half so black as the melancholy that wrapt his mind. He looked as if he had never smiled—as if some unutterable thought, dark as night and bitter as death, had built its nest within his bosom, and brooded therein eternally; he did not mention his name; but one of the villagers recognised him as Henry Vernon, the son of a baronet who possessed a mansion about three miles distant from the town for which he was bound. This mansion was almost abandoned by the family; but Henry had, in a romantic fit, visited it about three years before, and Sir Peter had been down there during the previous spring for about a couple of months.

The boat did not make so much way as was expected; the breeze failed them as they got out to sea, and they were fain with oar as well as sail to try to weather the promontory that jutted out between them and the spot they desired to reach. They were yet far distant when the shifting wind began to exert its strength, and to blow with violent though unequal blasts. Night came on pitchy dark, and the howling waves rose and broke with frightful violence, menacing to overwhelm the tiny bark that dared resist their fury. They were forced to lower every sail, and take to their oars; one man was obliged to bale out the water, and Vernon himself took an oar, and rowing with desperate energy, equalled the force of the more practised boatmen. There had been much talk between the sailors before the tempest came on; now, except a brief command, all were silent. One thought of his wife and children, and silently cursed the caprice of the stranger that endangered in its effect, not only his life, but their welfare; the other feared less, for he was a daring lad, but he worked hard, and had no time for speech; while Vernon bitterly regretting the thoughtlessness which had made him cause others to share a peril, unimportant as far as he himself was concerned, now tried to cheer them with a voice full of animation and courage, and now pulled yet more strongly at the oar he held. The only person who did not seem wholly intent on the work he was about, was the man who baled; every now and then he gazed intently round, as if the sea held afar off, on its tumultuous waste, some object that he strained his eyes to discern. But all was blank, except as the crests of the high waves showed themselves, or far out on the verge of the horizon, a kind of lifting of the clouds betokened greater violence for the blast. At length he exclaimed, 'Yes, I see it!—the larboard oar!—now! if we can make yonder light, we are saved!' Both the rowers instinctively turned their heads—but cheerless darkness answered their gaze.

'You cannot see it,' cried their companion, 'but we are nearing it; and, please God, we shall outlive this night.' Soon he took the oar from Vernon's hand, who, quite exhausted, was failing in his strokes. He rose and looked for the beacon which promised them safety; it glimmered with so faint a ray, that now he said, 'I see it'; and again, 'it is nothing': still, as they made way, it dawned upon his sight, growing more steady and distinct as it beamed across the lurid waters, which themselves became smoother, so that safety seemed to arise from the bosom of the ocean under the influence of that flickering gleam.

'What beacon is it that helps us at our need?' asked Vernon, as the men, now able to manage their oars with greater ease, found breath to answer his question.

'A fairy one, I believe,' replied the elder sailor, 'yet no less a true: it burns in an old tumble-down tower, built on the top of a rock which looks over the sea. We never saw it before this summer; and now each night it is to be seen—at least when it is looked for, for we cannot see it from our village—and it is such an out-of-the-way place that no one has need to go near it, except through a chance like this. Some say it is burnt by witches, some say by smugglers; but this I know, two parties have been to search, and found nothing, but the bare walls of the tower. All is deserted by day, and dark by night; for no light was to be seen while we were there, though it burned sprightly enough when we were out at sea.'

'I have heard say,' observed the younger sailor, 'it is burnt by the ghost of a maiden who lost her sweetheart in these parts; he being wrecked, and his body found at the foot of the tower: she goes by the name among us of the "Invisible Girl".'

The voyagers had now reached the landing-place at the foot of the tower. Vernon cast a glance upward—the light was still burning. With some difficulty, struggling with the breakers, and blinded by night, they contrived to get their little bark to shore, and to draw her up on the beach. They then scrambled up the precipitous pathway, overgrown by weeds and underwood, and, guided by the more experienced fisherman, they found the entrance to the tower;

door or gate there was none, and all was dark as the tomb, and silent and almost as cold as death.

'This will never do,' said Vernon; 'surely our hostess will show her light, if not herself, and guide our darkling steps by some sign of life and comfort.'

'We will get to the upper chamber,' said the sailor, 'if I can but hit upon the broken-down steps; but you will find no trace of the Invisible Girl nor her light either, I warrant.'

'Truly a romantic adventure of the most disagreeable kind,' muttered Vernon, as he stumbled over the unequal ground; 'she of the beacon-light must be both ugly and old, or she would not be so peevish and inhospitable.'

With considerable difficulty, and after divers knocks and bruises, the adventurers at length succeeded in reaching the upper storey; but all was blank and bare, and they were fain to stretch themselves upon the hard floor, when weariness, both of mind and body, conduced to steep their senses in sleep.

Long and sound were the slumbers of the mariners. Vernon but forgot himself for an hour; then throwing off drowsiness, and finding his rough couch uncongenial to repose, he got up and placed himself at the hole that served for a window—for glass there was none, and there being not even a rough bench, he leant his back against the embrasure, as the only rest he could find. He had forgotten his danger, the mysterious beacon, and its invisible guardian: his thoughts were occupied on the horrors of his own fate, and the unspeakable wretchedness that sat like a nightmare on his heart.

It would require a good-sized volume to relate the causes which had changed the once happy Vernon into the most woeful mourner that ever clung to the outer trappings of grief, as slight though cherished symbols of the wretchedness within. Henry was the only child of Sir Peter Vernon, and as much spoiled by his father's idolatry as the old baronet's violent and tyrannical temper would permit. A young orphan was educated in his father's house, who in the same way was treated with generosity and kindness, and yet who lived in deep awe of Sir Peter's authority, who was a widower; and these two children were all he had to exert his power over, or to whom to extend his affection. Rosina was a cheerful-tempered girl, a little timid, and careful to avoid displeasing her protector; but so docile, so kind-hearted, and so affectionate, that she felt even less than Henry the discordant spirit of his parent. It is a tale often told; they were playmates and companions in childhood, and lovers in after days. Rosina was frightened to imagine that this secret affection, and the vows they pledged, might be disapproved of by Sir Peter. But sometimes she consoled herself by thinking that perhaps she was in reality her Henry's destined bride, brought up with him under the design of their future union; and Henry, while he felt that this was not the case, resolved to wait only until he was of age to declare and accomplish his wishes in making the sweet Rosina his wife. Meanwhile he was careful to avoid premature discovery of his intentions, so to secure his beloved girl from persecution and insult. The old gentleman was very conveniently blind; he lived always in the country, and the lovers spent their lives together, unrebuked and uncontrolled. It was enough that Rosina played on her mandoline, and sang Sir Peter to sleep every day after dinner; she was the sole female in the house above the rank of servant, and had her own way in the disposal of her time. Even when Sir Peter frowned, her innocent caresses and sweet voice were powerful to smooth the rough current of his temper. If ever human spirit lived in an earthly paradise, Rosina did at this time: her pure love was made happy by Henry's constant presence; and the confidence they felt in each other, and the security with which they looked forward to the future, rendered their path one of roses under a cloudless sky. Sir Peter was the slight drawback that only rendered their *tête-à-tête* more delightful, and gave value to the sympathy they each bestowed on the other. All at once an ominous personage made its appearance in Vernon Place, in the shape of a widow sister of Sir Peter, who, having succeeded in killing her husband and children with the effects of her vile temper, came, like a harpy, greedy for new prey under her brother's roof. She too soon detected the attachment of the unsuspicious pair. She made all speed to impart her discovery to her brother, and at once to restrain and inflame his rage. Through her contrivance Henry was suddenly despatched on his travels abroad, that the coast might be clear for the persecution of Rosina; and then the richest of the lovely girl's many admirers, whom, under Sir Peter's single reign, she was allowed, nay, almost commanded, to dismiss, so desirous was he of keeping her for his own comfort, was selected, and she was ordered to marry him. The scenes of violence to which she was now exposed, the bitter taunts of the odious Mrs Bainbridge, and the reckless fury of Sir Peter were the more frightful and overwhelming from their novelty. To all she could only oppose a silent, tearful, but immutable steadiness of purpose: no threats, no rage could extort from her more than a touching prayer that they would not hate her, because she could not obey.

'There must be something we don't see under all this,' said Mrs Bainbridge; 'take my word for it, brother, she corresponds secretly with Henry. Let us take her down to your seat in Wales, where she will have no pensioned beggars to assist her; and we shall see if her spirit be not bent to our purpose.'

Sir Peter consented, and they all three took up their abode in the solitary and dreary-looking house before alluded to as belonging to the family. Here poor Rosina's sufferings grew intolerable. Before, surrounded by well-known scenes, and in perpetual inter-course with kind and familiar faces, she had not despaired in the end of conquering by her patience the cruelty of her persecutors— nor had she written to Henry, for his name had not been men-tioned by his relatives, nor their attachment alluded to, and she felt an instinctive wish to escape the dangers about her without his being annoyed, or the sacred secret of her love being laid bare, and wronged by the vulgar abuse of his aunt or the bitter curses of his father. But when she was taken to Wales, and made a prisoner in her apartment, when the flinty mountains about her seemed feebly to imitate the stony hearts she had to deal with, her courage began to fail. The only attendant permitted to approach her was Mrs Bainbridge's maid; and under the tutelage of her fiend-like mistress, this woman was used as a decoy to entice the poor prisoner into confidence, and then to be betrayed. The simple, kind-hearted Rosina was a facile dupe, and at last, in the excess of her despair, wrote to Henry, and gave the letter to this woman to be forwarded. The letter in itself would have softened marble; it did not speak of their mutual vows, it but asked him to intercede with his father, that he would restore her to the place she had formerly held in his affections, and cease from a cruelty that would destroy her. 'For I may die,' wrote the hapless girl, 'but marry another—never!' That single word, indeed, had sufficed to betray her secret, had it not been already discovered; as it was, it gave increased fury to Sir Peter, as his sister triumphantly pointed it out to him, for it need hardly be said that while the ink of the address was yet wet, and the seal still warm, Rosina's letter was carried to this lady. The culprit was summoned before them. What ensued none could tell; for their own sakes the cruel pair tried to palliate their part. Voices were high, and the soft murmur of Rosina's tone was lost in the howling of Sir Peter and the snarling of his sister. 'Out of doors you shall go,' roared the old man; 'under my roof you shall not spend another night.' And the words infamous seductress, and worse, such as had never met the poor girl's ear before, were caught by listening servants; and to each angry speech of the baronet, Mrs Bainbridge added an envenomed point worse than all.

More dead than alive, Rosina was at last dismissed. Whether guided by despair, whether she took Sir Peter's threats literally, or whether his sister's orders were more decisive, none knew, but Rosina left the house; a servant saw her cross the park, weeping, and wringing her hands as she went. What became of her none could tell; her disappearance was not disclosed to Sir Peter till the following day, and then he showed by his anxiety to trace her steps and to find her, that his words had been but idle threats. The truth was, that though Sir Peter went to frightful lengths to prevent the marriage of the heir of his house with the portionless orphan, the object of his charity, yet in his heart he loved Rosina, and half his violence to her rose from anger at himself for treating her so ill. Now remorse began to sting him, as messenger after messenger came back without tidings of his victim. He dared not confess his worst fears to himself; and when his inhuman sister, trying to harden her conscience by angry words, cried, 'The vile hussy has too surely made away with herself out of revenge to us,' an oath the most tremendous, and a look sufficient to make even her tremble, commanded her silence. Her conjecture, however, appeared too true: a dark and rushing stream that flowed at the extremity of the park had doubtless received the lovely form, and quenched the life of this unfortunate girl. Sir Peter, when his endeavours to find her proved fruitless, returned to town, haunted by the image of his victim, and forced to acknowledge in his own heart that he would willingly lay down his life, could he see her again, even though it were as the bride of his son—his son, before whose questioning he quailed like the veriest coward; for when Henry was told of the death of Rosina, he suddenly returned from abroad to ask the cause—to visit her grave, and mourn her loss in the groves and valleys which had been the scenes of their mutual happiness. He made a thousand inquiries, and an ominous silence alone replied. Growing more earnest and more anxious, at length he drew from servants and dependants, and his odious aunt herself, the whole dreadful truth. From that moment despair struck his heart, and misery named him her own. He fled from his father's presence; and the recollection that one whom he ought to revere was guilty of so dark a crime, haunted him, as of old the Eumenides tormented the souls of men given up to their torturings. His first, his only wish, was to visit Wales, and to learn if any new discovery had been made, and whether it were possible to recover the mortal remains of the lost Rosina, so to satisfy the unquiet longings of his miserable heart. On this expedition was he bound when he made his appearance at the village before named; and now, in the deserted tower, his thoughts were busy with images of despair and death, and what his beloved one had suffered before her gentle nature had been goaded to such a deed of woe.

While immersed in gloomy reverie, to which the monotonous roaring of the sea made fit accompaniment, hours flew on, and Vernon was at last aware that the light of morning was creeping from out its eastern retreat, and dawning over the wild ocean, which still broke in furious tumult on the rocky beach. His companions now roused themselves, and prepared to depart. The food they had brought with them was damaged by sea-water, and their hunger, after hard labour and many hours' fasting, had become ravenous. It was impossible to put to sea in their shattered boat; but there stood a fisher's cot about two miles off, in a recess in the bay, of which the promontory on which the tower stood formed one side; and to this they hastened to repair. They did not spend a second thought on the light which had saved them, nor its cause, but left the ruin in search of a more hospitable asylum. Vernon cast his eyes round as he quitted it, but no vestige of an inhabitant met his eye, and he began to persuade himself that the beacon had been a creation of fancy merely. Arriving at the cottage in question, which was inhabited by a fisherman and his family, they made a homely breakfast, and then prepared to return to the tower, to refit their boat, and, if possible, bring her round. Vernon accompanied them, together with their host and his son. Several questions were asked concerning the Invisible Girl and her light, each agreeing that the apparition was novel, and not one being able to give even an explanation of how the name had become affixed to the unknown cause of this singular appearance; though both of the men of the cottage affirmed that once or twice they had seen a female figure in the adjacent wood, and that now and then a stranger girl made her appearance at another cot a mile off, on the other side of the promontory, and bought bread; they suspected both these to be the same, but could not tell. The inhabitants of the cot, indeed, appeared too stupid even to feel curiosity, and had never made any attempt at discovery. The whole day was spent by the sailors in repairing the boat; and the sound of hammers, and the voices of the men at work, resounded along the coast, mingled with the dashing of the waves. This was no time to explore the ruin for one who, whether human or supernatural, so evidently withdrew herself from intercourse with every living being. Vernon, however, went over the tower, and searched every nook in vain. The dingy bare walls bore no token of serving as a shelter; and even a little recess in the wall of the staircase, which he had not before observed, was equally empty and desolate. Quitting the tower, he wandered in the pine wood that surrounded it, and, giving up all thought of solving the mystery, was soon engrossed by thoughts that touched his heart more nearly, when suddenly there appeared on the ground at his feet the vision of a slipper.

Since Cinderella so tiny a slipper had never been seen; as plain as shoe could speak, it told a tale of elegance, loveliness, and youth. Vernon picked it up. He had often admired Rosina's singularly small foot, and his first thought was a question whether this little slipper would have fitted it. It was very strange!—it must belong to the Invisible Girl. Then there was a fairy form that kindled that light—a form of such material substance that its foot needed to be shod; and yet how shod?—with kid so fine, and of shape so exquisite, that it exactly resembled such as Rosina wore! Again the recurrence of the image of the beloved dead came forcibly across him; and a thousand home-felt associations, childish yet sweet, and lover-like though trifling, so filled Vernon's heart, that he threw himself his length on the ground, and wept more bitterly than ever the miserable fate of the sweet orphan.

In the evening the men quitted their work, and Vernon returned with them to the cot where they were to sleep, intending to pursue their voyage, weather permitting, the following morning. Vernon said nothing of his slipper, but returned with his rough associates. Often he looked back; but the tower rose darkly over the dim waves, and no light appeared. Preparations had been made in the cot for their accommodation, and the only bed in it was offered Vernon; but he refused to deprive his hostess, and, spreading his cloak on a heap of dry leaves, endeavoured to give himself up to repose. He slept for some hours; and when he awoke, all was still, save that the hard breathing of the sleepers in the same room with him interrupted the silence. He rose, and, going to the window, looked out over the now placid sea towards the mystic tower. The light was burning there, sending its slender rays across the waves. Congratulating himself on a circumstance he had not anticipated, Vernon softly left the cottage, and, wrapping his cloak round him, walked with a swift pace round the bay towards the tower. He reached it; still the light was burning. To enter and restore the maiden her shoe, would be but an act of courtesy; and Vernon intended to do this with such caution as to come unaware, before its wearer could, with her accustomed arts, withdraw herself from his eyes; but, unluckily, while yet making his way up the narrow pathway, his foot dislodged a loose fragment, that fell with crash and sound down the precipice. He sprung forward, on this, to retrieve by speed the advantage he had lost by this unlucky accident. He reached the door; he entered: all was silent, but also all was dark. He paused in the room below; he felt sure that a slight sound met his ear. He ascended the steps, and entered the upper chamber; but blank obscurity met his penetrating gaze, the starless night admitted not even a twilight glimmer through the only aperture. He closed his eyes, to try, on opening them again, to be able to catch some faint, wandering ray on the visual nerve; but it was in vain. He groped round the room; he stood still, and held his breath; and then, listening intently, he felt sure that another occupied the chamber with him, and that its atmosphere was slightly agitated by another's respiration. He remembered the recess in the staircase; but before he approached it he spoke—he hesitated a moment what to say. 'I must believe,' he said, 'that misfortune alone can cause your seclusion; and if the assistance of a man—of a gentleman—'

An exclamation interrupted him; a voice from the grave spoke his name—the accents of Rosina syllabled, 'Henry!—is it indeed Henry whom I hear?'

He rushed forward, directed by the sound, and clasped in his arms the living form of his own lamented girl—his own Invisible Girl he called her; for even yet, as he felt her heart beat near his, and as he entwined her waist with his arm, supporting her as she almost sank to the ground with agitation, he could not see her; and, as her sobs prevented her speech, no sense but the instinctive one that filled his heart with tumultuous gladness, told him that the slender, wasted form he pressed so fondly was the living shadow of the Hebe beauty he had adored.

The morning saw this pair thus strangely restored to each other on the tranquil sea, sailing with a fair wind for L——, whence they were to proceed to Sir Peter's seat, which, three months before, Rosina had quitted in such agony and terror. The morning light dispelled the shadows that had veiled her, and disclosed the fair person of the Invisible Girl. Altered indeed she was by suffering and woe, but still the same sweet smile played on her lips, and the tender light of her soft blue eyes were all her own. Vernon drew out the slipper, and showed the cause that had occasioned him to resolve to discover the guardian of the mystic beacon; even now he dared not inquire how she had existed in that desolate spot, or wherefore she had so sedulously avoided observation, when the right thing to have been done was to have sought him immediately, under whose care, protected by whose love, no danger need be feared. But Rosina shrunk from him as he spoke, and a deathlike pallor came over her cheek, as she faintly whispered, 'Your father's curse—your father's dreadful threats!' It appeared, indeed, that Sir Peter's violence, and the cruelty of Mrs Bainbridge, had succeeded in impressing Rosina with wild and unvanquishable terror. She had fled from their house without plan or forethought—driven by frantic horror and overwhelming fear, she had left it with scarcely any money, and there seemed to her no possibility of either returning or proceeding onward. She had no friend except Henry in the wide world; whither could she go?—to have sought Henry would have sealed their fates to misery; for, with an oath, Sir Peter had declared he would rather see them both in their coffins than married. After wandering about, hiding by day, and only venturing forth at night, she had come to this deserted tower, which seemed a place of refuge. How she had lived since then she could hardly tell: she had lingered in the woods by day, or slept in the vault of the tower, an asylum none were acquainted with or had discovered: by night she burned the pinecones of the wood, and night was her dearest time; for it seemed to her as if security came with darkness. She was unaware that Sir Peter had left that part of the country, and was terrified lest her hiding-place should be revealed to him. Her only hope was that Henry would return— that Henry would never rest till he had found her. She confessed that the long interval and the approach of winter had visited her with dismay; she feared that, as her strength was failing, and her form wasting to a skeleton, that she might die, and never see her own Henry more.

An illness, indeed, in spite of all his care, followed her restoration to security and the comforts of civilised life; many months went by before the bloom revisiting her cheeks, and her limbs regaining their roundness, she resembled once more the picture drawn of her in her days of bliss before any visitation of sorrow. It was a copy of this portrait that decorated the tower, the scene of her suffering, in which I had found shelter. Sir Peter, overjoyed to be relieved from the pangs of remorse, and delighted again to see his orphan ward, whom he really loved, was now as eager as before he had been averse to bless her union with his son. Mrs Bainbridge they never saw again. But each year they spent a few months in their Welsh mansion, the scene of their early wedded happiness, and the spot where again poor Rosina had awoke to life and joy after her cruel persecutions. Henry's fond care had fitted up the tower, and decorated it as I saw; and often did he come over, with his 'Invisible Girl', to renew, in the very scene of its occurrence, the remembrance of all the incidents which had led to their meeting again, during the shades of night, in that sequestered ruin.

THE DYLLUAN

by George Borrow

GEORGE HENRY BORROW *(1803–1881),
master of languages, inveterate traveller, accomplished pugilist,
Bible thumper and champion of the gypsies, is to this day
remembered in Wales with special affection. As a child he was
particularly adept at languages and apart from the major
European tongues could also speak fluent Welsh and Romany.
In his youth he spent much of his time with the gypsies and
was known among them as 'Lavengro', the Word Master.
After the death of his father he was for a time a notedly
unsuccessful hack-writer in London and then took to tramping
the highways of England. Often he travelled with his friends
the gypsies and two of his books,* Lavengro *(1851)* and
Romany Rye *(1857) reflect his intimate knowledge of their
manners and customs. For a time he was an agent of the
Bible Society in Russia, Spain and Morocco and then settled
in Norfolk. In 1854 he went on a tour of Wales which not
only made him a great many friends along the way, but
produced perhaps his finest and best remembered work,* Wild
Wales: Its People, Language, and Scenery *(1862). Being
able to speak the Welsh language he delved deeply into the
lore and secrets of the country and his book is unsurpassed
as a mine of knowledge and instruction. Two stories from the
book particularly caught my eye, 'The Devil's Bridge and 'The
Dylluan', but as the first has been anthologised several times
previously I have selected the latter, which seems to me a
fable worthy of Aesop.*

Much rain fell about the middle of the month; in the intervals of the showers I occasionally walked by the banks of the river which speedily became much swollen; it was quite terrible both to the sight and ear near the 'Robbers Leap'; there were breakers above the higher stones at least five feet high and a roar around almost sufficient 'to scare a hundred men'.

The pool of Catherine Lingo was strangely altered; it was no longer the quiet pool which it was in summer, verifying the words of the old Welsh poet that the deepest pool of the river is always the stillest in the summer and of the softest sound, but a howling turbid gulf, in which branches of trees, dead animals and rubbish were whirling about in the wildest confusion.

The nights were generally less rainy than the days, and some-times by the pallid glimmer of the moon I would take a stroll along some favourite path or road.

One night as I was wandering slowly along the path leading through the groves of Pen y Coed I was startled by an unearthly cry—it was the shout of the dylluan or owl, as it flitted over the tops of the trees on its nocturnal business.

Oh, that cry of the dylluan! what a strange wild cry it is; how unlike any other sound in nature! a cry which no combination of letters can give the slightest idea of. What resemblance does Shakespeare's to-whit-to-whoo bear to the cry of the owl? none whatever; those who hear it for the first time never know what it is, however accustomed to talk of the cry of the owl and to-whit-to-whoo. A man might be wandering through a wood with Shakespeare's owl-chorus in his mouth, but were he then to hear for the first time the real shout of the owl he would assuredly stop short and wonder whence that unearthly cry could proceed.

Yet no doubt that strange cry is a fitting cry for the owl, the strangest in its habits and look of all birds, the bird whom by all nations the strangest tales are told. Oh, what strange tales are told of the owl, especially in connection with its long-lifedness; but of all the strange wild tales connected with the age of the owl, strangest of all is the old Welsh tale. When I heard the owl's cry in the groves of Pen y Coed that tale rushed into my mind. I had heard it from the singular groom who had taught me to gabble

Welsh in my boyhood, and had subsequently read it in an old tattered Welsh storybook, which by chance fell into my hands. The reader will perhaps be obliged by my relating it.

The eagle of the alder grove, after being long married and having had many children by his mate, lost her by death, and became a widower. After some time he took it into his head to marry the owl of the Cowlyd Coomb; but fearing he should have issue by her, and by that means sully his lineage, he went first of all to the oldest creatures in the world in order to obtain information about her age.

First he went to the stag of Ferny-side Brae, whom he found sitting by the old stump of an oak, and inquired the age of the owl. The stag said: 'I have seen this oak an acorn which is now lying on the ground without either leaves or bark: nothing in the world wore it up but my rubbing myself against it once a day when I got up, so I have seen a vast number of years, but I assure you that I have never seen the owl older or younger than she is today. However, there is one older than myself, and that is the salmon-trout of Glyn Llifon'.

To him went the eagle and asked him the age of the owl and got for answer: 'I have a year over my head for every gem on my skin and for every egg in my roe, yet have I always seen the owl look the same; but there is one older than myself, and that is the ousel of Cilgwry.'

Away went the eagle to Cilgwry, and found the ousel standing upon a little rock, and asked him the age of the owl. Quoth the ousel: 'You see that the rock below me is not larger than a man can carry in one of his hands: I have seen it so large that it would have taken a hundred oxen to drag it, and it has never been worn save by my drying my beak upon it once every night, and by my striking the tip of my wing against it in rising in the morning, yet never have I known the owl older or younger than she is today. However, there is one older than I, and that is the toad of Cors Fochnod; and unless he knows her age no one knows it.'

To him went the eagle and asked the age of the owl, and the toad replied: 'I have never eaten anything save what I have sucked from the earth, and have never eaten half my fill in all the days of my life; but do you see those two great hills beside the cross? I have seen the place where they stand level ground, and nothing produced those heaps save what I discharged from my body, who have ever eaten so very little—yet never have I known the owl anything else but an old hag who cried Too-hoo-hoo, and scared children with her voice even as she does at present.'

So the eagle of Gwernabwy; the stag of Ferny-side Brae; the salmon-trout of Glyn Llifon; the ousel of Cilgwry; the toad of Cors Fochnod, and the owl of Coomb Cowlyd are the oldest creatures in the world; the oldest of them all being the owl.

THE CURSE OF PANTANNAS

by Sir John Rhys

SIR JOHN RHYS *(1840–1915) is one of the three great collectors of Welsh folklore whose work is represented in this anthology. With his fellow countryman, the Reverend Elias Owen, and the American statesman, Wirt Sikes, Sir John was responsible for committing to paper a vast literature of oral folk-tales which would otherwise have been lost for all time. John Rhys was a gentle, pious man born in Cardigan-shire, who first became a village schoolmaster in Anglesey before entering Jesus College, Oxford. For a time he also studied in France and Germany, thereafter becoming inspector of schools in Wales in 1871. From this period onwards his general interest in folklore developed into a passion for ground research and by the close of the century he was widely re-garded as the most distinguished authority on Celtic phil-ology. In introducing his masterly work,* Celtic Folklore— Welsh and Manx *(1900) he admitted to having been spurred on in his researches by reading J. F. Campbell's* Popular Tales of the West Highlands[1] *to see if Wales boasted a similar rich vein of folklore. 'It is a cause of regret to me,' he went on, 'that I did not commence my enquiries earlier ... but my education, such as it was, had been of a nature to discourage all interest in anything that savoured of heathen lore and superstition.' Nevertheless, Sir John was determined in his work, managed to locate many old men and women who had heard stories as young children, and in assembling their patch-*

---

[1] A story from this book, 'The Sea Maiden', is to be found in Peter Haining's companion volume of Scottish Tales of fantasy and horror, *The Clans of Darkness* (U.K.: Gollancz, 1971; U.S.: Taplinger, 1971).

work of tales and partly remembered legends, produced a collection of paramount importance. From this book I am now delighted to be able to include a remarkable tale of those most cherished of Welsh fantasy figures, the fairies.

In one of the centuries gone by, there lived a husbandman on the farm of Pantannas, near Merthyr Tidfil; and at that time the fairies used to pay frequent visits to several of the fields which belonged to him. He cherished in his bosom a considerable hatred for the 'noisy, boisterous, and pernicious tribe', as he called them, and often did he long to be able to discover some way to rid the place of them. At last he was told by an old witch that the way to get rid of them was easy enough, and that she would tell him how to attain what he so greatly wished, if he gave her one evening's milking on his farm, and one morning's. He agreed to her conditions, and from her he received advice, which was to the effect that he was to plough all the fields where they had their favourite resorts, and that, if they found the green sward gone, they would take offence, and never return to trouble him with their visits to the spot.

The husbandman followed the advice to the letter, and his work was crowned with success. Not a single one of them was now to be seen about the fields, and, instead of the sound of their sweet music, which used to be always heard rising from the Coarse Meadow Land, the most complete silence now reigned over their favourite resort.

He sowed his land with wheat and other grain; the verdant spring had now thrust winter off its throne, and the fields appeared splendid in their vernal and green livery.

But one evening, when the sun had retired to the chambers of the west, and when the farmer of Pantannas was returning home, he was met by a diminutive being in the shape of a man, with a red coat on. When he had come right up to him, he unsheathed his little sword, and, directing the point towards the farmer, he said:

> Vengeance cometh,
> Fast it approacheth.

The farmer tried to laugh, but there was something in the surly and stern looks of the little fellow which made him feel exceedingly uncomfortable.

A few nights afterwards, as the family were retiring to rest, they were very greatly frightened by a noise, as though the house was falling to pieces; and, immediately after the noise, they heard a voice uttering loudly the threatening words—and nothing more:

Vengeance cometh.

When, however, the corn was reaped and ready to be carried to the barn, it was, all of a sudden, burnt up one night, so that neither an ear nor a straw of it could be found anywhere in the fields; and now nobody could have set the corn on fire but the fairies.

As one may naturally suppose, the farmer felt very much on account of this event, and he regretted in his heart having done according to the witch's direction, and having thereby brought upon him the anger and hatred of the fairies.

The day after the night of the burning of the corn, as he was surveying the destruction caused by the fire, behold the little fellow, who had met him a few days before, met him again, and, with a challenging glance, he pointed his sword towards him, saying:

It but beginneth.

The farmer's face turned as white as marble, and he stood calling the little fellow to come back; but the dwarf proved very unyielding and reluctant to turn to him; but, after long entreaty, he turned back, asking the farmer, in a surly tone, what he wanted, when he was told by the latter that he was quite willing to allow the fields, in which their favourite resorts had been, to grow again into a green sward, and to let them frequent them as often as they wished, provided they would no further wreak their anger on him.

'No,' was the determined reply, 'the word of the king has been given, that he will avenge himself on thee to the utmost of his power; and there is no power on the face of creation that will cause it to be withdrawn.'

The farmer began to weep at this, and, after a while, the little fellow said that he would speak to his lord on the matter, and that he would let him know the result, if he would come there to meet him at the hour of sunset on the third day after.

The farmer promised to meet him; and, when the time appointed for meeting the little man came, he found him awaiting him, and he was told by him that his lord had seriously considered his request, but that, as the king's word was ever immutable, the threatened vengeance was to take effect on the family. On account, however, of his repentance, it would not be allowed to happen in his time or that of his children.

That calmed the disturbed mind of the farmer a good deal. The fairies began again to pay frequent visits to the place, and their melodious singing was again heard at night in the fields around.

A century passed by without seeing the threatened vengeance carried into effect; and, though the Pantannas family were reminded now and again that it was certain sooner or later to come, nevertheless, by long hearing the voice that said:

Vengeance cometh,

they became so accustomed to it, that they were ready to believe that nothing would ever come of the threat.

The heir of Pantannas was paying his addresses to the daughter of a neighbouring landowner who lived at the farm house called Pen Craig Daf, and the wedding of the happy pair was to take place in a few weeks, and the parents on both sides appeared exceedingly content with the union that was about to take place between the two families.

It was Christmas time, and the intended wife paid a visit to the family of her would-be husband. There they had a feast of roast goose prepared for the occasion.

The company sat round the fire to relate amusing tales to pass the time, when they were greatly frightened by a piercing voice, rising, as it were, from the bed of the river, and shrieking:

The time for revenge is come.

They all went out to listen if they could hear the voice a second time, but nothing was to be heard save the angry noise of the water as it cascaded over the dread cliffs of the *kerwyni*; they had not long, however, to wait till they heard again the same voice rising above the noise of the waters, as they boiled over the shoulders of the rock, and crying:

The time is come.

They could not guess what it meant, and so great was their fright and astonishment, that no one could utter a word to another. Shortly they returned to the house, when they believed that beyond doubt the building was being shaken to its foundations by some noise outside. When all were thus paralysed by fear, behold a little woman made her appearance on the table, which stood near the window.

'What dost thou, ugly little thing, want here?' asked one of those present.

'I have nothing to do with thee, O man of the meddling tongue,' said the little woman, 'but I have been sent here to recount some things that are about to happen to this family and another family in the neighbourhood, things that might be of interest to them; but, as I have received such an insult from the black fellow that sits in the corner, the veil that hides them from their sight shall not be lifted by me.'

'Pray,' said another of those present, 'if thou hast in thy possession any knowledge with regard to the future of any one of us that would interest us to hear, bring it forth.'

'No, I will but merely tell you that a certain maiden's heart is like a ship on the coast, unable to reach the harbour because the pilot has lost heart.'

As soon as she had cried out the last word, she vanished, no one knew whither or how.

During her visit, the cry rising from the river had stopped, but soon afterwards it began again to proclaim:

The time of vengeance is come;

nor did it cease for a long while. The company had been possessed by too much terror for one to be able to address another, and a sheet of gloom had, as it were, been spread over the face of each. The time for parting came, and Rhyderch the heir went to escort Gwerfyl, his lady-love, home towards Pen Craig Daf, a journey from which he never returned.

Before bidding one another 'Good-bye', they are said to have sworn to each other eternal fidelity, even though they should never see one another from that moment forth, and that nothing should make the one forget the other.

It is thought probable that the young man Rhyderch, on his way back towards home, got into one of the rings of the fairies, that they allured him into one of their caves in the Ravens' Rift, and that there he remained.

It is high time for us now to turn back towards Pantannas and Pen Craig Daf. The parents of the unlucky youth were almost beside themselves: they had no idea where to go to look for him, and, though they searched every spot in the place, they failed completely to find him or any clue to his history.

A little higher up the country, there dwelt, in a cave underground, an aged hermit called Gweiryd, who was regarded also as a sorcerer. They went a few weeks afterwards to ask him whether he could give them any information about their lost son; but it was of little avail. What that man told them did but deepen the wound and give the event a still more hopeless aspect. When they had told him of the appearance of the little woman, and the doleful cry heard rising from the river on the night when their son was lost, he informed them that it was the judgement threatened to the family by the fairies that had overtaken the youth, and that it was useless for them to think of ever seeing him again: possibly he might make his appearance after generations had gone by, but not in their lifetime.

Time rolled on, weeks grew into months, and months into years, until Rhyderch's father and mother were gathered to their ancestors. The place continued the same, but the inhabitants constantly changed, so that the memory of Rhyderch's disappearance was fast dying away. Nevertheless there was one who expected his return all the while, and hoped, as it were against hope, to see him once more. Every morn, as the gates of the dawn opened beyond the castellated heights of the east, she might be seen, in all weathers, hastening to the top of a small hill, and, with eyes full of tears of longing, gazing in every direction to see if she could behold any sign of her beloved's return; but in vain. At noon, she might be seen on the same spot again; she was also there at the hour when the sun was wont to hide himself, like a red-hot ball of fire below the horizon. She gazed until she was nearly blind, and she wept forth her soul from day to day for the darling of her heart. At last they that looked out at the windows began to refuse their service, and the almond tree commenced to crown her head with its virgin bloom. She continued to gaze, but he came not. Full of days, and ripe for the grave, death put an end to all her hopes and all her expectations. Her mortal remains were buried in the graveyard of the old Chapel of the Fan.

Years passed away like smoke, and generations like the shadows of the morning, and there was no longer anybody alive who remembered Rhyderch, but the tale of his sudden missing was frequently in people's mouths. And we ought to have said that after the event no one of the fairies was seen about the neighbourhood, and the sound of their music ceased from that night.

Rhyderch had been allured by them, and they took him away into their cave. When he had stayed there only a few days, as he thought, he asked for permission to return, which was readily granted him by the king. He issued from the cave when it was a fine noon, with the sun beaming from the bosom of a cloudless firmament. He walked on from the Ravens' Rift until he came near the site of the Fan Chapel; but what was his astonishment to find no chapel there! Where, he wondered, had he been, and how long away? So with mixed feelings he directed his steps towards Pen Craig Daf, the home of his beloved one, but she was not there nor any one whom he knew either. He could get no word of the history of his sweetheart, and those who dwelt in the place took him for a madman.

He hastened then to Pantannas, where his astonishment was still greater. He knew nobody there, and nobody knew anything about him. At last the man of the house came in, and he remembered hearing his grandfather relating how a youth had suddenly disappeared, nobody knew whither, some hundreds of years previously. Somehow or other the man of the house chanced to knock his walking-stick against Rhyderch, when the latter vanished in a shower of dust. Nothing more was ever heard of him.

THE TREASURE GHOST

by Elias Owen

E L I A S   O W E N *(1837–1906), the second of the tri-*
umverate of great Welsh folklorists, was a humble country
clergyman who collected much of his material with the simple
objective of presenting it at the Welsh National Eisteddfod.
Born in Llanyblodwel, he spent several years as a vicar in
Caernarvonshire, before being appointed Inspector of Schools
for the Diocese of St Asaph. He had been an enthusiastic
reader of the pioneer Welsh folklore magazine Y Brython
(1858–1863), and inspired by its example, began to listen
out himself for tales as he travelled about. His two prime
sources were the local clergymen he visited and the old people
to whom they introduced him. For years he painstakingly
recorded all that he learned and then in 1887 presented the
material as a lecture, 'The Folklore of North Wales', at the
Eisteddfod. It swept the board to win the coveted silver medal
for Reverend Owen. Despite this recognition, it was to be
nearly ten years before the work appeared in book form, and
then only when enough subscribers had been found to meet
the printer's bill! However, immediately after its publication
in 1896, Welsh Folk Lore *(as the book was re-titled) was*
accepted as a major work of research and has retained its
importance to this day. The book is not completely exhaustive
of all Welsh folklore, but it is particularly detailed in the area
of the 'Bwcoid'—apparitions and spirits—and consequently
I have selected a story from that section called 'The Treasure
Ghost'. The story is also of considerable interest in that it is
one of the few authentic ghost tales which contains a spirit
which actually speaks.

For some time it had been widely reported that a poor un-married woman, who was a member of the Methodist Society, had seen and conversed with the apparition of a gentleman who had made a strange discovery to her. A preacher of her church being desirous to ascertain if there was any truth in the story, sent for the woman, and asked her to give him an exact account of the whole affair as near the truth as she possibly could.

The woman then related that she got her living by spinning hemp and line; that it was customary for the farmers and gentle-men of that neighbourhood to grow a little hemp or line in a corner of their fields for their own consumption, and as she was a good hand at spinning the materials, she used to go from house to house to inquire for work. If they employed her, it was agreed that she should have meat, and drink, and lodging (if she had occasion to sleep with them), for her work, and what they pleased to give her besides.

On the occasion in question she happened to call at the Welsh Earl of Powis's country seat, called Redcastle, to inquire for work, as she usually had done before. The Earl and his wife were at this time in London, and had left the steward and his wife, with other servants, to take care of their country residence in their absence. The steward's wife set her to work, and in the evening told her that she must stay all night with them, as they had more work for her to do next day.

When bedtime arrived, two or three of the servants in company, each with a lighted candle in her hand, conducted the woman to her lodging. They led her to a ground room, with a boarded floor, and two sash windows. The room was grandly furnished, and had a genteel bed in one corner of it. They had made the woman a good fire, and had placed her a chair and a table before it, and a large lighted candle upon the table. They told her that this was her bed-room, and she might go to sleep when she pleased. They then wished her a good night and withdrew altogether, pulling the door quickly after them, so as to secure the brass lock that was upon it.

When the servants were gone, the woman gazed awhile at the fine furniture, under no small astonishment that they should put such a poor person as her in so good a room and bed, with all the apparatus of fire, chair, table and candle. However, after gazing about her some little time, she sat down and took a small Welsh Bible out of her pocket, which she always carried about with her, and from which she usually read a chapter—chiefly in the New Testament—before she went to bed.

While she was reading the woman heard the room door open, and turning her head, saw a figure of a man enter in a gold-laced hat and coat. There was about him a misty look and a coldness filled the air.

After a moment, the figure walked down by the sash window to the corner of the room and then returned. When he came to the first window on his return (the bottom of which was nearly breast-high), he rested his elbow on the bottom of the window, and the side of his face upon the palm of his hand, and stood in that leaning posture for some time, with his side partly towards her. The woman looked at him earnestly and in some fear to see if she knew him, but, though from her frequent intercourse with them, she had a personal knowledge of all the present family, he appeared a stranger to her. She supposed afterwards that he stood in this manner to encourage her to speak; but as she did not, after some little time he walked off, pulling the door after him as the servants had done before.

She began now to be much alarmed, concluding it to be an apparition, and that they had put her there on purpose. (This was really the case. The room, it seems, had been disturbed for a long time, so that nobody could sleep peacefully in it, and as she passed for a very serious woman, the servants took it into their heads to put the Methodist and Spirit together, to see what they would make of it.)

Startled at this thought, the woman rose from her chair, and kneeled down by the bedside to say her prayers. While she was praying the figure came in again, walked round the room, and came close behind her. She had it on her mind to speak, but when she attempted it she was so very much agitated that she could not utter a word. He walked out of the room again, pulling the door after him as before.

She begged that God would strengthen her and not suffer her to be tried beyond what she was able to bear. She recovered her spirits, and thought she felt more confidence and resolution, and determined if he came in again she would speak to him, if possible.

Presently the ghost came in once more, walked round, and came behind her as before. She turned her head and said, 'Pray sir, who are you, and what do you want?'

At this the man put up his finger and spoke in a hollow, unearthly voice: 'Take up the candle and follow me, and I will tell you.'

The woman got up, took up the candle, and followed him out of the room. He led her through a long boarded passage till they came to the door of another room, which he opened and went in. It was a small room, or what might be called a large closet. The woman hesitated at the door.

'Walk in, I will not hurt you,' said the apparition. So she walked in and the man went on, 'Observe what I do.' He stooped forward and one of the boards of the floor lifted, and there appeared under it a box with an iron handle on the lid.

He then stepped to one side of the room, and showed the woman a crevice in the wall, where, he said, a key was hidden that could open it. He said, 'This box and key must be taken out, and sent to the Earl in London' (naming the Earl, and his place of residence in the city). 'Will you see it done?' The woman shook her head in much fear.

'Do, and I will trouble the house no more.' With that, the figure disappeared instantly and the woman was left alone.

Recovering her wits, she stepped back quickly to her room and set up a shout. The steward and his wife, and the other servants came immediately, all clinging together, with a number of lights in their hands. (It seems they had been waiting all the time to see the issue of the interview betwixt the woman and the apparition.)

They asked her what was the matter? She told them the foregoing circumstances, and showed them the box. The steward dared not touch it, but his wife had more courage, and with the help of the other servants, lugged it out, and found the key. The wife said it appeared to be pretty heavy, but she did not know what it contained; perhaps money, or writings of consequence to the family, or both.

The servants then took it away with them, and the woman went to bed and slept peaceably till the morning.

It appeared afterwards that they sent the box to the Earl in London, with an account of the manner of its discovery and by whom; and the Earl sent down orders immediately to his steward to inform the poor woman who had been the occasion of this discovery, that if she would come and reside in his family, she should be comfortably looked after for the remainder of her days; or, if she did not choose to reside constantly with them, if she would let them know when she wanted assistance, she should be liberally supplied at his Lordship's expense as long as she lived.

And it was a known fact in the neighbourhood that she had been so supplied by his Lordship's family from that time forth—and no more was the Ghost of the Treasure seen or heard.

THE CORPSE CANDLE

by Wirt Sikes

WIRT SIKES *(1831–1896) is the third of the great folklore collectors whose work and memory is still acknowledged today. As an outsider to the country, albeit a resident for some years, he brought great objectivity to his study and his writings are models of enquiry and evaluation. Born in Washington, Sikes entered the civil service after a brilliantly successful college career, and progressed rapidly in his work. He received several postings to foreign embassies before being sent to Wales in 1875. Here he established the Consular office in Cardiff and became a well-known and popular member of local society. His interest and love for Wales was soon evident and his researches into local customs and legends were eagerly and widely supported. He joined the Cardiff Naturalists' Society and from there began his journeys into the country to locate material at first hand. (One book to result from this was* Rambles and Studies in Old South Wales *published in 1881.) He was particularly interested in two areas of the supernatural, the Fairy Legends and the 'Canwyll Corph' or Corpse Candles. As we have already encountered fairies in previous items, the Corpse Candles seem a natural selection from Mr Sikes' pen. Here, then, is his account of this peculiarly Welsh tradition taken from the best of his books,* British Goblins. *This work, published in 1880, takes its place beside those of Sir John Rhys and the Reverend Elias Owen as required reading for all students of Welsh legend and lore.*

Perhaps the most picturesque of the several death-omens popular in Wales is the Canwyll Corph, or Corpse Candle. It is also, according to my observation, the most extensively believed in at the present day. Its details are varied and extremely interesting. The idea of a goblin in the form of a lighted tallow candle is ludicrous enough, at first sight; and indeed I know several learned Welsh gentlemen who venture to laugh at it; but the superstition grows more and more grim and less risible the better one becomes acquainted with it. It is worth noting here that the canwyll, or candle, is a more poetic thing among the Welsh—has a higher literary place, so to speak—than among English-speaking peoples. In the works of their ancient poets the candle is mentioned in passages where we should use the word light or lamp—as in this verse, which is attributed to Aneurin (sixth century):

The best candle for man is prudence.

The candle is the favourite figure for mental guidance among the Welsh;[1] there is no book in the Welsh language so popular as a certain work of religious counsel by a former Vicar of Llandovery, called *The Candle of the Cymry*. The Corpse Candle is always and invariably a death-warning. It sometimes appears as a stately flambeau, stalking along unsupported, burning with a ghastly blue flame. Sometimes it is a plain tallow 'dip' in the hand of a ghost, and when the ghost is seen distinctly it is recognised as the ghost of some person yet living, who will now soon die. This, it will be noticed, is a variation upon the wraith, or Lledrith. Sometimes the goblin is a light which issues from a person's mouth or nostrils. According to the belief of some sections, the size of the candle indicates the age of the person who is about to die, being large when it is a full-grown person whose death is foretold, small when it is a child, still smaller when an infant. Where two candles together are seen, one of which is large and the other small, it is a mother and child who are to die. When the flame is white, the doomed person is a woman; when red, a man.

Among the accounts of the Corpse Candle which have come under my notice none are more interesting than those given me by a good dame whom I encountered at Caerau, near Cardiff. Caerau is a

[1] Stephens, *Lit. of the Kymry*, 287. (New Ed., 1876).

little village of perhaps one hundred souls, crouched at the foot of a steep hill on whose summit are the ancient earthworks of a Roman camp. On this summit also stands the parish church, distinctly visible from Cardiff streets, so ponderous is its square tower against the sky. To walk there is a pleasant stroll from the late Marquis of Bute's statue in the centre of the seaport town. I am thus particular merely for emphasis of the fact that this superstition is not confined to remote and out-of-the-way districts. Caerau is rural, and its people are all poor people, perhaps; but its church is barely three miles from the heart of a busy seaport. In this church I met the voluble Welshwoman who gave me the accounts referred to. One was to this effect: One night her sister was lying very ill at the narrator's house, and she was alone with her children, her husband being in the lunatic asylum at Cardiff. She had just put the children to bed, and had set her candle on the floor preparatory to going to bed herself, when there came a 'swish' along the floor, like the rustling of grave-clothes, and the candle was blown out. The room, however, to her surprise, remained glowing with a feeble light as from a very small taper, and looking behind her she beheld 'old John Richards', who had been dead ten years. He held a Corpse Candle in his hand, and he looked at her in a chill and steadfast manner which caused the blood to run cold in her veins. She turned and woke her eldest boy, and said to him, 'Don't you see old John Richards?' The boy asked 'Where?' rubbing his eyes. She pointed out the ghost, and the boy was so frightened at sight of it that he cried out 'O wi! O Dduw! I wish I may die!' The ghost then disappeared, the Corpse Candle in its hand; the candle on the floor burned again with a clear light, and next day the sick sister died.

Another account ran somewhat thus: The narrator's mother-in-law was ill with a cancer of the breast. 'Jenny fach,' she said to the narrator one night, 'sleep by me—I feel afraid.' 'Hach!' said Jenny, thinking the old woman was foolishly nervous; but she stayed. As she was lying in bed by the side of her mother-in-law, she saw at the foot of the bed the faint flame of a Corpse Candle, which shed no light at all about the room; the place remained as dark as it was before. She looked at it in a sort of stupor for a short time, and then raised herself slowly up in the bed and reached out to see if she could grasp the candle. Her fingers touched it, but it immediately went out in a little shower of pale sparkles that fell downward. At that moment her mother-in-law uttered a groan, and expired.

'Do you know Thomas Mathews, sir?' she asked me; 'he lives at Crwys now, but he used to live here at Caerau.' 'Crwys?' I repeated, not at once comprehending. 'Oh, you must know Crwys, sir; it's just the other side of Cardiff, towards Newport.' 'Can you spell it for me?'[2] The woman blushed. ' 'Deed, sir,' said she, 'I ought to be a scholar, but I've had so much trouble with my old man that I've quite forgot my spellin'.' However, the story of Thomas Mathews was to the effect that he saw a Corpse Candle come out of his father's mouth and go to his feet, and away a bit, then back again to the mouth, which it did not exactly enter, but blended as it were with the sick man's body. I asked if the candle was tallow at any point in its excursion, to which I was gravely answered that it was the spirit of tallow. The man died not long after, in the presence of my informant, who described the incident with a dramatic force and fervour peculiarly Celtic, concluding with the remark: 'Well, well, there's only one way to come into the world, but there's a many ways to go out of it.'

The light issuing from the mouth is a fancy frequently encountered. In the 'Liber Landavensis' it is mentioned that one day as St Samson was celebrating the holy mysteries, St Dubricius with two monks saw a stream of fire to proceed glittering from his mouth.[3] In old woodcuts, the souls of the dying are represented as issuing from the mouth in the form of small human figures; and the Tyrolese peasants still fancy the soul is seen coming out of the mouth of a dying man like a white cloud.[4] From the mouth of a patient in a London hospital some time since the nurses observed issuing a pale bluish flame, and soon after the man died. The frightened nurses—not being acquainted with the corpse-candle theory of such things—imagined the torments of hell had already

---

[2] It is pronounced Croo-iss.
[3] *Liber Landavensis*, 299.
[4] Tylor, *Primitive Culture*, 391.

begun in the still living body. A scientific explanation of the phenomenon ascribed it to phosphuretted hydrogen, a result of incipient
decomposition.[5]

It is ill jesting with the Corpse Candle. Persons who have endeavoured to stop it on its way have come severely to grief thereby.
Many have been struck down where they stood, in punishment of
their audacity, as in the case of William John, a blacksmith of Lan-
boydi. He was one night going home on horseback, when he saw a
Corpse Candle, and his natural caution being at the moment somewhat overcome by potables, he resolved to go out of his way to
obstruct its passage. As the candle drew near he saw a corpse upon
a bier, the corpse of a woman he knew, and she held the candle
between her forefingers, and dreadfully grinned at him. Then he
was struck from his horse, and lay in the road a long time insensible, and was ill for weeks thereafter. Meantime, the woman whose
spectral corpse he had seen, died and was buried, her funeral passing by that road.

A clergyman's son in Carmarthenshire (subsequently himself a
preacher), who in his younger days was somewhat vicious, came
home one night late from a debauch, and found the doors locked.
Fearing to disturb the folk, and fearing also their reproaches and
chidings for his staying out so late (as many a young fellow has felt
before and since), he went to the man-servant, who slept in an out-
room, as is sometimes the custom in Welsh rural districts. He could
not awake the man-servant, but while standing over him, he saw
a small light issue from the servant's nostrils, which soon became
a Corpse Candle. He followed it out. It came to a foot-bridge
which crossed a rivulet. Here the young man became inspired
with the idea of trying an experiment with the Corpse Candle. He
raised the end of the foot-bridge off the bank, and watched to see
what the ghostly light would do. When it came to the rivulet it
seemed to offer to go over, but hesitated, as if loth to cross except
upon the bridge. So the young man put the bridge back in its
place, and stayed to see how the candle would act. It came on the
bridge, and as it passed the young man it struck him, as with

5 'Transactions Cardiff Nat. Soc.', iv. 5.

a handkerchief. But though the blow was thus light and phantom-like, it doubled the young man up and left him a senseless heap on the ground, where he lay till morning, when he recovered and went home. It is needless to add that the servant died.

Morris Griffith was once schoolmaster in the parish of Pontfaen, in Pembrokeshire, but subsequently became a Baptist preacher of the Gospel. He tells this story: 'As I was coming from a place called Tre-Davydd, and was come to the top of the hill, I saw a great light down in the valley, which I wondered at; for I could not imagine what it meant. But it came to my mind that it was a light before a burying, though I never could believe before that there was such a thing. The light which I saw then was a very red light, and it stood still for about a quarter of an hour in the way which went towards Llanferch-Llawddog church. I made haste to the other side of the hill, that I might see it farther; and from thence I saw it go along to the churchyard, where it stood still for a little time and entered into the church. I remained waiting to see it come out, and it was not long before it came out, and went to a certain part of the churchyard, where it stood a little time, and then vanished out of my sight. A few days afterwards, being in school with the children about noon, I heard a great noise overhead, as if the top of the house was coming down. I ran out to see the garret, and there was nothing amiss. A few days afterwards, Mr Higgon of Pontfaen's son died. When the carpenter came to fetch the boards to make the coffin (which were in the garret), he made exactly such a stir, in handling the boards in the garret, as was made before by some spirit, who foreknew the death that was soon to come to pass. In carrying the body to the grave, the burying stood where the light had stood for about a quarter of an hour, because there was some water crossing the way, and the people could not go over it without wetting their feet, there-fore they were obliged to wait till those that had boots helped them over. The child was buried in that very spot of ground in the churchyard, where I saw the light stop after it came out of the church. This is what I can boldly testify, having seen and heard what I relate—a thing which before I could not believe.'

Another man, Joshua Coslet, suddenly met a Corpse Candle as he was going through Heol Bwlch y Gwynt (Windgap Lane) in Llandilo Fawr parish. It was a small light when near him, but increased as it went farther from him. He could easily see that there was some dark shadow passing along with the candle, and the shadow of a man carried it, holding it 'between his three forefingers over against his face'. He might perhaps have seen more, but he was afraid to look too earnestly upon it. Not long after, a burying passed through Heol Bwlch y Gwynt. Another time he saw the likeness of a candle carried in a skull. 'There is nothing unlikely or unreasonable in either of these representations,' says the Prophet Jones, their historian.

A Carmarthenshire tradition relates that one day, when the coach which runs between Llandilo and Carmarthen was passing by Golden Grove, the property of the Earl of Cawdor, three Corpse Candles were observed on the surface of the water gliding down the stream which runs near the road. All the passengers saw them. A few days after, some men were about crossing the river near there in a coracle, when one of them expressed his fear at venturing, as the river was flooded, and he remained behind. Thus the fatal number crossed the river—three—three Corpse Candles having foretold their fate; and all were drowned.

Tradition ascribes the origin of all these death-portents to the efforts of St David. This saint appears to have been a great and good man, and a zealous Catholic, who, as a contemporary of the historical Arthur, is far enough back in the dim past to meet the views of romantic minds. And a prelate who by his prayers and presence could enable King Arthur to overthrow the Saxons in battle, or who by his pious learning could single-handed put down the Pelagian heresy in the Cardiganshire synod, was surely strong enough to invoke the Gwrach y Rhibyn, the Cyhyraeth, the Corpse Candle, and all the dreadful brood. This the legend relates he did by a special appeal to Heaven. Observing that the people in general were careless of the life to come, and could not be brought to mind it, and make preparation for it, St David prayed that Heaven would give a sign of the immortality of the soul, and of a life to come by a passage of death.

Since that day, Wales, and particularly that part of Wales included in the bishopric of St David, has had these phantoms. More materialistic minds consider these portents to be a remainder of those practices by which the persecuted Druids performed their rites and long kept up their religion in the land which Christianity had claimed: a similar origin, in fact, is here found for goblin omens as for fairies.

THE CHRONIC ARGONAUTS

by H. G. Wells

HERBERT GEORGE WELLS *(1866–1946) is still today considered this century's most important writer of Science Fiction and Fantasy. His unique imagination, uncanny ability at prophecy and his wide-ranging ideas have also given him an enduring place in the wider realms of world literature. Born into humble circumstances, he worked initially as a draper's assistant but gave this up for teaching. In his spare time he wrote prolifically—journalism, philosophy and fiction—and the early success which these items earned him secured his future as a man of letters. The variety of his work is well known to most readers as is the exuberance with which he threw himself into the propagation of utopian ideals and scientific progress. In the realms of Science Fiction,* The Time Machine *(1895),* The War of the Worlds *(1898)* and The Shape of Things to Come *(1933) are probably his best-known works. The first of these,* The Time Machine, *is widely considered as Wells' masterpiece and its history has strong Welsh connections. As a youngster he spent many holidays in the country and it was here that he first began 'thinking out' the idea of a time machine. The result of these deliberations was this short story, 'The Chronic Argonauts', which he completed in 1888 when he was only twenty-two. It appeared just once in* The Science Schools Journal *published by the Royal College of Science and was then several times re-written both as fact and fiction before finally emerging in the full-length form we know it today in 1895. This publication marks the story's first appearance in book form and only the most perfunctory glance will show its importance to students of Wells' work. It is also a tale which embodies some interesting elements of Welsh fantasy and as such is an important contribution to this collection.*

THE STORY FROM AN ESOTERIC POINT OF VIEW

Being the Account of Dr Nebogipfel's Sojourn in Llyddwdd

About half-a-mile outside the village of Llyddwdd by the road that goes up over the eastern flank of the mountain called Pen-y-pwll to Rwstog is a large farm-building known as the Manse. It derives this title from the fact that it was at one time the residence of the minister of the Calvinistic Methodists. It is a quaint, low, irregular erection, lying back some hundred yards from the railway, and now fast passing into a ruinous state.

Since its construction in the latter half of the last century this house has undergone many changes of fortune, having been abandoned long since by the farmer of the surrounding acres for less pretentious and more commodious headquarters. Among others Miss Carnot, 'the Gallic Sappho' at one time made it her home, and later on an old man named Williams became its occupier. The foul murder of this tenant by his two sons was the cause of its remaining for some considerable period uninhabited; with the inevitable consequence of its undergoing very extensive dilapidation.

The house had got a bad name, and adolescent man and Nature combined to bring swift desolation upon it. The fear of the Williamses which kept the Llyddwdd lads from gratifying their propensity to invade its deserted interior, manifested itself in unusually destructive resentment against its external breakables. The missiles with which they at once confessed and defied their spiritual dread, left scarcely a splinter of glass, and only battered relics of the old-fashioned leaden frames, in its narrow windows, while numberless shattered tiles about the house, and four or five black apertures yawning behind the naked rafters in the roof, also witnessed vividly to the energy of their trajection. Rain and wind thus had free way to enter the empty rooms and work their will there, old Time aiding and abetting. Alternately soaked and desiccated, the planks of flooring and wainscot warped apart strangely, split here and there, and tore themselves away in paroxysms of rheumatic pain from the rust-devoured nails that had once held them firm. The plaster of walls and ceiling, growing green-black with a rain-fed crust of lowly life, parted slowly from the fermenting laths; and large fragments thereof falling down inexplicably in tranquil hours, with loud concussion and clatter, gave strength to the popular superstition that old Williams and his sons were fated to re-enact their fearful tragedy until the final judgment. White roses and daedal creepers, that Miss Carnot had first adorned the walls with, spread now luxuriantly over the lichen-filmed tiles of the roof, and in slender graceful sprays timidly invaded the ghostly cobweb-draped apartments. Fungi, sickly pale, began to displace and uplift the bricks in the cellar floor; while on the rotting wood everywhere they clustered, in all the glory of the purple and mottled crimson, yellow-brown and hepatite. Woodlice and ants, beetles and moths, winged and creeping things innumerable, found each day a more congenial home among the ruins; and after them in ever-increasing multitudes swarmed the blotchy toads. Swallows and martins built every year more thickly in the silent, airy, upper chambers. Bats and owls struggled for the crepuscular corners of the lower rooms. Thus, in the Spring of the year eighteen hundred and eighty-seven, was Nature taking over, gradually but certainly, the tenancy of the old Manse. 'The house was falling into decay,' as men who do not appreciate the application of human derelicts to other beings' use would say, 'surely and swiftly.' But it was destined nevertheless to shelter another human tenant before its final dissolution.

There was no intelligence of the advent of a new inhabitant in quiet Llyddwdd. He came without a solitary premonition out of the vast unknown into the sphere of minute village observation and gossip. He fell into the Llyddwdd world, as it were, like a thunderbolt falling in the daytime. Suddenly, out of nothingness, he *was*. Rumour, indeed, vaguely averred that he was seen to arrive by a certain train from London, and to walk straight without hesitation to the old Manse, giving neither explanatory word nor sign to mortal as to his purpose there: but then the same fertile source of information also hinted that he was first beheld skimming down the slopes of steep Pen-y-pwll with exceeding swiftness, riding, as it appeared to the intelligent observer, upon an instrument not unlike a sieve and that he entered the house by the chimney. Of these conflicting reports, the former was the first to be generally circulated, but the latter, in view of the bizarre presence and eccentric ways of the newest inhabitant, obtained wider credence. By whatever means he arrived, there can be no doubt that he was in, and in possession of the Manse, on the first of May; because on the morning of that day he was inspected by Mrs Morgan ap Lloyd Jones, and subsequently by the numerous persons her report brought up the mountain slope, engaged in the curious occupation of nailing sheet-tin across the void window sockets of his new domicile—'blinding his house', as Mrs Morgan ap Lloyd Jones not inaptly termed it.

He was a small-bodied, sallow faced little man, clad in a close-fitting garment of some stiff, dark material, which Mr Parry Davies the Llyddwdd shoemaker, opined was leather. His aquiline nose, thin lips, high cheek-ridges, and pointed chin, were all small and mutually well proportioned; but the bones and muscles of his face were rendered excessively prominent and distinct by his extreme leanness. The same cause contributed to the sunken appearance of the large eager-looking grey eyes, that gazed forth from under his phenomenally wide and high forehead. It was this latter feature that most powerfully attracted the attention of an observer. It seemed to be great beyond all preconceived ratio to the rest of his countenance. Dimensions, corrugations, wrinkles, venation, were alike abnormally exaggerated. Below it his eyes glowed like lights in some cave at a cliff's foot. It so over-powered and suppressed the rest of his face as to give an *unhuman* appearance almost, to what would otherwise have been an unquestionably handsome pro-file. The lank black hair that hung unkempt before his eyes served to increase rather than conceal this effect, by adding to unnatural altitude a suggestion of hydrocephalic projection: and the idea of something ultra human was furthermore accentuated by the temporal arteries that pulsated visibly through his transparent yellow skin. No wonder, in view even of these things, that among the highly and over-poetical Cymric of Llyddwdd the sieve theory of arrival found considerable favour.

It was his bearing and actions, however, much more than his personality, that won over believers to the warlock notion of matters. In almost every circumstance of life the observant villagers soon found his ways were not only not *their* ways, but altogether inexplicable upon any theory of motives they could conceive. Thus, in a small matter at the beginning, when Arthur Price Williams, eminent and famous in every tavern in Caernarvonshire for his social gifts, endeavoured, in choicest Welsh and even choicer English, to inveigle the stranger into conversation over the sheet-tin performance, he failed utterly. Inquisitional supposition, straightforward enquiry, offer of assistance, suggestion of method, sarcasm, irony, abuse, and at last, gage of battle, though shouted with much effort from the road hedge, went unanswered and apparently unheard. Missile weapons, Arthur Price Williams found, were equally unavailing for the purpose of introduction, and the gathered crowd dispersed with unappeased curiosity and suspicion. Later in the day, the swarth apparition was seen striding down the mountain road towards the village, hatless, and with such swift width of step and set resolution of countenance, that Arthur Price Williams, beholding him from afar from the Pig and Whistle doorway was seized with dire consternation, and hid behind the Dutch oven in the kitchen till he was past. Wild panic also smote the school-house as the children were coming out, and drove them indoors like leaves before a gale. He was merely seeking the provision shop, however, and erupted thencefrom after a prolonged stay, loaded with a various armful of blue parcels, a loaf, herrings, pigs' trotters, salt pork, and a black bottle, with which he returned in the same swift projectile gait to the Manse. His way of shopping was to name, and to name simply, without solitary other word of explanation, civility or request, the article he required.

The shopkeeper's crude meteorological superstitions and inquisitive commonplaces, he seemed not to hear, and he might have been esteemed deaf if he had not evinced the promptest attention to the faintest relevant remark. Consequently it was speedily rumoured that he was determined to avoid all but the most necessary human intercourse. He lived altogether mysteriously, in the decaying manse, without mortal service or companionship, presumably sleeping on planks or litter, and either preparing his own food or eating it raw. This, coupled with the popular conception of the haunting patricides, did much to strengthen the popular supposition of some vast gulf between the newcomer and common humanity. The only thing that was inharmonious with this idea of severance from mankind was a constant flux of crates filled with grotesquely contorted glassware, cases of brazen and steel instruments, huge coils of wire, vast iron and fire-clay implements, of inconceivable purpose, jars and phials labelled in black and scarlet—POISON, huge packages of books, and gargantuan rolls of cartridge paper, which set in towards his Llyddwdd quarters from the outer world. The apparently hieroglyphic inscriptions on these various consignments revealed at the profound scrutiny of Pugh Jones that the style and title of the new inhabitant was Dr Moses Nebogipfel, Ph.D., F.R.S., N.W.R., PAID: at which discovery much edification was felt, especially among the purely Welsh-speaking community. Further than this, these arrivals, by their evident unfitness for any allowable mortal use, and inferential diabolicalness, filled the neighbourhood with a vague horror and lively curiosity, which were greatly augmented by the extraordinary phenomena, and still more extraordinary accounts thereof, that followed their reception in the Manse.

The first of these was on Wednesday, the fifteenth of May, when the Calvinistic Methodists of Llyddwdd had their annual commemoration festival; on which occasion, in accordance with custom, dwellers in the surrounding parishes of Rwstog, Pen-y-garn, Caergyllwdd, Llanrdd, and even distant Llanrwst flocked into the village. Popular thanks to Providence were materialised in the usual way, by means of plum-bread and butter, mixed tea, *terza*, consecrated flirtations, kiss-in-the-ring, rough-and-tumble football, and vituperative political speechmaking. About half-past eight the fun began to tarnish, and the assembly to break up; and by nine numerous couples and occasional groups were wending their way in the darkling along the hilly Llyddwdd and Rwstog road. It was a calm warm night; one of those nights when lamps, gas and heavy sleep seem stupid ingratitude to the Creator. The zenith sky was an ineffable deep lucent blue, and the evening star hung golden in the liquid darkness of the west. In the north-north-west, a faint phosphorescence marked the sunken day. The moon was just rising, pallid and gibbous over the huge haze-dimmed shoulder of Pen-y-pwll. Against the wan eastern sky, from the vague outline of the mountain slope, the Manse stood out black, clear and solitary. The stillness of the twilight had hushed the myriad murmurs of the day. Only the sounds of footsteps and voices and laughter, that came fitfully rising and falling from the roadway, and an intermittent hammering in the darkened dwelling, broke the silence. Suddenly a strange whizzing, buzzing whirr filled the night air, and a bright flicker glanced across the dim path of the wayfarers. All eyes were turned in astonishment to the old Manse. The house no longer loomed a black featureless block but was filled to overflowing with light. From the gaping holes in the roof, from chinks and fissures amid tiles and brickwork, from every gap which Nature or man had pierced in the crumbling old shell, a blinding blue-white glare was streaming, beside which the rising moon seemed a disc of opaque sulphur. The thin mist of the dewy night had caught the violet glow and hung, unearthly smoke, over the colourless blaze. A strange turmoil and outcrying in the old Manse now began, and grew ever more audible to the clustering spectators, and therewith came clanging loud impacts against the window-guarding tin. Then from the gleaming roof-gaps of the house suddenly vomited forth a wonderous swarm of heteromerous living things—swallows, sparrows, martins, owls, bats, insects in visible multitudes, to hang for many minutes a noisy, gyring, spreading cloud over the black gables and chimneys . . . and then slowly to thin out and vanish away in the night.

As this tumult died away the throbbing humming that had first arrested attention grew once more in the listener's hearing, until at last it was the only sound in the long stillness. Presently, however, the road gradually awoke again to the beating and shuffling of feet, as the knots of Rwstog people, one by one, turned their blinking eyes from the dazzling whiteness and, pondering deeply, continued their homeward way.

The cultivated reader will have already discerned that this phenomenon, which sowed a whole crop of uncanny thoughts in the minds of these worthy folk, was simply the installation of the electric light in the Manse. Truly, this last vicissitude of the old house was its strangest one. Its revival to mortal life was like the raising of Lazarus. From that hour forth, by night and day, behind the tin-blinded windows, the tamed lightning illuminated every corner of its quickly changing interior. The almost frenzied energy of the lank-haired, leather-clad little doctor swept away into obscure holes and corners and common destruction, creeper sprays, toadstools, rose leaves, birds' nests, birds' eggs, cobwebs, and all the coatings and lovingly fanciful trimmings with which that maternal old dotard, Dame Nature, had tricked out the decaying house for its lying in state. The magneto-electric apparatus whirred incessantly amid the vestiges of the wainscoted dining-room, where once the eighteenth-century tenant had piously read morning prayer and eaten his Sunday dinner; and in the place of his sacred symbolical sideboard was a nasty heap of coke. The oven of the bakehouse supplied substratum and material for a forge, whose snorting, panting bellows, and intermittent, ruddy spark-laden blast made the benighted, but Bible-lit Welsh women murmur in liquid Cymric, as they hurried by: 'Whose breath kindleth coals, and out of his mouth is a flame of fire.' For the idea these good people formed of it was that a tame, but occasionally restive, leviathan had been added to the terrors of the haunted house. The constantly increasing accumulation of pieces of machinery, big brass castings, block tin, casks, crates, and packages of innumerable articles, by their demands for space, necessitated the sacrifice of most of the slighter partitions of the house, and the beams and flooring of the upper chambers were also mercilessly sawn away by the tireless scientist in such a way as to convert them into mere shelves and corner brackets of the atrial space between cellars and rafters. Some of the sounder planking was utilised in the making of a rude broad table, upon which files and heaps of geometrical diagrams speedily accumulated. The production of these latter seemed to be the object upon which the mind of Dr Nebogipfel was so inflexibly set. All other circumstances of his life were made entirely subsidiary to this one occupation. Strangely complicated traceries of lines they were—plans, elevations, sections by surfaces and solids, that, with the help of logarithmic mechanical apparatus and involved curvigraphical machines, spread swiftly under his expert hands over yard after yard of paper. Some of these symbolised shapes he despatched to London, and they presently returned, *realised,* in forms of brass and ivory, and nickel and mahogany. Some of them he himself translated into solid models of metal and wood; occasionally casting the metallic ones in moulds of sand, but often laboriously hewing them out of the block for greater precision of dimension. In this second process, among other appliances, he employed a steel circular saw set with diamond powder and made to rotate with extraordinary swiftness, by means of steam and multiplying gear. It was this latter thing, more than all else, that filled Llyddwdd with a sickly loathing of the Doctor as a man of blood and darkness. Often in the silence of midnight—for the newest inhabitant heeded the sun but little in his incessant research—the awakened dwellers around Pen-y-pwll would hear, what was at first a complaining murmur, like the groaning of a wounded man, '*gurr*-urr-urr-URR', rising by slow gradations in pitch and intensity to the likeness of a voice in despairing passionate protest, and at last ending abruptly in a sharp piercing shriek that rang in the ears for hours afterwards and begot numberless gruesome dreams.

The mystery of all these unearthly noises and inexplicable phenomena, the Doctor's inhumanly brusque bearing and evident uneasiness when away from his absorbing occupation, his entire and jealous seclusion, and his terrifying behaviour to certain officious intruders, roused popular resentment and curiously to the highest, and a plot was already on foot to make some sort of popular inquisition (probably accompanied by an experimental ducking) into his proceedings, when the sudden death of the hunchback Hughes in a fit, brought matters to an unexpected crisis. It happened in broad daylight, in the roadway just opposite the Manse. Half a dozen people witnessed it. The unfortunate creature was seen to fall suddenly and roll about on the pathway, struggling violently, as it appeared to the spectators, with some invisible assailant. When assistance reached him he was purple in the face and his blue lips were covered with a glairy foam. He died almost as soon as they laid hands on him.

Owen Thomas, the general practitioner, vainly assured the excited crowd which speedily gathered outside the Pig and Whistle, whither the body had been carried, that death was unquestionably natural. A horrible zymotic suspicion had gone forth that the deceased was the victim of Dr Nebogipfel's imputed aerial powers. The contagion was with the news that passed like a flash through the village and set all Llyddwdd seething with a fierce desire for action against the worker of this iniquity. Downright superstition, which had previously walked somewhat modestly about the village, in the fear of ridicule and the Doctor, now appeared boldly before the sight of all men, clad in the terrible majesty of truth. People who had hitherto kept entire silence as to their fears of the imp-like philosopher suddenly discovered a fearsome pleasure in whispering dread possibilities to kindred souls, and from whispers of possibilities their sympathy-fostered utterances soon developed into unhesitating asserverations in loud and even high-pitched tones. The fancy of a captive leviathan, already alluded to, which had up to now been the horrid but secret joy of a certain conclave of ignorant old women, was published to all the world as indisputable fact; it being stated, on her own authority, that the animal had, on one occasion, chased Mrs Morgan ap Lloyd Jones almost into Rwstog. The story that Nebogipfel had been heard within the Manse chanting, in conjunction with the Williamses, horrible blasphemy, and that a 'black flapping thing, of the size of a young calf', had thereupon entered the gap in the roof, was universally believed in. A grisly anecdote, that owed its origination to a stumble in the churchyard, was circulated, to the effect that the Doctor had been caught ghoulishly tearing with his long white fingers at a new-made grave. The numerously attested declaration that Nebogipfel and the murdered Williams had been seen hanging the sons on a ghostly gibbet, at the back of the house, was due to the electric illumination of a fitfully wind-shaken tree. A hundred like stories hurtled thickly about the village and darkened the moral atmosphere. The Reverend Elijah Ulysses Cook, hearing of the tumult, sallied forth to allay it, and narrowly escaped drawing on himself the gathering lightning.

By eight o'clock (it was Monday the twenty-second of July) a grand demonstration had organised itself against the 'necromancer'. A number of bolder hearts among the men formed the nucleus of the gathering, and at nightfall Arthur Price Williams, John Peters, and others brought torches and raised their spark-raining flames aloft with curt ominous suggestions. The less adventurous village manhood came straggling late to the rendezvous, and with them the married women came in groups of four or five, greatly increasing the excitement of the assembly with their shrill hysterical talk and active imaginations. After these the children and young girls, overcome by undefinable dread, crept quietly out of the too silent and shadowy houses into the yellow glare of the pine knots, and the tumultuary noise of the thickening people. By nine, nearly half the Llyddwdd population was massed before the Pig and Whistle. There was a confused murmur of many tongues, but above all the stir and chatter of the growing crowd could be heard the coarse, cracked voice of the blood-thirsty old fanatic, Pritchard, drawing a congenial lesson from the fate of the four hundred and fifty idolators of Carmel.

Just as the church clock was beating out the hour, an occultly originated movement up hill began, and soon the whole assembly, men, women, and children, was moving in a fear-compacted mass, towards the ill-fated doctor's abode. As they left the brightly-lit public house behind them, a quavering female voice began singing one of those grim-sounding canticles that so satisfy the Calvinistic ear. In a wonderfully short time, the tune had been caught up, first by two or three, and then by the whole procession, and the manifold shuffling of heavy shoon grew swiftly into rhythm with the beats of the hymn. When, however, their goal rose, like a blazing star, over the undulation of the road, the volume of the chanting suddenly died away, leaving only the voices of the ringleaders, shouting indeed now somewhat out of tune, but, if anything, more vigorously than before. Their persistence and example nevertheless failed to prevent a perceptible breaking and slackening of the pace, as the Manse was neared, and when the gate was reached, the whole crowd came to a dead halt. Vague fear for the future had begotten the courage that had brought the villagers thus far: fear for the present now smothered its kindred birth. The intense blaze from the gaps in the death-like silent pile lit up rows of livid, hesitating faces: and a smothered, frightened sobbing broke out among the children. 'Well,' said Arthur Price Williams, addressing Jack Peters, with an expert assumption of the modest discipleship, 'what do we do *now*, Jack?' But Peters was regarding the Manse with manifest dubiety, and ignored the question. The Llyddwdd witch-find seemed to be suddenly aborting.

At this juncture old Pritchard suddenly pushed his way forward, gesticulating weirdly with his bony hands and long arms. '*What!*' he shouted, in broken notes, 'fear ye to smite when the Lord hateth? *Burn* the warlock!' And seizing a flambeau from Peters, he flung open the rickety gate and strode on down the drive, his torch leaving a coiling trail of scintillant sparks on the night wind. 'Burn the warlock,' screamed a shrill voice from the wavering crowd, and in a moment the gregarious human instinct had prevailed. With an outburst of incoherent, threatening voice, the mob poured after the fanatic.

Woe betide the Philosopher now! They expected barricaded doors; but with a groan of a conscious insufficiency, the hinge-rusted portals swung at the push of Pritchard. Blinded by the light, he hesitated for a second on the threshold, while his followers came crowding up behind him.

Those who were there say that they saw Dr Ncbogipfel, standing in the toneless electric glare, on a peculiar erection of brass and ebony and ivory; and that he seemed to be smiling at them, half pityingly and half scornfully, as it is said martyrs are wont to smile. Some assert, moreover, that by his side was sitting a tall man, clad in ravenswing, and some even aver that this second man— whom others deny—bore on his face the likeness of the Reverend Elijah Ulysses Cook, while others declare that he resembled the description of the murdered Williams. Be that as it may, it must now go unproven for ever, for suddenly a wonderous thing smote the crowd as it swarmed in through the entrance. Pritchard pitched headlong on the floor senseless. While shouts and shrieks of anger, changed in mid utterance to yells of agonising fear, or to the mute gasp of heart-stopping horror: and then a frantic rush was made for the doorway.

For the calm, smiling doctor, and his quiet, black-clad companion, and the polished platform which upbore them, had vanished before their eyes!

How an Esoteric Story Became Possible

A silvery-foliaged willow by the side of a mere. Out of the cress-spangled waters below, rise clumps of sedge-blades, and among them glows the purple fleur-de-lys, and sapphire vapour of forget-me-nots. Beyond is a sluggish stream of water reflecting the intense blue of the moist Fenland sky; and beyond that a low osier-fringed eyot. This limits all the visible universe, save some scattered pollards and spear-like poplars showing against the violet distance. At the foot of the willow reclines the Author watching a copper butterfly fluttering from iris to iris.

Who can fix the colours of the sunset? Who can take a cast of flame? Let him essay to register the mutations of mortal thought as it wanders from a copper butterfly to the disembodied soul, and thence passes to spiritual motions and the vanishing of Dr Moses Nebogipfel and the Rev. Elijah Ulysses Cook from the world of sense.

As the author lay basking there and speculating, as another once did under the Budh tree, on mystic transmutations, a presence became apparent. There was a somewhat on the eyot between him and the purple horizon—an opaque reflecting entity, making itself dimly perceptible by reflection in the water to his averted eyes. He raised them in curious surprise.

What was it?

He stared in stupefied astonishment at the apparition, doubted, blinked, rubbed his eyes, stared again, and believed. It was solid, it cast a shadow, and it upbore two men. There was white metal in it that blazed in the noontide sun like incandescent magnesium, ebony bars that drank in the light, and white parts that gleamed like polished ivory. Yet withal it seemed unreal. The thing was not square as a machine ought to be, but all awry: it was twisted and seemed falling over, hanging in two directions, as those queer crystals called triclinic hang; it seemed like a machine that had been crushed or warped; it was suggestive and not confirmatory, like the machine of a disordered dream. The men, too, were dream-like. One was short, intensely sallow, with a strangely-shaped head, and clad in a garment of dark olive green, the other was, grotesquely out of place, evidently a clergyman of the Established Church, a fair-haired, pale-faced respectable-looking man.

Once more doubt came rushing in on the author. He sprawled back and stared at the sky, rubbed his eyes, stared at the willow wands that hung between him and the blue, closely examined his hands to see if his eyes had any new things to relate about them, and then sat up again and stared at the eyot. A gentle breeze stirred the osiers; a white bird was flapping its way through the lower sky. The machine of the vision had vanished! It was an illusion—a projection of the subjective—an assertion of the immateriality of mind. 'Yes,' interpolated the sceptic faculty, 'but *how comes it that the clergyman is still there?*'

The clergyman had not vanished. In intense perplexity the author examined this black-coated phenomenon as he stood regarding the world with hand-shaded eyes. The author knew the periphery of that eyot by heart, and the question that troubled him was, 'Whence?' The clergyman looked as Frenchmen look when they land at Newhaven—intensely travel-worn; his clothes showed rubbed and seamy in the bright day. When he came to the edge of the island and shouted a question to the author, his voice was broken and trembled. 'Yes,' answered the author, 'it is an island. *How did you get there?*'

But the clergyman, instead of replying to this asked a very strange question.

He said 'Are you in the nineteenth century?' The author made him repeat that question before he replied. 'Thank heaven,' cried the clergyman rapturously. Then he asked very eagerly for the exact date.

'August the ninth, eighteen hundred and eighty-seven,' he repeated after the author. 'Heaven be praised!' and sinking down on the eyot so that the sedges hid him, he audibly burst into tears.

Now the author was mightily surprised at all this, and going a certain distance along the mere, he obtained a punt, and getting into it he hastily poled to the eyot where he had last seen the clergyman. He found him lying insensible among the reeds, and carried him in his punt to the house where he lived, and the clergyman lay there insensible for ten days.

Meanwhile, it became known that he was the Rev. Elijah Cook, who had disappeared from Llyddwdd with Dr Moses Nebogipfel three weeks before.

On August 19th, the nurse called the author out of his study to speak to the invalid. He found him perfectly sensible, but his eyes were strangely bright, and his face was deadly pale. 'Have you found out who I am?' he asked.

'You are the Rev. Elijah Ulysses Cook, Master of Arts, of Pembroke College, Oxford, and Rector of Llyddwdd, near Rwstog, in Caernarvon.'

He bowed his head. 'Have you been told anything of how I came here?'

'I found you among the reeds,' I said. He was silent and thoughtful for a while. 'I have a deposition to make. Will you take it? It concerns the murder of an old man named Williams, which occurred in 1862, this disappearance of Dr Moses Nebogipfel, the abduction of a ward in the year 4003—'

The author stared.

'The year of our Lord 4003,' he corrected. 'She would come. Also several assaults on public officials in the years 17,901 and 2.'

The author coughed.

'The years 17,901 and 2, and valuable medical, social, and physiographical data for all time.'

After a consultation with the doctor, it was decided to have the deposition taken down, and this is which constitutes the remainder of the story of the Chronic Argonauts.

On August 29th, 1887, the Rev Elijah Cook died. His body was conveyed to Llyddwdd, and buried in the churchyard there.

THE ESOTERIC STORY
BASED ON THE CLERGYMAN'S DEPOSITIONS

The Anachronic Man

Incidentally it has been remarked in the first part, how the Reverend Elijah Ulysses Cook attempted and failed to quiet the superstitious excitement of the villagers on the afternoon of the memorable twenty-second of July. His next proceeding was to try and warn the unsocial philosopher of the dangers which impended. With this intent he made his way from the rumour-pelted village, through the silent, slumbrous heat of the July afternoon, up the slopes of Pen-y-pwll, to the old Manse. His loud knocking at the heavy door called forth dull resonance from the interior, and produced a shower of lumps of plaster and fragments of decaying touchwood from the rickety porch, but beyond this the dreamy stillness of the summer mid-day remained unbroken. Everything was so quiet as he stood there expectant, that the occasional speech of the haymakers a mile away in the fields, over towards Rwstog, could be distinctly heard. The reverend gentleman waited, then knocked again, and waited again, and listened, until the echoes and the patter of rubbish had melted away into the deep silence, and the creeping in the blood-vessels of his ears had become oppressively audible, swelling and sinking with sounds like the confused murmuring of a distant crowd, and causing a suggestion of anxious discomfort to spread slowly over his mind.

Again he knocked, this time loud, quick blows with his stick, and almost immediately afterwards, leaning his hand against the door, he kicked the panels vigorously. There was a shouting of echoes, a protesting jarring of hinges, and then the oaken door yawned and displayed, in the blue blaze of the electric light, vestiges of partitions, piles of planking and straw, masses of metal, heaps of papers and overthrown apparatus, to the rector's astonished eyes. 'Doctor Nebogipfel, excuse my intruding,' he called out, but the only response was a reverberation among the black beams and shadows that hung dimly above. For almost a minute he stood there, leaning forward over the threshold, staring at the glittering mechanisms, diagrams, books, scattered indiscriminately with broken food, packing cases, heaps of coke, hay, and microcosmic lumber, about the undivided house cavity; and then, removing his hat and treading stealthily, as if the silence were a sacred thing, he stepped into the apparently deserted shelter of the Doctor.

His eyes sought everywhere, as he cautiously made his way through the confusion, with a strange anticipation of finding Nebogipfel hidden somewhere in the sharp black shadows among the litter, so strong in him was an indescribable sense of perceiving presence. This feeling was so vivid that, when, after an abortive exploration, he seated himself upon Nebogipfel's diagram-covered bench, it made him explain in a forced hoarse voice to the stillness—'He is not here. I have something to say to him. I must wait for him.' It was so vivid, too, that the trickling of some grit down the wall in the vacant corner behind him made him start round in a sudden perspiration. There was nothing visible there, but turning his head back, he was stricken rigid with horror by the swift, noiseless apparition of Nebogipfel, ghastly pale, and with red stained hands, crouching upon a strange-looking metallic platform, and with his deep grey eyes looking intently into the visitor's face.

Cook's first impulse was to yell out his fear, but his throat was paralysed, and he could only stare fascinated at the bizarre countenance that had thus clashed suddenly into visibility. The lips were quivering and the breath came in short convulsive sobs. The un-human forehead was wet with perspiration, while the veins were swollen, knotted and purple. The Doctor's red hands, too, he noticed, were trembling, as the hands of slight people tremble after intense muscular exertion, and his lips closed and opened as if he, too, had a difficulty in speaking as he gasped, 'Who—what do you do here?'

Cook answered not a word, but stared with hair erect, open mouth, and dilated eyes, at the dark red unmistakeable smear that streaked the pure ivory and gleaming nickel and shining ebony of the platform.

'What are you doing here?' repeated the doctor, raising himself. 'What do you want?'

Cook gave a convulsive effort. 'In Heaven's name, *what* are you?' he gasped; and then black curtains came closing in from every side, sweeping the squatting, dwarfish phantasm that reeled before him into rayless, voiceless night.

The Reverend Elijah Ulysses Cook recovered his perceptions to find himself lying on the floor of the old Manse, and Doctor Nebogipfel, no longer blood-stained and with all trace of his agitation gone, kneeling by his side and bending over him with a glass of brandy in his hand. 'Do not be alarmed, sir,' said the philosopher with a faint smile, as the clergyman opened his eyes. 'I have not treated you to a disembodied spirit, or anything nearly so extraordinary . . . may I offer you this?'

The clergyman submitted quietly to the brandy, and then stared perplexed into Nebogipfel's face, vainly searching his memory for what occurrences had preceded his insensibility. Raising himself at last, into a sitting posture, he saw the oblique mass of metals that had appeared with the doctor, and immediately all that happened flashed back upon his mind. He looked from this structure to the recluse, and from the recluse to the structure.

'There is absolutely no deception, sir,' said Nebogipfel with the slightest trace of mockery in his voice. 'I lay no claim to work in matters spiritual. It is a *bona fide* mechanical contrivance, a thing emphatically of this sordid world. Excuse me—just one minute.' He rose from his knees, stepped upon the mahogany platform, took a curiously curved lever in his hand and pulled it over. Cook rubbed his eyes. *There* certainly was no deception. The doctor and the machine had vanished.

The reverend gentleman felt no horror this time, only a slight nervous shock, to see the doctor presently re-appear 'in the twinkling of an eye' and get down from the machine. From that he walked in a straight line with his hands behind his back and his face downcast, until his progress was stopped by the intervention of a circular saw; then, turning round sharply on his heel, he said:

'I was thinking while I was . . . away . . . Would you like to come? I should greatly value a companion.'

The clergyman was still sitting, hatless, on the floor. 'I am afraid,' he said slowly, 'you will think me stupid—'

'Not at all,' interrupted the doctor. 'The stupidity is mine. You desire to have all this explained ... wish to know where I am going first. I have spoken so little with men of this age for the last ten years or more that I have ceased to make due allowances and concessions for other minds. I will do my best, but that I fear will be very unsatisfactory. It is a long story ... do you find that floor comfortable to sit on? If not, there is a nice packing case over there, or some straw behind you, or this bench—the diagrams are done with now, but I am afraid of the drawing pins. You may sit on the Chronic Argo!'

'No, thank you,' slowly replied the clergyman, eyeing that deformed structure thus indicated, suspiciously; 'I am *quite* comfortable here.'

'Then I will begin. Do you read fables? Modern ones?'

'I am afraid I must confess to a good deal of fiction,' said the clergyman deprecatingly. 'In Wales the ordained ministers of the sacraments of the Church have perhaps *too* large a share of leisure—'

'Have you read the Ugly Duckling?'

'Hans Christian Andersen's—yes—in my childhood.'

'A wonderful story—a story that has ever been full of tears and heart swelling hopes for me, since first it came to me in my lonely boyhood and saved me from unspeakable things. That story, if you understand it well, will tell you almost all that you should know of me to comprehend how that machine came to be thought of in a mortal brain ... Even when I read that simple narrative for the first time, a thousand bitter experiences had begun the teaching of my isolation among the people of my birth—I knew the story was for me. The ugly duckling that proved to be a swan, that lived through all contempt and bitterness, to float at last sublime. From that hour forth, I dreamt of meeting with my kind, dreamt of encountering that sympathy I knew was my profoundest need. Twenty years I lived in that hope, lived and worked, lived and wandered, loved even, and at last, despaired. Only once among all those millions of wondering, astonished, indifferent, contemptuous, and insidious faces that I met with in that passionate wandering, looked *one* upon me as I desired . . . looked—'

He paused. The Reverend Cook glanced up into his face, expecting some indication of the deep feeling that had sounded in his last words. It was downcast, clouded, and thoughtful, but the mouth was rigidly firm.

'In short, Mr Cook, I discovered that I was one of those superior Cagots called a genius—a man born out of my time—a man thinking the thoughts of a wiser age, doing things and believing things that men now *cannot* understand, and that in the years ordained to me there was nothing but silence and suffering for my soul—unbroken solitude, man's bitterest pain. I knew I was an Anachronic Man; my age was still to come. One filmy hope alone held me to life, a hope to which I clung until it had become a certain thing. Thirty years of unremitting toil and deepest thought among the hidden things of matter and form and life, and then *that*, the Chronic Argo, *the ship that sails through time*, and now I go to join my generation, to journey through the ages till my time has come.'

The Chronic Argo

Dr Nebogipfel paused, looked in sudden doubt at the clergyman's perplexed face. 'You think that sounds mad,' he said, 'to travel through time?'

'It certainly jars with accepted opinions,' said the clergyman, allowing the faintest suggestion of controversy to appear in his intonation, and speaking apparently to the Chronic Argo. Even a clergyman of the Church of England you see can have a suspicion of illusions at times.

'It certainly *does* jar with accepted opinions,' agreed the philosopher cordially. 'It does more than that—it defies accepted opinions to mortal combat. Opinions of all sorts, Mr Cook—Scientific Theories, Laws, Articles of Belief, or, to come to elements, Logical Premises, Ideas, or whatever you like to call them—all are, from the infinite nature of things, so many diagrammatic caricatures of the ineffable—caricatures altogether to be avoided save where they are necessary in the shaping of results—as chalk outlines are necessary to the painter and plans and sections to the engineer. Men, from the exigencies of their being, find this hard to believe.'

The Rev. Elijah Ulysses Cook nodded his head with the quiet smile of one whose opponent has unwittingly given a point.

'It is as easy to come to regard ideas as complete reproductions of entities as it is to roll off a log. Hence it is that almost all civilised men believe in the *reality* of the Greek geometrical conceptions.'

'Oh! pardon me, sir,' interrupted Cook. 'Most men know that a geometrical point has no existence in matter, and the same with a geometrical line. I think you underrate . . .'

'Yes, yes, *those* things are recognised,' said Nebogipfel calmly; 'but now . . . a cube. Does that exist in the material universe?'

'Certainly.'

'An instantaneous cube?'

'I don't know what you intend by that expression.'

'Without any other sort of extension; a body having length, breadth, and thickness, exists?'

'What other sort of extension *can* there be?' asked Cook, with raised eyebrows.

'Has it never occurred to you that no form can exist in the material universe that has no extension in time? . . . Has it never glimmered upon your consciousness that nothing stood between men and a geometry of four dimensions—length, breadth, thickness, and *duration*—but the inertia of opinion, the impulse from the Levantine philosophers of the bronze age?'

'Putting it that way,' said the clergyman, 'it does look as though there was a flaw somewhere in the notion of tridimensional being; but' . . . He became silent, leaving that sufficiently eloquent 'but' to convey all the prejudice and distrust that filled his mind.

'When we take up this new light of a fourth dimension and re-examine our physical science in its illumination,' continued Nebogipfel, after a pause, 'we find ourselves no longer limited by hopeless restriction to a certain beat of time—to our own generation. Locomotion along lines of duration—chronic navigation comes within the range, first, of geometrical theory, and then of practical mechanics. There *was* a time when men could only move horizontally and in their appointed country. The clouds floated above them, unattainable things, mysterious chariots of those fearful gods who dwelt among the mountain summits. Speaking practically, men in those days were restricted to motion in two dimensions; and even there circumambient ocean and hypoborean fear bound him in. But those times were to pass away. First, the keel of Jason cut its way between the Symplegades, and then in the fulness of time, Columbus dropped anchor in a bay of Atlantis. Then man burst his bidimensional limits, and invaded the third dimension, soaring with Montgolfier into the clouds, and sinking with a diving bell into the purple treasure-caves of the waters. And now another step, and the hidden past and unknown future are before us. We stand upon a mountain summit with the plains of the ages spread below.'

Nebogipfel paused and looked down at his hearer.

The Reverend Elijah Cook was sitting with an expression of strong distrust on his face. Preaching much had brought home certain truths to him very vividly, and he always suspected rhetoric. 'Are those things figures of speech,' he asked; 'or am I to take them as precise statements? Do you speak of travelling through time in the same way as one might speak of Omnipotence making His pathway on the storm, or do you—a—mean what you say?'

Dr Nebogipfel smiled quietly. 'Come and look at these diagrams,' he said, and then with elaborate simplicity he commenced to explain again to the clergyman the new quadridimensional geometry. Insensibly Cook's aversion passed away, and seeming impossibility grew possible, now that such tangible things as diagrams and models could be brought forward in evidence. Presently he found himself asking questions, and his interest grew deeper and deeper as Nebogipfel slowly and with precise clearness unfolded the beautiful order of his strange invention. The moments slipped away unchecked, as the Doctor passed on to the narrative of his research, and it was with a start of surprise that the clergyman noticed the deep blue of the dying twilight through the open doorway.

'The voyage,' said Nebogipfel concluding his history, 'will be full of undreamt-of dangers—already in one brief essay I have stood in the very jaws of death—but it is also full of the divinest promise of undreamt-of joy. Will you come? Will you walk among the people of the Golden Years? . . .'

But the mention of death by the philosopher had brought flooding back to the mind of Cook, all the horrible sensations of that first apparition.

'Dr Nebogipfel . . . one question?' He hesitated. 'On your hands . . . *Was it blood?*'

Nebogipfel's countenance fell. He spoke slowly.

'When I had stopped my machine, I found myself in this room as it used to be. *Hark!*'

'It is the wind in the trees towards Rwstog.'

'It sounded like the voices of a multitude of people singing . . . when I had stopped I found myself in this room as it used to be. An old man, a young man, and a lad were sitting at a table—reading some book together. I stood behind them unsuspected. "Evil spirits assailed him," read the old man; "but it is written, 'to him that overcometh shall be given life eternal'. They came as entreating friends, but he endured through all their snares. They came as principalities and powers, but he defied them in the name of the King of Kings. Once even it is told that in his study, while he was translating the New Testament into German, the Evil One himself appeared before him . . ." Just then the lad glanced timorously round, and with a fearful wail fainted away . . .

'The others sprang at me . . . It was a fearful grapple . . . The old man clung to my throat, screaming "Man or Devil, I defy thee . . ."

'I could not help it. We rolled together on the floor . . . the knife his trembling son had dropped came to my hand . . . Hark!'

He paused and listened, but Cook remained staring at him in the same horror-stricken attitude he had assumed when the memory of the blood-stained hands had rushed back over his mind.

'Do you hear what they are crying? *Hark!*'

Burn the warlock! Burn the murderer!

'Do you hear? There is no time to be lost.'

Slay the murderer of cripples. Kill the devil's claw!

'Come! Come!'

Cook, with a convulsive effort, made a gesture of repugnance and strode to the doorway. A crowd of black figures roaring towards him in the red torchlight made him recoil. He shut the door and faced Nebogipfel.

The thin lips of the Doctor curled with a contemptuous sneer. 'They will kill you if you stay,' he said; and seizing his unresisting vistior by the wrist, he forced him towards the glittering machine. Cook sat down and covered his face with his hands.

In another moment the door was flung open, and old Pritchard stood blinking on the threshold.

A pause. A hoarse shout changing suddenly into a sharp shrill shriek.

A thunderous roar like the bursting forth of a great fountain of water.

The voyage of the Chronic Argonauts had begun.

EDITOR'S NOTE: *It was at this point that the first draft of 'The Time Machine' closed. Wells told his readers, in a footnote, that the unanswered questions about how the story finally ended and what befell to Cook and Nebogipfel, 'has been written—and will or will never be read, according as Fate may have decreed to the curious reader'. What indeed happened thereafter is now literary history.*

THE GIFT OF TONGUES

by Arthur Machen

ARTHUR LLEWELLYN MACHEN *(1863–1947) is for me the finest of all Welsh fantasy fiction writers. His works like* The Great God Pan, The Hill of Dreams, Black Crusade *and the magnificent short stories to be found in* The Three Imposters *and* The House of Souls *put him head and shoulders above all others. His work has the bizarre style of an Oscar Wilde, the malignance of an Edgar Allan Poe and the supernatural authority of* The Mabinogion, *all of which he undoubtedly knew intimately. Machen seems destined to have become a writer of fantasy, being born at Caerlon-on-Usk, the mythical court of King Arthur. The son of an impoverished clergyman, he was brought up at an isolated rectory and in his loneliness turned to tales of folklore and legend. By his own admission superstition became a reality to him, and the brooding countryside around 'gave me a vague, indefinable sense of awe and mystery and terror'. Machen early discovered the work of Thomas de Quincey and vowed to follow him to London and journalism. To the English capital city he took his deeply entrenched and firmly held beliefs about Welsh folklore—the fairies, dwarfs, witches and Little People—and these elements he poured lavishly into his most successful works. Widely regarded though he is today, Machen spent much of his life in penury and earned no more than £1,000 from all his eighteen books. Apart from his knowledge of Welsh folklore, he was also intrigued and fascinated by the Black Arts and several of his books display a very real knowledge of the occult. The vast majority of his work is set against a Welsh background and few elements of the country's lore have escaped his pen. In selecting an item by him to appear in this collection I have purposely avoided all the well-known and easily obtainable stories and picked a minor and unreprinted item from the 1930s. As the most famous fantasy writer herein, it seems only right that he should utilise for his theme that most controversial of all Welsh topics—the Welsh language.*

More than a hundred years ago a simple German maid-of-all-work caused a great sensation. She became subject to seizures of a very singular character, of so singular a character that the family inconvenienced by these attacks were interested and, perhaps a little proud of a servant whose fits were so far removed from the ordinary convulsion. The case was thus. Anna, or Gretchen, or whatever her name might be, would suddenly become oblivious of soup, sausage, and the material world generally.

But she neither screamed, nor foamed, nor fell to earth after the common fashion of such seizures. She stood up, and from her mouth rolled sentence after sentence of splendid sound, in a sonorous tongue, filling her hearers with awe and wonder. Not one of her listeners understood a word of Anna's majestic utterances, and it was useless to question her in her uninspired moments, for the girl knew nothing of what had happened.

At length, as it fell out, some scholarly personage was present during one of these extraordinary fits; and he at once declared that the girl was speaking Hebrew, with a pure accent and perfect intonation. And, in a sense, the wonder was now greater than ever. How could the simple Anna speak Hebrew? She had certainly never learnt it. She could barely read and write her native German. Everyone was amazed, and the occult mind of the day began to formulate theories and to speak of possession and familiar spirits. Unfortunately (as I think, for I am a lover of all insoluble mysteries), the problem of the girl's Hebrew speech was solved; solved, that is, to a certain extent.

The tale got abroad, and so it became known that some years before Anna had been servant to an old scholar. The personage was in the habit of declaiming Hebrew as he walked up and down his

study and the passages of his house, and the maid had unconsciously stored the chanted words in some cavern of her soul; in
that receptacle, I suppose, which we are content to call the subconsciousness. I must confess that the explanation does not strike
me as satisfactory in all respects. In the first place, there is the
extraordinary tenacity of memory; but I suppose that other
instances of this, though rare enough, might be cited. Then, there is
the association of this particular storage of the subconsciousness
with a species of seizure; I do not know whether any similar
instance can be cited.

Still, minor puzzles apart, the great mystery was mysterious no
more: Anna spoke Hebrew because she had heard Hebrew and,
in her odd fashion, had remembered it.

To the best of my belief, cases that offer some points of similarity
are occasionally noted at the present day. Persons ignorant of
Chinese deliver messages in that tongue; the speech of Abyssinia is
heard from lips incapable, in ordinary moments, of anything but
the pleasing idiom of the United States of America, and untaught
Cockneys suddenly become fluent in Basque.

But all this, so far as I am concerned, is little more than
rumour; I do not know how far these tales have been subjected to
strict and systematic examination. But in any case, they do not
interest me so much as a very odd business that happened on the
Welsh border more than sixty years ago. I was not very old at
the time, but I remember my father and mother talking about the
affair, just as I remember them talking about the Franco-Prussian
War in the August of 1870, and coming to the conclusion that the
French seemed to be getting the worst of it. And later, when I
was growing up and the mysteries were beginning to exercise their
fascination upon me, I was able to confirm my vague recollections
and to add to them a good deal of exact information. The odd
business to which I am referring was the so-called 'Speaking with
Tongues' at Bryn Sion Chapel, Treowen, Monmouthshire, on a
Christmas Day of the early 'seventies.

Treowen is one of a chain of horrible mining villages that wind in and out of the Monmouthshire and Glamorganshire valleys. Above are the great domed heights, quivering with leaves (like the dear Zacynthus of Ulysses), on their lower slopes, and then mounting by far stretches of deep bracken, glittering in the sunlight, to a golden land of gorse, and at last to wild territory, bare and desolate, that seems to surge upward for ever. But beneath, in the valley, are the black pits and the blacker mounds, and heaps of refuse, vomiting chimneys, mean rows and ranks of grey houses faced with red brick; all as dismal and detestable as the eye can see.

Such a place is Treowen; uglier and blacker now than it was sixty years ago; and all the worse for the contrast of its vileness with those glorious and shining heights above it. Down in the town there are three great chapels of the Methodists and Baptists and Congregationalists; architectural monstrosities all three of them, and a red brick church does not do much to beautify the place. But above all this, on the hillside, there are scattered white-washed farms, and a little hamlet of white, thatched cottages, remnants all of a pre-industrial age, and here is situate the old meeting-house called Bryn Sion, which means, I believe, the Brow of Zion. It must have been built about 1790–1800, and, being a simple, square building, devoid of crazy ornament, is quite inoffensive.

Here came the mountain farmers and cottagers, trudging, some of them, long distances on the wild tracks and paths of the hillside; and here ministered, from 1860 to 1880, the Reverend Thomas Beynon, a bachelor, who lived in the little cottage next to the chapel, where a grove of beech-trees was blown into a thin straggle of tossing boughs by the great winds of the mountain.

Now, Christmas Day falling on a Sunday in this year of long ago, the usual service was held at Bryn Sion Chapel, and, the weather being fine, the congregation was a large one—that is, something between forty and fifty people. People met and shook hands and wished each other 'Merry Christmas', and exchanged the news of the week and prices at Newport market, till the elderly, white-bearded minister, in his shining black, went into the chapel. The deacons followed him and took their places in the big pew by the open fireplace, and the little meeting-house was almost full. The minister had a windsor chair, a red hassock, and a pitch-pine table in a sort of raised pen at the end of the chapel, and from this place he gave out the opening hymn. Then followed a long portion of Scripture, a second hymn, and the congregation settled themselves to attend to the prayer.

It was at this moment that the service began to vary from the accustomed order. The minister did not kneel down in the usual way; he stood staring at the people, very strangely, as some of them thought. For perhaps a couple of minutes he faced them in dead silence, and here and there people shuffled uneasily in their pews. Then he came down a few paces and stood in front of the table with bowed head, his back to the people. Those nearest to the ministerial pen or rostrum heard a low murmur coming from his lips. They could not make out the words.

Bewilderment fell upon them all, and, as it would seem, a con-fusion of mind, so that it was difficult afterwards to gather any clear account of what actually happened that Christmas morning at Bryn Sion Chapel. For some while the mass of the congregation heard nothing at all; only the deacons in the Big Seat could make out the swift mutter that issued from their pastor's lips; now a little higher in tone, now sunken so as to be almost inaudible. They strained their ears to discover what he was saying in that low, continued utterance; and they could hear words plainly, but they could not understand. It was not Welsh.

It was neither Welsh—the language of the chapel—nor was it English. They looked at one another, those deacons, old men like their minister most of them; looked at one another with some-thing of strangeness and fear in their eyes. One of them, Evan Tudor, Torymynydd, ventured to rise in his place and to ask the preacher, in a low voice, if he were ill. The Reverend Thomas Beynon took no notice; it was evident that he did not hear the question: swiftly the unknown words passed his lips.

'He is wrestling with the Lord in prayer,' one deacon whispered to another, and the man nodded—and looked frightened.

And it was not only this murmured utterance that bewildered

those who heard it; they, and all who were present, were amazed at the pastor's strange movements. He would stand before the middle of the table and bow his head, and go now to the left of the table, now to the right of it, and then back again to the middle. He would bow down his head, and raise it, and look up, as a man said afterwards, as if he saw the heavens opened. Once or twice he turned round and faced the people, with his arms stretched wide open, and a swift word on his lips, and his eyes staring and seeing nothing, nothing that anyone else could see. And then he would turn again. And all the while the people were dumb and stricken with amazement; they hardly dared to look at each other; they hardly dared to ask themselves what could be happening before them. And then, suddenly, the minister began to sing.

It must be said that the Reverend Thomas Beynon was celebrated all through the valley and beyond it for his 'singing religious eloquence', for that singular chant which the Welsh call the *hwyl*. But his congregation had never heard so noble, so awful a chant as this before. It rang out and soared on high, and fell, to rise again with wonderful modulations; pleading to them and calling them and summoning them; with the old voice of the *hwyl*, and yet with a new voice that they had never heard before: and all in those sonorous words that they could not understand. They stood up in their wonder, their hearts shaken by the chant; and then the voice died away. It was as still as death in the chapel. One of the deacons could see that the minister's lips still moved; but he could hear no sound at all. Then the minister raised up his hands as if he held something between them; and knelt down, and rising, again lifted his hands. And there came the faint tinkle of a bell from the sheep grazing high up on the mountain side.

The Reverend Thomas Beynon seemed to come to himself out of a dream, as they said. He looked about him nervously, perplexed, noted that his people were gazing at him strangely, and then, with a stammering voice, gave out a hymn and afterwards ended the service. He discussed the whole matter with the deacons and heard what they had to tell him. He knew nothing of it himself and had no explanation to offer. He knew no languages, he declared, save Welsh and English. He said that he did not believe there was evil in what had happened, for he felt that he had been in Heaven before the Throne. There was a great talk about it all, and that queer Christmas service became known as the Speaking with Tongues of Bryn Sion.

Years afterwards, I met a fellow-countryman, Edward Williams, in London, and we fell talking, in the manner of exiles, of the land and its stories. Williams was many years older than myself, and he told me of an odd thing that had once happened to him.

'It was years ago,' he said, 'and I had some business—I was a mining-engineer in those days—at Treowen, up in the hills. I had to stay over Christmas, which was on a Sunday that year, and talking to some people there about the *hwyl*, they told me that I ought to go up to Bryn Sion if I wanted to hear it done really well. Well, I went, and it was the queerest service I ever heard of. I don't know much about the Methodists' way of doing things, but before long it struck me that the minister was saying some sort of Mass. I could hear a word or two of the Latin service now and again, and then he sang the Christmas Preface right through: "*Quia per incarnati Verbi mysterium*"—you know.'

Very well; but there is always a loophole by which the reasonable, or comparatively reasonable, may escape. Who is to say that the old preacher had not strayed long before into some Roman Catholic Church at Newport or Cardiff on a Christmas Day, and there heard Mass with exterior horror and interior love?

THE COFFIN

by Caradoc Evans

DAVID CARADOC EVANS *(1878–1945) has his
name writ large across modern Welsh literature. He was an
outrageous, talented, dedicated and, above all, enduring writer,
whose work is now much emulated but never equalled. Professor Gwyn Jones of the University of Wales, and a noted
writer himself, has perceptively and aptly called him a 'legend-
laden person sprung from dragon seed'. Born in Llanfihangel-
ar-Arth, Cardiganshire, Caradoc Evans devoted his life to
writing and in particular to the people and manners of West
Wales. His plays and short stories are noted for their controversial nature and for a number of years his work was banned
in many Welsh libraries. (One librarian was so incensed by his
books that he actually burned all of them in the public in-
cinerator!) The protests invariably stemmed from Evans'
views of hypocrisy, lust and greed among the peasantry of his
part of the country and hilarious stories are still told of how
he unobtrusively added to the complaints with still more
alarming accusations of his own making! His finest works are
perhaps* My People *(1915),* Capel Sion *(1917) and* My
Neighbours *(1919), not to mention his volumes of short
stories. He is also well remembered for championing the Welsh
short story for the best part of half a century. The craftsman-
ship which he brought to all his works is particularly evident
in the story here, which deals lovingly with another topic so
dear to the Welsh heart—dying.*

Captain Shacob owned *Rhondda,* the rowing-boat from which he
fished and in which he took folk on the sea at Ferryside. A plump

widow named Ann who had sailed in his boat for pleasure said to him: 'My son, Little Ben, is a prentice to the carpenter; be you a father to him. My husband, Big Ben, is in the graveyard; be you my second husband.' She also told him that she rented a house and ten acres of fertile land on the bank of Avon Towy.

Shacob sold his boat and married Ann, whose fields he trimmed at what time he was not repairing the ditches on the public roads. Now Ann fattened wondrously; her flesh almost choking her, she was wont in hot weather to throw up her hands and scream that she was dying. On arising on a July day, she went into a fit and fell back upon her bed. At mid-day she would not sup of the gingered and sugared bread and water which her husband offered her, nor again in the evening.

'Eat, woman fach,' said Shacob.

'Let me perish on an empty belly,' answered Ann.

Having milked his cow, tended his two pigs, and shooed his fowls to roost, Shacob walked to the workshop of Lloyd the carpenter. He stood at the threshold of the workshop, his hands, like the claws of a very old crow, grasping the top of the half door, his eyes wearing the solemn aspect of the man who is soon to revel in the mournful joy that Death brings to us Welsh people; his long underlip curling over his purple-stained chin like the petal of a rose, Shacob stood at the door as if he were the reporter of sacred messages in the chapel.

This is what he saw inside the workshop: the crutched figure of the carpenter, whose mouth, from the corners of which dribbled tiny streams of tobacco juice, was like the ungainly cut in a turnip lantern; the hairy face of the cobbler, much of whose wooden leg was thrust into the earth through the shavings and sawdust with which the ground was strewn; the bright countenance of the broken-out preacher, whose skin was of the freshness of that of a sucking pig; the head of Little Ben, whose nose had been twisted at birth, bending over a bird-cage.

The preacher was declaring that Jonah was not swallowed by a fish, even though the fish was a whale whereat the cobbler, driving his leg farther into the earth, cried: 'Atheist!'

'Hoit!' said Shacob.

None of the company heard him, so low was his voice.

Presently Little Ben looked up, and after his gaze had rested for a while upon his stepfather's hands he set to improve the perch-rod of his cage.

'Hoity-ho!' Shacob sounded.

'Why do you stand there like a thirsty ox at the gate?' asked the carpenter. 'You have seen millions of whales at Ferryside. Sure, indeed, they can take in a man at a gulp.'

'Hist-hist,' said Shacob. 'Ann is going for the sail.'

'For two shillings—for one shilling and a morsel of butter,' said the preacher, 'I'll make a memorial song to the dead.'

'Don't let him,' cried the cobbler. 'Be you warned by me.' He struggled to free his leg. 'Little Ben, pull her out.'

'I am about the coffin,' Shacob announced.

'How can I make the coffin,' Lloyd replied, 'when I am hay-making all the week? Why didn't you come a month back? And Ann is so stout that it will be a longish job.'

'Where else can I go?' Shacob wailed.

'That's it!' the carpenter growled. 'Take your custom from me. Don't bring your breaks here any more if you talk like that. Go away with your wheelbarrow and spade and pickaxe and shovel.'

'The perished—the stout and the thin—must be housed,' the preacher proclaimed.

'Hay must be gathered and stacked and thatched before the corn harvest,' Lloyd answered. 'How are the animals to live in the winter? Tell me that.'

'All the dead—tenors and basses, praying men and men who cry "Amen", old and young, big and little—must be housed.' So sang the preacher in his pulpit manner.

The cobbler moved before he was freed and fell upon the floor, his wooden leg breaking in two.

'The Big Man's punishment for discussing the Beybile with you,' he reproached the preacher. 'The breath in your body is the smoke of hell fire.'

'I have not the timber to make Ann a coffin,' said Lloyd. 'No; not for stout Ann.'

'There are many trees,' said Shacob.

'Great will be the cost of the coffin.'

'I'll sell the cow,' Shacob began.

'Hearken! if I make the coffin, you must pay the day after the funeral. You shall not make a debt of it.'

The preacher blessed Lloyd. 'You are behaving in a most religious spirit. Houses of stone-masons crumble, but the houses of carpenters will be placed in the lofts of the White Palace.'

Husband, stepson and carpenter then passed through the village and the deeply-rutted, cart-wide lane to Shacob's house, which is in the midst of marshland.

As the three unlatched their clogs at the foot of the stairway, Shacob shouted: 'Ann, here is Lloyd Carpenter. Are you perished?'

Ann made an answer, whereupon they went up to her. Lloyd drew back the bedclothes and bade the woman straighten her limbs; then he measured her length, her breadth, and her depth. 'Write you down two inches extra every way for the swellings,' he commanded Little Ben.

'We ought to write four,' said the youth.

'Clap your head. Have I ever made a coffin too small?'

'If it only fits,' said Ben, 'how can the angel flap his wings when he comes to call mammo up? Mammo, you need the angel?'

'Why, iss, son bach,' Ann replied. 'Are you not ashamed, carpenter, to deprive me of the angel?'

'It is the large cost that is in my think,' murmured Lloyd.

'Drat your think! I will not go into a coffin that will smother the angel. Have I not suffered enough?'

'It will be many shillings more. Maybe ten. Maybe fifteen. O iss, a pound.'

'Be good,' said Shacob. 'It is well to obey the perished.'

For three days Ben and Lloyd laboured, and as the coffin was carried on the shoulders of four men, the haymakers who came to the hedges were amazed at its vastness.

By the side of the bed it was put. 'For,' said Lloyd, 'she will be a heavy corpse and easier to roll down than lift.'

At the end of the year the carpenter said to Ann's husband: 'Give me now the coffin money.'

'On the day after the funeral,' said Shacob.

'I will have the petty sessions on you, I will, drop dead and blind. I'll poison your well. And your cow. And your pigs. Is it my blame that Ann is alive?'

'It shall be as you pledged. Broken-out preacher heard you.'

'Tut-tut. He is a bad man. He disputes the Beybile. That is why he was broken out from the capel.'

But Shacob was soon puzzle-headed. Ann fancied to see herself in the coffin, and holding a mirror she tried to enter it, but the breadth of it was too narrow. She made such a great dole that Shacob hurried to discover Lloyd's iniquity. 'Little Ben,' he shouted at the door of the workshop, 'come forth from the workshop of the sinner. Bring your bird-cage and coat and tools. Have a care you bring nothing that is his.'

The youth obeyed and remained like a sentry by his stepfather.

'There's glad I am I did not pay you,' cried Shacob. 'If I had, the law would find a thief.'

'Be quiet, robber,' Lloyd returned.

'Who made Ann's coffin too small? Come out, neighbours bach, and listen. Who made Ann's coffin too small? Who tried to cheat the perished dead?'

Many people came to hear Shacob reviling Lloyd and were very sorry that the carpenter answered in this fashion: 'Reit. 'Oreit. Little Ben, go you in and find the paper with the figures.'

'And keep it tightly,' Shacob counselled his stepson. 'Nothing new must be put in it. Don't you be tempted by Lloyd because he was your master. We are honest.'

After Lloyd had measured Ann, and while he was measuring the coffin, Little Ben went under his mother's bed and wrote anew on another paper and in accordance with the fresh measurements.

'Carpenter,' he said shyly, 'you are wrong. Study the figures. I cannot work for a scampist master.'

'Why do I want a useless coffin?' Ann shrieked. 'A mess I would be in if I perished now. And what would be said if I reached the Palace in a patched coffin? Ach y fy!'

That night Little Ben, who was unable to sleep for his mother's plight, stole into Lloyd's workshop and brought away screws and nails and a few planks of timber, and with these he enlarged the coffin.

In the ten years that followed the trouble between Lloyd and Shacob brewed into bitter hatred; it attracted one to the other, when they fought as fiercely as poachers fight for the possession of a ferret. Shacob died, and there was peace for a little while, but in the after-season Lloyd did not subdue his rage. 'Shacob is gone,' he whined. 'Cobbler Wooden Leg is gone and Broken-out Preacher. The next will be Ann. Oh, there will be a champion riot if I don't get my money.' His spoken and unspoken prayer was that the Big Man would allow him to live longer than Ann. Every summer evening he watched the weather signs, and if they foretold heat, he said joyfully to himself: 'Like a poof she'll go off tomorrow.'

As Ann fattened so Ben enlarged the coffin with iron staples and leathern hinges. This he did many times. The fame of his skill became a byword, and folk brought to him clocks, sewing-machines, and whatsoever that wanted much cunning to be set in proper order.

He had married, and his four children were a delight to Ann, who often tumbled into her coffin and closing her eyes said to them: 'Like this grand-mammo will go to the Palace.' The children pranced about with glee, and by and by they played hide and seek in it.

On a day when Ben said: 'If I stretch the box any more your perished corpse will fall through the bottom, mammo; even now it will have to be well roped before you are lifted,' before sunset a horrible thing happened: three children hid in the coffin and the fourth swooped down upon them, and the sides of it fell apart.

Ben viewed what had been done. 'It won't repair,' he told his tearful mother. 'I'll make you another, mammo fach.'

He laughed as he separated the pieces, for those that belonged to Lloyd he was returning to Lloyd.

A STRAY FROM CATHAY

by John Wyndham

JOHN WYNDHAM HARRIS *(1903–1969),
author of the modern Science Fiction classic* The Day of The
Triffids, *was born in England but came of Welsh parentage
and wrote frequently of his devotion to the country and its
legends. His boyhood was much influenced by the works of
H. G. Wells, so it is perhaps not surprising that he began
writing Science Fiction when he was in his late teens. His
early work, published under the name of John Beynon Harris,
appeared primarily in American magazines where readers were
quick to recognise his skill. Then when his stories began to
appear in British publications, he was hailed (in 1937) as 'probably the best of our modern science fiction writers'. The years
of the Second World War interrupted his work, however,
and when he returned to writing, he found the market depressed.
Instead he decided to try fantasy fiction and met with one
rejection after another until he conceived and executed the
unique* Revolt of the Triffids *in 1951. (The book was later
retitled* The Day of the Triffids *in 1954.) From then until
his death, John Wyndham, as he now called himself, enjoyed
enormous success, and apart from sequels to* The Day of the
Triffids, *he also wrote several novels which were filmed,
including the ingenious* The Midwich Cuckoos. *He further
produced a number of outstanding short tales of horror of
which the next item happens to be a favourite of mine. It not
only demonstrates John Wyndham's mastery of the fantasy
genre, but also his knowledge of the country's strange 'dragon-
lore'.*

The parcel, waiting provocatively on the dresser, was the first thing that Hwyl noticed when he got in from work.

'From Dai, is it?' he inquired of his wife.

'Yes, indeed. Japanese the stamps are,' she told him.

He went across to examine it. It was the shape a small hatbox might be, about ten inches each way, perhaps. The address: Mr and Mrs Hwyl Hughes, Ty Derwen, Llynllawn, Llangolwgcoch, Brecknockshire, S. Wales, was lettered carefully, for the clear understanding of foreigners. The other label, also hand-lettered, but in red, was quite clear, too. It said: EGGS—Fragile—With great CARE.

'There is funny to send eggs so far,' Hwyl said. 'Plenty of eggs we are having. Might be chocolate eggs, I think?'

'Come you to your tea, man.' Bronwen told him. 'All day I have been looking at that old parcel, and a little longer it can wait now.'

Hwyl sat down at the table and began his meal. From time to time, however, his eyes strayed again to the parcel.

'If it is real eggs they are, careful you should be,' he remarked. 'Reading in a book I was once how in China they keep eggs for years. Bury them in the earth, they do, for a delicacy. There is strange for you, now. Queer they are in China, and not like Wales, at all.'

Bronwen contented herself with saying that perhaps Japan was not like China, either.

When the meal had been finished and cleared, the parcel was transferred to the table. Hwyl snipped the string and pulled off the brown paper. Within was a tin box which, when the sticky tape holding its lid had been removed, proved to be full to the brim with sawdust. Mrs Hughes fetched a sheet of newspaper, and prudently covered the table-top. Hwyl dug his fingers into the sawdust.

'Something there, there is,' he announced.

'There is stupid you are. Of course there is something there,' Bronwen said, slapping his hand out of the way.

She trickled some of the sawdust out on to the newspaper, and then felt inside the box herself. Whatever it was, it felt much too large for an egg. She poured out more sawdust and felt again.

This time, her fingers encountered a piece of paper. She pulled it out and laid it on the table; a letter in Dafydd's handwriting. Then she put in her hand once more, got her fingers under the object, and lifted it gently out.

'Well, indeed! Look at that now! Did you ever?' she exclaimed. 'Eggs, he was saying, is it?'

They both regarded it with astonishment for some moments.

'So big it is. Queer, too,' said Hwyl, at last.

'What kind of bird to lay such an egg?' said Bronwen.

'Ostrich, perhaps?' suggested Hwyl.

But Bronwen shook her head. She had once seen an ostrich's egg in a museum, and remembered it well enough to know that it had little in common with this. The ostrich's egg had been a little smaller, with a dull, sallow-looking, slightly dimpled surface. This was smooth and shiny, and by no means had the same dead look: it had a lustre to it, a nacreous kind of beauty.

'A pearl, could it be?' she said, in an awed voice.

'There is silly you are,' said her husband. 'From an oyster as big as Llangolwgcoch Town Hall, you are thinking?'

He burrowed into the tin again, but "Eggs", it seemed, had been a manner of speaking; there was no other, nor room for one.

Bronwen put some of the sawdust into one of her best vegetable-dishes, and bedded the egg carefully on top of it. Then they sat down to read their son's letter:

S.S. Tudor Maid,
Kobe.

Dear Mam and Dad,

I expect you will be surprised about the enclosed I was too. It is a funny looking thing I expect they have funny birds in China after all they have Pandas so why not. We found a small sampan about a hundred miles off the China coast that had bust its mast and should never have tried and all except two of them were dead they are all dead now. But one of them that wasn't dead then was holding this egg-thing all wrapped up in a padded coat like it was a baby only I didn't know it was an egg then not till later. One of them died coming aboard but this other one lasted two days longer in spite of all I could do for him which was my best. I was sorry nobody here can speak Chinese because he was a nice little chap and lonely and knew he was a goner but there it is. And when he saw it was nearly all up he gave me this egg and talked very faint but I'd not have understood anyway. All I could do was take it and hold it careful the way he had and tell him I'd look after it which he couldn't understand either. Then he said something else and looked very worried and died poor chap.

So here it is. I know it *is* an egg because when I took him a boiled egg once he pointed to both of them to show me but nobody on board knows what kind of egg. But seeing I promised him I'd keep it safe I am sending it to you to keep for me as this ship is no place to keep anything safe anyway and hope it doesn't get cracked on the way too.

Hoping this finds you as it leaves me and love to all and you special.

Dai.

'Well, there is strange for you, now,' said Mrs Hughes, as she finished reading. 'And *looking* like an egg it is, indeed—the shape of it,' she conceded. 'But the colours are not. There is pretty they are. Like you see when oil is on the road in the rain. But never an egg like that have I seen in my life. Flat the colour is on eggs, and not to shine.'

Hwyl went on looking at it thoughtfully.

'Yes. There is beautiful,' he agreed, 'but what use?'

'Use, is it, indeed!' said his wife. 'A trust it is, and sacred, too. Dying the poor man was, and our Dai gave him his word. I am thinking of how we will keep it safe for him till he will be back, now.'

They both contemplated the egg awhile.

'Very far away, China is,' Bronwen remarked, obscurely.

Several days passed, however, before the egg was removed from display on the dresser. Word quickly went round the valley about it, and the callers would have felt slighted had they been unable to see it. Bronwen felt that continually getting it out and putting it away again would be more hazardous than leaving it on exhibition.

Almost everyone found the sight of it rewarding. Idris Bowen who lived three houses away was practically alone in his divergent view.

'The shape of an egg, it has,' he allowed. 'But careful you should be, Mrs Hughes. A fertility symbol it is, I am thinking, and stolen, too, likely.'

'Mr Bowen—' began Bronwen, indignantly.

'Oh, by the men in that boat, Mrs Hughes. Refugees from China they would be, see. Traitors to the Chinese people. And running away with all they could carry, before the glorious army of the workers and peasants could catch them, too. Always the same, it is, as you will be seeing when the revolution comes to Wales.'

'Oh, dear, dear! There is funny you are, Mr Bowen. Propaganda you will make out of an old boot, I think,' said Bronwen.

Idris Bowen frowned.

'Funny, I am not, Mrs Hughes. And propaganda there is in an honest boot, too,' he told her as he left with dignity.

By the end of a week practically everyone in the village had seen the egg and been told no, Mrs Hughes did not know what kind of a creature had laid it, and the time seemed to have come to store it away safely against Dafydd's return. There were not many places in the house where she could feel sure that it would rest undisturbed, but, on consideration, the airing-cupboard seemed as likely as any, so she put it back on what sawdust was left in the tin, and stowed it in there.

It remained there for a month, out of sight, and pretty much out of mind until a day when Hwyl returning from work discovered his wife sitting at the table with a disconsolate expression on her face, and a bandage on her finger. She looked relieved to see him.

'Hatched, it is,' she observed.

The blankness of Hwyl's expression was irritating to one who had a single subject on her mind all day.

'Dai's egg,' she explained, 'Hatched out, it is, I am telling you.'

'Well, there is a thing for you, now!' said Hwyl. 'A nice little chicken, is it?'

'A chicken it is not, at all. A monster, indeed, and biting me it is, too.' She held out her bandaged finger.

She explained that this morning she had gone to the airing-cupboard to take out a clean towel, and as she put her hand in, something had nipped her finger, painfully. At first she had thought that it might be a rat that had somehow got in from the yard, but then she had noticed that the lid was off the tin, and the shell of the egg there was all broken to pieces.

'How is it to see?' Hwyl asked.

Bronwen admitted that she had not seen it well. She had had a glimpse of a long, greeny-blue tail protruding from behind a pile of sheets, and then it had looked at her over the top of them, glaring at her from red eyes. On that, it had seemed to her more the kind of a job a man should deal with, so she had slammed the door, and gone to bandage her finger.

'Still there, then, is it?' said Hwyl.

She nodded.

'Right you. Have a look at it, we will, now then,' he said, decisively.

He started to leave the room, but on second thoughts turned back to collect a pair of heavy working-gloves. Bronwen did not offer to accompany him.

Presently there was a scuffle of his feet, an exclamation or two, then his tread descending the stairs. He came in, shutting the door behind him with his foot. He set the creature he was carrying on the table, and for some seconds it crouched there, blinking, but otherwise unmoving.

'Scared, he was, I think,' Hwyl remarked.

In the body, the creature bore some resemblance to a lizard—a large lizard, over a foot long. The scales of its skin, however, were much bigger, and some of them curled up and stood out here and there, in a fin-like manner. And the head was quite unlike a lizard's, being much rounder, with a wide mouth, broad nostrils, and, overall a slightly pushed-in effect, in which were set a pair of goggling red eyes. About the neck, and also making a kind of mane, were curious, streamer-like attachments with the suggestion of locks of hair which had permanently cohered. The colour was mainly green, shot with blue, and having a metallic shine to it, but there were brilliant red markings about the head and in the lower parts of the locks. There were touches of red, too, where the legs joined the body, and on the feet, where the toes finished in sharp yellow claws. Altogether, a surprisingly vivid and exotic creature.

It eyed Bronwen Hughes for a moment, turned a baleful look on Hwyl, and then started to run about the table-top, looking for a way off. The Hughes watched it for a moment or two, and then regarded one another.

'Well, there is nasty for you, indeed,' observed Bronwen.

'Nasty it may be. But beautiful it is, too, look,' said Hwyl.

'Ugly old face to have,' Bronwen remarked.

'Yes, indeed. But fine colours, too, see. Glorious, they are, like technicolor, I am thinking,' Hwyl said.

The creature appeared to have half a mind to leap from the table. Hwyl leaned forward and caught hold of it. It wriggled, and tried to get its head round to bite him, but discovered he was holding it too near the neck for that. It paused in its struggles. Then, suddenly, it snorted. Two jets of flame and a puff of smoke came from its nostrils. Hwyl dropped it abruptly, partly from alarm, but more from surprise. Bronwen gave a squeal, and climbed hastily on to her chair.

The creature itself seemed a trifle astonished. For a few seconds it stood turning its head and waving the sinuous tail that was quite as long as its body. Then it scuttled across to the hearthrug, and curled itself up in front of the fire.

'By dammo! There was a thing for you!' Hwyl exclaimed, regarding it a trifle nervously. 'Fire there was with it, I think. I will like to understand that, now.'

'Fire indeed, and smoke too,' Bronwen agreed. 'There is shocking it was, and not natural, at all.'

She looked uncertainly at the creature. It had so obviously settled itself for a nap that she risked stepping down from the chair, but she kept on watching it, ready to jump up again if it should move. Then:

'Never did I think I will see one of those. And not sure it is right to have in the house, either,' she said.

'What is it you are meaning, now?' Hwyl asked, puzzled.

'Why, a dragon, indeed,' Bronwen told him.

'Dragon!' he exclaimed. 'There is foolish—' Then he stopped. He looked at it again, and then down at the place where the flame had scorched his glove. 'No, by dammo!' he said. 'Right, you. A dragon it is, I believe.'

They both regarded it with some apprehension.

'Glad, I am, not to live in China,' observed Bronwen.

Those who were privileged to see the creature during the next day or two supported almost to a man the theory that it was a dragon. This, they established by poking sticks through the wire-netting of the hutch that Hwyl had made for it until it obliged with a resentful huff of flame. Even Mr Jones, the Chapel, did not doubt its authenticity, though on the propriety of its presence in his community he preferred to reserve judgment for the present.

After a short time, however, Bronwen Hughes put an end to the practice of poking it. For one thing, she felt responsible to Dai for its well-being, for another, it was beginning to develop an irritable disposition, and a liability to emit flame without cause; for yet another, and although Mr Jones' decision on whether it could be considered as one of God's creatures or not was still pending, she felt that in the meantime it deserved equal rights with other dumb animals. So she put a card on the hutch saying: PLEASE NOT TO TEASE, and most of the time was there to see that it was heeded.

Almost all Llynllawn, and quite a few people from Llangolwg-coch, too, came to see it. Sometimes they would stand for an hour or more, hoping to see it huff. If it did, they went off satisfied that it was a dragon; but if it maintained a contented, non-fire-breathing mood, they went and told their friends that it was really no more than a little old lizard, though, big, mind you.

Idris Bowen was an exception to both categories. It was not

until his third visit that he was privileged to see it snort, but even then he remained unconvinced.

'Unusual, it is, yes,' he admitted. 'But a dragon it is not. Look you at the dragon of Wales, or the dragon of St George, now. To huff fire is something, I grant you, but wings, too, a dragon must be having, or a dragon he is not.'

But that was the kind of cavilling that could be expected from Idris, and disregarded.

After ten days or so of crowded evenings, however, interest slackened. Once one had seen the dragon and exclaimed over the brilliance of its colouring, there was little to add, beyond being glad it was in the Hughes' house rather than one's own, and wondering how big it would eventually grow. For, really, it did not do much but sit and blink, and perhaps give a little huff of flame if you were lucky. So, presently, the Hughes' home became more their own again.

And, no longer pestered by visitors, the dragon showed an equable disposition. It never huffed at Bronwen, and seldom at Hwyl. Bronwen's first feeling of antagonism passed quickly, and she found herself growing attached to it. She fed it, and looked after it, and found that on a diet consisting chiefly of minced horseflesh and dog-biscuits it grew with astonishing speed. Most of the time, she let it run free in the room. To quiet the misgiving of callers she would explain:

'Friendly, he is, and pretty ways he has with him, if there is not teasing. Sorry for him, I am, too, for bad it is to be an only child, and an orphan worse still. And less than an orphan, he is, see. Nothing of his own sort he is knowing, not likely, either. So very lonely he is being, poor thing, I think.'

But, inevitably, there came an evening when Hwyl, looking thoughtfully at the dragon, remarked:

'Outside you, soon. There is too big for the house you are getting, see.'

Bronwen was surprised to find how unwilling she felt about that.

'Very good and quiet, he is,' she said. 'There is clever he is to tuck his tail away not to trip people, too. And clean with the house he is, also, and no trouble. Always out to the yard at proper times. Right as clockwork.'

'Behaving well, he is, indeed,' Hwyl agreed. 'But growing so fast, now. More room he will be needing, see. A fine hutch for him in the yard, and with a run to it, I think.'

The advisability of that was demonstrated a week later when Bronwen came down one morning to find the end of the wooden hutch charred away, the carpet and rug smouldering, and the dragon comfortably curled up in Hwyl's easy chair.

'Settled, it is, and lucky indeed not to burn in our bed. Out you,' Hwyl told the dragon. 'A fine thing to burn a man's house for him, and not grateful, either. For shame, I am telling you.'

The insurance-man who came to inspect the damage thought similarly.

'Notified, you should have,' he told Bronwen. 'A fire-risk, he is, you see.'

Bronwen protested that the policy made no mention of dragons.

'No, indeed,' the man admitted, 'but a normal hazard he is not, either. Inquire, I will, from Head Office how it is, see. But better to turn him out before more trouble, and thankful, too.'

So, a couple of days later, the dragon was occupying a large hutch, constructed of asbestos sheets, in the yard. There was a wire-netted run in front of it, but most of the time Bronwen locked the gate, and left the backdoor of the house open so that he could come and go as he liked. In the morning he would trot in, and help Bronwen by huffing the kitchen fire into a blaze, but apart from that he had learnt not to huff in the house. The only times he was any bother to anyone were the occasions when he set his straw on fire in the night so that the neighbours got up to see if the house was burning, and were somewhat short about it the next day.

Hwyl kept a careful account of the cost of feeding him, and hoped that it was not running into more than Dai would be willing to pay. Otherwise, his only worries were his failure to find a cheap, non-inflammable bedding-stuff, and speculation on how big the dragon was likely to grow before Dai should return to take him off his hands. Very likely all would have gone smoothly until that happened, but for the unpleasantness with Idris Bowen.

The trouble which blew up unexpectedly one evening was really of Idris' own finding. Hwyl had finished his meal, and was peacefully enjoying the last of the day beside his door, when Idris happened along, leading his whippet on a string.

'Oh, hullo you, Idris,' Hwyl greeted him, amiably.

'Hullo you, Hwyl,' said Idris. 'And how is that phoney dragon of yours, now then?'

'Phoney, is it, you are saying?' repeated Hwyl, indignantly.

'Wings a dragon is wanting, to be a dragon,' Idris insisted firmly.

'Wings to hell, man! Come you and look at him now then, and please to tell me what he is if he is no dragon.'

He waved Idris into the house, and led him through into the yard. The dragon, reclining in its wired run, opened an eye at them, and closed it again.

Idris had not seen it since it was lately out of the egg. Its growth impressed him.

'There is big he is now,' he conceded. 'Fine, the colours of him, and fancy, too. But still no wings to him, so a dragon he is not.'

'What, then, is it he is?' demanded Hwyl.

How Idris would have replied to this difficult question was never to be known, for at that moment the whippet jerked its string free from his fingers, and dashed, barking, at the wire-netting. The dragon was startled out of its snooze. It sat up suddenly, and snorted with surprise. There was a yelp from the whippet which bounded into the air, and then set off round and round the yard, howling. At last, Idris managed to corner it, and pick it up. All down the right side its hair had been scorched off, making it look very peculiar. Idris' eyebrows lowered.

'Trouble you want, is it? And trouble you will be having, by God!' he said.

He put the whippet down again, and began to take off his coat.

It was not clear whether he had addressed, and meant to fight, Hwyl or the dragon, but either intention was forestalled by Mrs Hughes coming to investigate the yelping.

'Oh! Teasing the dragon is it!' she said. 'There is shameful,

indeed. A lamb the dragon is, as people know well. But not to tease.
It is wicked you are, Idris Bowen, and to fight does not make right,
either. Go you from here, now then.'

Idris began to protest, but Bronwen shook her head and set her
mouth.

'Not listening to you, I am, see. A fine brave man, to tease a
helpless dragon. Not for weeks now has the dragon huffed. So go
you, and quick.'

Idris glowered. He hesitated, and pulled on his jacket again. He
collected his whippet, and held it in his arms. After a final dis-
paraging glance at the dragon, he turned.

'Law I will have to you,' he announced ominously, as he left.

Nothing more, however, was heard of legal action. It seemed as if
Idris had either changed his mind or been advised against it, and
that the whole thing would blow over. But three weeks later was
the night of the Union Branch meeting.

It had been a dull meeting, devoted chiefly to passing a number
of resolutions suggested to it by its headquarters, as a matter of
course. Then, just at the end, when there did not seem to be any
other business, Idris Bowen rose.

'Stay, you!' said the Chairman to those who were preparing to
leave, and he invited Idris to speak.

Idris waited for persons who were half-in and half-out of their
overcoats to subside, then:

'Comrades—' he began.

There was immediate uproar. Through the mingled approbation
and cries of 'Order' and 'Withdraw' the Chairman smote energetically with his gavel until quiet was restored.

'Tendencious, that is,' he reproved Idris. 'Please to speak half-
way, and in good order.'

Idris began again:

'Fellow workers. Sorry indeed, I am, to have to tell you of a
discovery I am making. A matter of disloyalty, I am telling you:
grave disloyalty to good friends and com— and fellow workers,
see.' He paused, and went on:

'Now, every one of you is knowing of Hwyl Hughes' dragon, is it? Seen him yourselves you have likely, too. Seen him myself, I have, and saying he was no dragon. But now then, I am telling you, wrong I was, wrong, indeed. A dragon he is and not to doubt, though no wings.

'I am reading in the Encyclopedia in Merthyr Public Library about two kinds of dragons, see. Wings the European dragon has, indeed. But wings the Oriental dragon has not. So apologising now to Mrs Hughes, I am, and sorry.'

A certain restiveness becoming apparent in the audience was quelled by a change in his tone.

'But—' he went on, 'but another thing, too, I am reading there, and troubled inside myself with it, I am. I will tell you. Have you looked at the feet of this dragon, is it? Claws there is, yes, and nasty, too. But how many, I am asking you? And five, I am telling you. Five with each foot.' He paused dramatically, and shook his head. 'Bad, is that, bad, indeed. For, look you, Chinese a five-toed dragon is, yes—but five-toed is not a People's dragon; five-toed is an *Imperial* dragon, see. A symbol, it is, of the oppression of Chinese workers and peasants. And shocking to think that in our village we are keeping such an emblem. What is it that the free people of China will be saying of Llynllawn when they will hear of this, I am asking? What is it Mao Tse Tung, glorious leader of the heroic Chinese people in their magnificent fight for peace, will be thinking of South Wales and this imperialist dragon?' He was continuing, when differences of view in the audience submerged his voice.

Again the Chairman called the meeting to order. He offered Hwyl the opportunity to reply, and after the situation had been briefly explained, the dragon was, on a show of hands, acquitted of political implication by all but Idris' doctrinaire faction, and the meeting broke up.

Hwyl told Bronwen about it when he got home.

'No surprise there,' she said. 'Jones the Post is telling me, telegraphing Idris has been.'

'Telegraphing?' inquired Hwyl.

'Yes, indeed. Asking the *Daily Worker*, in London, how is the party-line on imperialist dragons, he was. But no answer yet, though.'

A few mornings later the Hughes were awakened by a hammering on their door. Hwyl went to the window and found Idris below. He asked what the matter was.

'Come you down here, and I will show you,' Idris told him.

After some argument, Hwyl descended. Idris led the way round to the back of his own house, and pointed.

'Look you there, now,' he said.

The door to Idris' henhouse was hanging by one hinge. The remains of two chickens lay close by. A large quantity of feathers was blowing about the yard.

Hwyl looked at the henhouse more closely. Several deep-raked scores stood out white on the creosoted wood. In other places there were darker smears where the wood seemed to have been scorched. Silently Idris pointed to the ground. There were marks of sharp claws, but no imprint of a whole foot.

'There is bad. Foxes is it?' inquired Hwyl.

Idris choked slightly.

'Foxes, you are saying. Foxes, indeed! What will it be but your dragon? And the police to know it, too.'

Hwyl shook his head.

'No,' he said.

'Oh,' said Idris. 'A liar, I am, is it? I will have the guts from you, Hwyl Hughes, smoking hot, too, and glad to do it.'

'You talk too easy, man,' Hwyl told him. 'Only how the dragon is still fast in his hutch, I am saying. Come you now, and see.'

They went back to Hwyl's house. The dragon was in his hutch, sure enough, and the door of it was fastened with a peg. Furthermore, as Hwyl pointed out, even if he had left it during the night, he could not have reached Idris' yard without leaving scratches and traces on the way, and there were none to be found.

They finally parted in a state of armistice. Idris was by no means convinced, but he was unable to get round the facts, and not at all impressed with Hwyl's suggestion that a practical joker could have produced the effect on the henhouse with a strong nail and a blowtorch.

Hwyl went upstairs again to finish dressing.

'There is funny it is, all the same,' he observed to Bronwen. 'Not seeing, that Idris was, but scorched the peg is, on the *outside* of the hutch. And how should that be, I wonder?'

'Huffed four times in the night the dragon has, five, perhaps,' Bronwen said. 'Growling, he is, too, and banging that old hutch about. Never have I heard him like that before.'

'There is queer,' Hwyl said, frowning. 'But never out of his hutch, and that to swear to.'

Two nights later Hwyl was awakened by Bronwen shaking his shoulder.

'Listen, now then,' she told him.

There was an unmistakable growling going on at the back of the house, and the sound of several snorts.

'Huffing, he is, see,' said Bronwen, unnecessarily.

There was a crash of something thrown with force, and the sound of a neighbour's voice cursing. Hwyl reluctantly decided that he had better get up and investigate.

Everything in the yard looked as usual, except for the presence of a large tin can which was clearly the object thrown. There was, however, a strong smell of burning, and a thudding noise, recognisable as the sound of the dragon tramping round and round in his hutch to stamp out the bedding caught alight again. Hwyl went across, and opened the door. He raked out the smouldering straw, fetched some fresh, and threw it in.

'Quiet, you,' he told the dragon. 'More of this, and the hide I will have off you, slow and painful, too. Bed, now then, and sleep.'

He went back to bed himself, but it seemed as if he had only just laid his head on the pillow when it was daylight, and there was Idris Bowen hammering on the front door again.

Idris was more than a little incoherent, but Hwyl gathered that something further had taken place at his house, so he slipped on jacket and trousers, and went down. Idris led the way down beside his own house, and threw open the yard door with the air of a conjuror. Hwyl stared for some moments without speaking.

In front of Idris' henhouse stood a kind of trap, roughly contrived of angle-iron and wire-netting. In it, surrounded by chicken feathers, and glaring at them from eyes like live topazes, sat a creature, blood-red all over.

'Now, there is a dragon for you, indeed,' Idris said. 'Not to have colours like you see on a merry-go-round at a circus, either. A serious dragon, that one, and proper—wings, too, see?'

Hwyl went on looking at the dragon without a word. The wings were folded at present, and the cage did not give room to stretch them. The red, he saw now, was darker on the back, and brighter beneath, giving it the rather ominous effect of being lit from below by a blast-furnace. It certainly had a more practical aspect than his own dragon, and a fiercer look about it, altogether. He stepped forward to examine it more closely.

'Careful, man,' Idris warned him, laying a hand on his arm.

The dragon curled back its lips, and snorted. Twin flames a yard long shot out of his nostrils. It was a far better huff than the other dragon had ever achieved. The air was filled with a strong smell of burnt feathers.

'A fine dragon that is,' Idris said again. 'A real Welsh dragon for you. Angry he is, see, and no wonder. A shocking thing for an imperialist dragon to be in his country. Come to throw him out, he has, and mincemeat he will be making of your namby-pamby, best-parlour dragon, too!'

'Better for him not to try,' said Hwyl, stouter in word than heart.

'And another thing, too. Red this dragon is, and so a real people's dragon, see.'

'Now then. Now then. Propaganda with dragons again, is it? Red the Welsh dragon has been two thousand years, and a fighter, too, I grant you. But a fighter for Wales, look; not just a loud-mouth talker of fighting for peace, see. If it is a good red Welsh dragon he is, then out of some kind of egg laid by your Uncle Joe, he is not; and thankful, too, I think,' Hwyl told him. 'And look you,' he added as an afterthought, 'this one it is who is stealing your chickens, not mine, at all.'

'Oh, let him have the old chickens, and glad,' Idris said. 'Here he is come to chase a foreign imperialist dragon out of his rightful territory, and a proper thing it is, too. None of your D. P. dragons are we wanting round Llynllawn, or South Wales, either."

'Get you to hell, man,' Hwyl told him. 'Sweet dispositioned my dragon is, no bother to anyone, and no robber of henhouses, either. If there is trouble at all, the law I will be having of you and your dragon for disturbing of the peace, see. So I am telling you. And goodbye, now.'

He exchanged another glance with the angry-looking, topaz eyes of the red dragon, and then stalked away, back to his own house.

That evening, just as Hwyl was sitting down to his meal, there was a knock at the front door. Bronwen went to answer it, and came back.

'Ivor Thomas and Dafydd Ellis wanting you. Something about the Union,' she told him.

He went to see them. They had a long and involved story about dues that seemed not to have been fully paid. Hwyl was certain that he was paid-up to date, but they remained unconvinced. The argument went on for some time before, with head-shaking and reluctance, they consented to leave. Hwyl returned to the kitchen. Bronwen was waiting, standing by the table.

'Taken the dragon off, they have,' she said, flatly.

Hwyl stared at her. The reason why he had been kept at the front door in pointless argument suddenly came to him. He crossed to the window, and looked out. The back fence had been pushed flat, and a crowd of men carrying the dragon's hutch on their shoulders was already a hundred yards beyond it. Turning round, he saw Bronwen standing resolutely against the backdoor.

'Stealing, it is, and you not calling,' he said, accusingly.

'Knocked you down, they would, and got the dragon just the same,' she said. 'Idris Bowen and his lot, it is.'

Hwyl looked out of the window again.

'What to do with him, now then?' he asked.

'Dragon fight, it is,' she told him. 'Betting, they were. Five to one on the Welsh dragon, and sounding very sure, too.'

Hwyl shook his head.

'Not to wonder, either. There is not fair, at all. Wings, that Welsh dragon has, so air attacks he can make. Unsporting, there is, and shameful indeed.'

He looked out of the window again. More men were joining the party as it marched its burden across the wasteground, towards the slag-heap. He sighed.

'There is sorry I am for our dragon. Murder it will be, I think. But go and see it, I will. So no tricks from that Idris to make a dirty fight dirtier.'

Bronwen hesitated.

'No fighting for you? You promise me?' she said.

'Is it a fool I am, girl, to be fighting fifty men, and more. Please to grant me some brains, now."

She moved doubtfully out of his way, and let him open the door. Then she snatched up a scarf, and ran after him, tying it over her head as she went.

The crowd that was gathering on a piece of flat ground near the foot of the slag-heap already consisted of something more like a hundred men than fifty, and there were more hurrying to join it. Several self-constituted stewards were herding people back to clear an oval space. At one end of it was the cage in which the red dragon crouched huddled, with a bad-tempered look. At the other, the asbestos hutch was set down, and its bearers withdrew. Idris noticed Hwyl and Bronwen as they came up.

'And how much is it you are putting on your dragon?' he inquired, with a grin.

Bronwen said, before Hwyl could reply:

'Wicked, it is, and ashamed you should be, Idris Bowen. Clip you your dragon's wings to fight fair, and we will see. But betting against a horseshoe in the glove, we are not.' And she dragged Hwyl away.

All about the oval the laying of bets went on, with the Welsh dragon gaining favour all the time. Presently Idris stepped out into the open, and held up his hands for quiet.

'Sport it is for you tonight. Super colossal attraction, as they are saying on the movies, and never again, likely. So put you your money, now. When the English law is hearing of this, no more dragon-fighting, it will be—like no more to cockfight.' A boo went up, mingled with the laughter of those who knew a thing or two about cock-fighting that the English law did not. Idris went on: 'So now the dragon championship, I am giving you. On my right, the Red Dragon of Wales, on his home ground. A people's dragon, see. For more than confidence, it is, that the colour of the Welsh dragon—' His voice was lost for some moments in controversial shouts. It re-emerged, saying: 'left, the decadent dragon of the imperialist exploiters of the suffering Chinese people who, in their glorious fight for peace under the heroic leadership—' But the rest of his introduction was also lost among the catcalls and cheers that were still continuing when he beckoned forward attendants from the ends of the oval, and withdrew.

At one end, two men reached up with a hooked pole, pulled over the contraption that enclosed the red dragon, and ran back hurriedly. At the far end, a man knocked the peg from the asbestos door, pulled it open, scuttled round behind the hutch, and no less speedily out of harm's way.

The red dragon looked round, uncertainly. It tentatively tried unfurling its wings. Finding that possible, it reared up on its hind legs, supporting itself on its tail, and flapped them energetically, as though to dispel the creases.

The other dragon ambled out of its hutch, advanced a few feet, and stood blinking. Against the background of the waste ground and slag-heap it looked more than usually exotic. It yawned largely, with a fine display of fangs, rolled its eyes hither and thither, and then caught sight of the red dragon.

Simultaneously, the red dragon noticed the other. It stopped flapping and dropped to all four feet. The two regarded one another. A hush came over the crowd. Both dragons remained motionless, except for a slight waving of the last foot or so of their tails.

The oriental dragon turned its head a little on one side. It snorted slightly, and shrivelled up a patch of weeds.

The red dragon stiffened. It suddenly adopted a pose gardant, one forefoot uplifted with claws extended, wings raised. It huffed with vigour, vapourised a puddle, and disappeared momentarily in a cloud of steam. There was an anticipatory murmur from the crowd.

The red dragon began to pace round, circling the other, giving a slight flap of its wings now and then.

The crowd watched it intently. So did the other dragon. It did not move from its position, but turned as the red dragon circled, keeping its head and gaze steadily towards it.

With the circle almost completed, the red dragon halted. It extended its wings widely, and gave a full-throated roar. Simultaneously, it gushed two streams of fire, and belched a small cloud of black smoke. The part of the crowd nearest to it moved back, apprehensively.

At this tense moment Bronwen Hughes began suddenly to laugh. Hwyl shook her by the arm.

'Hush, you! There is not funny, at all,' he said, but she did not stop at once.

The oriental dragon did nothing for a moment. It appeared to be thinking the matter over. Then it turned swiftly round and began to run. The crowd behind it raised a jeer, those in front waved their arms to shoo it back. But the dragon was unimpressed by arm-waving. It came on, with now and then a short spurt of flame from its nostrils. The people wavered, and then scattered out of its way. Half-a-dozen men started to chase after it with sticks, but soon gave up. It was travelling at twice the pace they could run.

With a roar, the red dragon leapt into the air, and came across the field, spitting flames like a strafing aircraft. The crowd scattered still more swiftly, tumbling over itself as it cleared a way.

The running dragon disappeared round the foot of the slag-heap, with the other hovering above it. Shouts of disappointment rose from the crowd, and a good part of it started to follow, to be in at the death.

But in a minute or two the running dragon came into view again. It was making a fine pace up the mountainside, with the red dragon still flying a little behind it. Everybody stood watching it wind its way up and up until, finally, it disappeared over the shoulder. For a moment the flying dragon still showed as a black silhouette above the skyline, then, with a final whiff of flame, it, too, disappeared—and the arguments about paying up began.

Idris left the wrangling to come across to the Hughes.

'So there is a coward your imperialist dragon is, then. And not one good huff, or a bite to him, either,' he said

Bronwen looked at him, and smiled.

'So foolish, you are, Idris Bowen, with your head full of propaganda and fighting. Other things than to fight, there is, even for dragons. Such a brave show your red dragon was making, such a fine show, oh, yes—and very like a peacock, I am thinking. Very like the boys in their Sunday suits in Llangolwgcoch High Street, too—all dressed up to kill, but not to fight.'

Idris stared at her.

'And our dragon,' she went on. 'Well, there is not a very new trick, either. Done a bit of it before now, I have, myself.' She cast a sidelong glance at Hwyl.

Light began to dawn on Idris.

'But—but it is *he* you were always calling your dragon,' he protested.

Bronwen shrugged.

'Oh, yes, indeed. But how to tell with dragons?' she asked.

She turned to look up the mountain.

'There is lonely, lonely the red dragon must have been these two thousand years—so not much bothering with your politics, he is, just now. More single with his mind, see. And interesting it will be, indeed, to be having a lot of baby dragons in Wales before long, I am thinking.'

THE STRANGER

by Richard Hughes

RICHARD HUGHES *(1900–   ) has had his work compared to that of Tolstoy and certainly with the first two volumes of his trilogy,* The Human Predicament *he has demonstrated himself as a master of English literature. A quiet, gentle man who lives on an isolated estuary near Portmeirion, he has reversed an early life of prolific writing to a sedate maturity from which has come perhaps his most incisive and brilliant work. From his childhood he recalls a fascination with Welsh fairy tales and legends which he used to retell to anyone who would listen. He started writing as a teenager, and much of this was done in a one-roomed cottage in North Wales near the Graves family home at Harlech, which he rented out of his school pocket-money for 4d per year! (Hughes and the poet Graves were at Oxford together and have been life-long friends.) In his University days he began to write plays, and his first,* The Sisters' Tragedy, *was staged in London by Lewis Casson while its author was still an undergradute. A year or two later* Danger *was the first play in the world written specifically for broadcasting. Then he turned to novels, and was immediately successful with* A High Wind in Jamaica *in 1929. Only three novels have followed,* In Hazard *(1938),* The Fox in the Attic *(1961) and* The Wooden Shepherdess *(1973). His other writings include some slim volumes of poetry, two collections of stories for children and one remarkable collection of short stories for adults. These tales often reflect his interest and love for Wales, and his deep understanding of her character. In 'The Stranger' (written while still at Oxford, and after-*

wards expanded into a play he called A Comedy of Good and Evil*) he shows perhaps more succinctly and with greater feeling than any other writer all there is to say about Welsh superstition and the people's fear of the Devil. It is both a masterful piece of black humour and a unique fantasy.*

I

The street in Cylfant was so steep that if you took a middling jump from the top of the village you would not touch ground again till you reached the bottom: but you would probably hurt yourself.

The houses sat each on other's left shoulder, all the way up, so that the smoke from Mrs Grocery-Jones' chimney blew in at Mrs Boot-Jones' basement, and out through her top windows into the cellar of the Post Office, and out through the Post Office Daughter's little bedroom casement into that of the Butchery Aunt (who was paralysed and lived downstairs): and so on, up the whole line like a flue, till it left soot on the stomachs of the sheep grazing on the hillside above.

But that does not explain why the Stranger came to Cylfant village, unless it was through curiosity: nor, indeed, what he was doing in such a Sabbath-keeping little Anabaptist hamlet at all, where he might have known he would meet with an accident: nor what he was doing so far from home.

Mr Williams was the rector of Cylfant, and perhaps thirty miles round: such an old fat man that he had difficulty in walking between his different churches on Sundays. His face was heavy, his eyes small but with a dream in them, and he kept sticky sweet things ready in his pocket. He was stone-deaf, so that now he roared like a bull, now whispered like a young lover. He might be heard roaring across a valley. He had one black suit, with patches on it; and one surplice, that he darned sometimes. He lived by letting the rectory in the summer: and when the Disestablishment Bill wiped away his stipend of eight pounds a year, he made up for it by taking in laundry: you would see him in front of the rectory, legs set well apart, both heavy arms plunged up to the elbows in suds, a towel pinned to both shoulders to save his black coat, roaring a greeting to all who might pass.

Cylfant was very proud of the smallness of his congregation: for in Wales to have many churchpeople in a village is a great disgrace. They are always the scallywags, the folk who have been expelled from their chapels; and who hope, even if they cannot expect heaven, that things will not be quite so uncomfortable for them in the next world as if they gave up religion altogether. There were only three families, except for the Squire's governess, that ever came to Cylfant church. Mr Williams hated verse, but he preached them pure poetry: he had such an imagination that if he meditated on the anatomy of angels there seemed to be strange flying things about his head; and the passionate roaring and whispering of his voice could hang Christ even on the polished brass altar-cross.

Presently he married the girl who played the harmonium: but she had one leg.

It was she, Minnie, that took in the Stranger. They were sitting one night in the rectory parlour, and Mr Williams was reading a book of sermons with great fixity of mind, in order to forget his Loss: for that day the little ring of his watch-chain had opened, and he had lost the gold cross that he had always carried. Minnie was sure that it had been there when they started to climb the village: but they had no lantern: the wind was a fleet howling darkness, so they could not search till the morning, even if it lay on their very doorstep. Mr Williams read three sermons at a gulp, and closed the book. It was always a thing of amazement that a man who read such dull sermons with such avidity could put so much thrill and beauty, so little of the moralities, into his own preaching.

He shut the book, and, giving a great sight, puffed out his cheeks, while he squinted along the broad shirt-front under his chin. Minnie went to turn down the lamp—as she always did, for reasons of thrift, when her husband was not actually reading; and all at once she heard a cry in the night, sharp as a child's, and full of terror and innocence. She opened the door, and saw a small huddled figure in the roadway. There was a little light shining from it, bluish and fitful: and she knew at once it was something more than natural. She set her wooden leg firmly against the doorstep, and, bending down, caught the Stranger up in her arms, and lifted him over the threshold. He lay there, blinking in the lamplight: a grotesque thing, with misshapen ears and a broad, flat nose. His limbs were knotted, but the skin at his joints was yellow and delicate as a snake's belly. He had crumpled wings, as fine as petrol upon water: even thus battered, their beauty could not but be seen. He seemed in pain: and there was a small cross-shaped weal burnt on his side, as if he had stumbled on a little red-hot iron.

'Poor little thing,' said Mr Williams, looking at it sideways from his chair. 'What is it?'

'It is more ugly than anything I have ever seen,' said Minnie. 'Perhaps it is an angel: for it was never born of woman.'

'We should be more humble, Minnie,' said her husband. 'Who are we that God should send His angels to try us?'

'At any rate, I think it is not,' said Minnie. 'We will see.'

She took up the book of sermons, and touched him on the forehead with it. He gave a shrill yell of pain.

'God forgive me for my cruelty,' she exclaimed. 'It must be a—'

'It is a stranger,' said Mr Williams quickly.

Minnie turned and looked at him.

'What shall we do?' she shouted in his ear. 'For if we harbour it we shall surely be damned. We must not help God's enemies.'

'We are taught to love our enemies,' whispered Mr Williams. 'And who is God's enemy is ours too.'

'But it can feel no gratitude,' said Minnie. 'It will return us evil for good.'

'If we do good in the hope of gratitude we have our reward,' roared Mr Williams.

'You mean you will keep him?' said Minnie.

'I mean'—the old man groaned—'I do not know what to do, indeed, whatever.'

But the visitor settled that question for them himself. He crawled over to the fireplace, and sitting himself on one of the reddest coals, smiled out at them with a grin that stretched from ear to ear.

II

That was how the little devil came to Cylfant rectory. He had great natural charm, and when the cross-shaped weal on his side was better—for it healed quickly under the action of fire—his spirits returned to him. One was led to forget the grotesque beauty of his form by the generous amiability of his expression. He took to the old rector at once; and Mr Williams himself could not but feel a secret liking for him. That night he followed them up to bed: Mr Williams had to shut and lock the bedroom door on him. But hardly were they inside when they saw a bluish light on the panel: and presently the little devil was sitting perched upon the bed-rail, watching with a sober interest Minnie unstrap her wooden leg: and even when she said her prayers—which she did in a shamefast fashion, for fear of giving him pain—he showed no embarrassment whatever. When they were both fast asleep, he took down Minnie's old peg from the shelf where she had laid it, and did something to it in the corner. He then lay down in a pool of moonlight, and was still sleeping soundly when the rector heaved himself out of bed in the morning. The old man woke Minnie, who scrambled out of bed, and began to strap on her leg preparatory to getting the breakfast: but a wonderful thing happened, for no sooner had she fitted her scarred stump into the leather socket than the leather changed to flesh, and the wood to flesh, and there she was with the most elegant and seductive leg that ever troubled a man's eye: and, moreover, there was a silk stocking on it, and a high-heeled Paris shoe on it, before she could recover from her surprise. As she drew on her old ringed black-and-white cotton oddment over the other stocky red ankle she thought that never had such a pair of legs been seen together on one body. She looked round in a guilty fashion: but her husband was balanced in front of the looking-glass shaving himself. He had not seen. She pulled on her dress all in a hurry and danced away downstairs. She let up the blinds and swept the floor; and all the time her new leg behaved as well as if she had known it all her life: but directly she flung open the front door to shake the mat, it began all at once to drag, and jib: she got pins and needles in it: it jumped and kicked like a thing quite out of control. And she saw the reason: for there in the roadway, where she had found the Stranger the night before, was the rector's gold cross.

'There is no mistaking,' said Minnie to herself, 'where *that* leg came from.'

And, indeed, there was not. She sidled up to the cross with difficulty, and recovered it: and all at once heard steps on the cobbles. It was Scraggy Evan, the postman. Minnie's first thought was to hide the leg, for it would take some explaining away. But it would not be hidden: the shameless thing thrust the delicate turn of its ankle right under Scraggy Evan's nose. Scraggy's cheery 'bore da!' was lost in a gasp, and poor Minnie fled into the house scarlet with shame, the damnable leg giving coquettish little kicks into the air as she went.

What Scraggy told the village we can only guess: but he must have told them something, or why should Mrs Williams have received so many callers that morning? The first came when breakfast was hardly over: and the Stranger was sitting quietly on the hob picking his teeth with his tail. Minnie had great presence of mind. She ran to her wood-box, and taking from it a red-flannel petticoat that she had been mending, wrapped the Stranger in it and crammed him quickly into a wooden box, begging him in a staccato whisper to lie still. Upon the face of Mr Williams there was a look of much courage and resignation. Devil or no, he was prepared to justify his guest to all comers. Minnie opened the door, and Mrs Grocery-Jones stood there.

'Good morning,' said she. 'I was calling to ask if you are driving over to Ynysllanbedrbachdeudraethgerylan today.'

She paused and sniffed, then sniffed again.

There was no doubt of it: somewhere sulphur was burning.

'We are not,' said Minnie. 'We are too busy here, indeed, with the plaguey wasps. Mr Williams has hardly smoked out one nest, but bad are they as they were before, indeed.'

Mrs Jones gave a gasp of surprise.

'Wasps in the winter-time?' she said.

'I did not say *wasps*,' said Minnie, 'I said the *wall-paper*, which the doctor thinks may have the scarlet-fever lurking in it, so have we fumigated the whole house.'

It was lucky, thought Minnie, that her husband was so deaf. He would never have forgiven her.

'Well, good gracious!' said Mrs Jones. As her eyes got used to the dim light she caught sight of a broad head with two beady yellow eyes, peering at her from a soap-box. 'And is that a cat you have there, Mrs Williams?'

'It is a *pig*!' she cried with sudden heat; for her new leg showed an obvious desire to kick Mrs Jones out of the house. 'It has the wind,' she explained, 'so we thought it would be best in the house, indeed.'

'Well, good gracious me!' repeated Mrs Jones.

Minnie's leg was quivering, but she managed to control it. Mrs Jones was staring past her at the pig, as if she could not take her eyes off it. As, indeed, she could not: for suddenly she shot half across the road, backward, with the force of a bullet: and when released she scrambled down the street, as she herself explained it, 'as if the devil was after me': and there was the Stranger, wrapped still in the red-flannel petticoat, sitting on the window-sill and grinning amiably at her back.

III

If Mr Williams had lived longer, a few curious things might have happened in Cylfant village: but he did not. There was a buzzing feeling in his head all that day, and when he went to bed at night he lay quietly on his back staring at the ceiling. It had turned a bright green. Presently, with his eyes open still, he began to snore. Minnie did not notice anything queer; and in the small hours of the morning, after two or three loud snores, he stopped altogether.

When he felt better, he found that his soul was outside his body. It was not at all the kind of thing he had expected it to be, but was fairly round, and made of some stuff like white of egg. He gathered it gently into his arms, and began to float about: his body had disappeared. Presently he was aware that the Stranger was still watching him.

'You'll be damned for this: double-damned even, for giving place to the devil—and you a priest.' He sighed. 'It is so hard,' he went on seriously, 'even for devils to conquer their better nature. Oh, I *try* hard enough. I surely try. The seeds of goodness have lurked in us ever since the Fall: try as we will, they *sprout*.

> 'With a fork drive Nature out,
> She will ever yet return.

'Temptation is always lurking ready for us: it is a long and a hard fight: the Forces of Evil against the Forces of Good. But we shall conquer in the end: with Wrong on our side, we *must* conquer.' There was an elation in his face that transcended all earthly ugliness. 'At last,' he went on, 'I have done a really immoral act: an act with no trace of good in it, either in motive or effect. You will be damned, and Minnie will be damned too, even if she has to hop to hell on the leg I gave her. But it was hard, hard.'

Old Williams floated over on to the other side.

'I am a sinful man,' he said; 'a very sinful man. Heaven was never my deserts, whatever.'

The devil looked at him in surprise.

'Oh, you were not!' he said earnestly. 'Indeed, you were not! You were the truest—'

He stopped suddenly. Williams was aware of the presence of some very unpleasant personality. He looked round: and behind him stood a tall figure with thin, tight lips and watery eyes, who began speaking at once—rapidly, as if by rote.

'As a matter of form,' said he, 'I claim this soul.'

'As a matter of form,' replied the devil in a singsong voice, 'he is mine.'

The angel rapped out: 'De qua causa?'

'De diabolo consortando,' chaunted the little devil, in even worse Latin.

'Quae sit evidentia?'

'Tuos voco oculos ipsos.'

'Quod vidi, vero, atque affirmo.—Satis,' continued the angel. 'Tuumst.' And he turned to go.

'Stop!' cried the Stranger suddenly, all his bad resolutions breaking down.

'Stop!' he cried, and began speaking rapidly. 'I'm a backslider, I know, but the strain is too much: there's no true devilry in me. Take him: take him: there never was better Christian in Wales, I swear it: and to that alone his damnation is due: pure charity—'

'What are you talking about?' snapped the angel petulantly. 'The case is settled: I have withdrawn my claim.'

'So do I!' cried the devil excitedly. 'I withdraw mine.'

The angel shrugged his wings.

'What's the use of making a scene?' he said. 'Never, in all my office, have I known a fiend break down and forget himself like this before. You are making an exhibition of yourself, sir! Besides, if we both withdraw, he can't go anywhere. It's none of my business.'

He shrugged his wings and soared away.

'*Heaven or Hell or the Land of Whipperginny,*' murmured Williams to himself, vague memories of Nashe rising to the surface of his astonishment. Together they watched the angel's purple pinions bearing him from sight: the Stranger cocked a snook at his straight back.

'Where now?' asked the rector.

'Where now? Heaven! Wait till he's out of sight.'

He turned and winked broadly at Williams, making a motion on his bare shanks as if to thrust his hand in a pocket.

'You come with me,' he said. 'I know how I can get things fixed for you!'

THE SCHOOL FOR WITCHES

by Dylan Thomas

D Y L A N M A R L A I S T H O M A S *(1914–1953)* '*The
Rimbaud of Cwymdonkin Drive*' *as he called himself, is
probably the one writer in this collection more readily identi-
fied than any other with Wales by readers around the world.
His legend, for such it is, of man of genius, poet, carouser,
and '*maker of word magic*' *has left a mark not only on his
native land but on the whole of modern poetry. The unique
lyrical talent he possessed flowered into some of the most
widely read and admired poetry of this century, culminating
in the play-in-verse,* Under Milk Wood *(1945). He was a
brilliant prose writer, too, bringing to his essays and works
of short fiction the same remarkable insight and bizarre
imagery. Wales and the Welsh flood into all his work, as
does his knowledge of history and legend. Many of his stories
are well known, reprinted in collection after collection, but
'*The School for Witches*' *does not fall into this category. It
dates from his formative years and appeared first in 1936.
It shows Thomas's profound knowledge of the tradition of
witchcraft in Wales (which records show was widespread
and of very long standing), and is doubtless based on oral
traditions which were related to him. All the word magic is
here, thickly laced with legend, in a triumph of the fantasy
writer's art.*

On Cader Peak there was a school for witches where the doctor's
daughter, teaching the unholy cradle and the devil's pin, had
seven country girls. On Cader Peak, half ruined in an enemy
weather, the house with a story held the seven girls, the cellar

echoing, and a cross reversed above the entrance to the inner rooms. Here the doctor, dreaming of illness, in the centre of the tubercular hill, heard his daughter cry to the power swarming under the West roots. She invoked a particular devil, but the gehenna did not yawn under the hill, and the day and the night continued with their two departures; the cocks crew and the corn fell in the villages and yellow fields as she taught the seven girls how the lust of man, like a dead horse, stood up to his injected mixtures. She was short and fat-thighed; her cheeks were red; she had red lips and innocent eyes. But her body grew hard as she called to the black flowers under the tide of roots; when she fetched the curdlers out of the trees to bore through the cows' udders, the seven staring stared at the veins hardening in her breast; she stood uncovered, calling the devil, and the seven uncovered closed round her in a ring.

Teaching them the intricate devil, she raised her arms to let him enter. Three years and a day had vanished since she first bowed to the moon, and, maddened by the mid light, dipped her hair seven times in the salt sea, and a mouse in honey. She stood, still untaken, loving the lost man; her fingers hardened on light as on the breastbone of the unentering devil.

Mrs Price climbed up the hill, and the seven saw her. It was the first evening of the new year, the wind was motionless on Cader Peak, and a half red, promising dusk floated over the rocks. Behind the midwife the sun sank as a stone sinks in a marsh, the dark bubbled over it, and the mud sucked it down into the bubble of the bottomless fields.

In Bethlehem there is a prison for mad women, and in Cathmarw by the parsonage trees a black girl screamed as she laboured. She was afraid to die like a cow on the straw, and to the noises of the rooks. She screamed for the doctor on Cader Peak as the tumultuous West moved in its grave. The midwife heard her. A black girl rocked in her bed. Her eyes were stones. Mrs Price climbed up the hill, and the seven saw her.

Midwife, midwife, called the seven girls. Mrs Price crossed herself. A chain of garlic hung at her throat. Carefully, she touched it. The seven cried aloud, and ran from the window to the inner rooms where the doctor's daughter, bent on uncovered knees, counselled the black toad, her familiar, and the divining cat slept by the wall. The familiar moved his head. The seven danced, rubbing the white wall with their thighs until the blood striped the thin symbols of fertility upon them. Hand in hand they danced among dark symbols, under the charts that marked the rise and fall of the satanic seasons, and their white dresses swung around them. The owls commenced to sing, striking against the music of the suddenly awaking winter. Hand in hand the dancers spun around the black toad and the doctor's daughter, seven stags dancing, their antlers shaking, in the confusion of the unholy room.

She is a very black woman, said Mrs Price, and curtsied to the doctor.

He woke to the midwife's story out of a dream of illness, remembering the broken quicked, the black patch and echo, and mutilated shadows of the seventh sense.

She lay with a black scissor-man.

He wounded her deep, said the doctor, and wiped a lancet on his sleeve.

Together they stumbled down the rocky hill.

A terror met them at the foot, the terror of the blind tapping their white sticks and the stumps of the arms on the solid darkness; two worms in the foil of a tree, bellies on the rubber sap and the glues of a wrong-grained forest, they, holding tight to hats and bags, crawled now up the path that led to the black birth. From right, from left, the cries of labour came in under the branches, piercing the dead wood, from the earth where a mole sneezed, and from the sky, out of the worms' sight.

They were not the only ones caught that night in the torrential blindness; to them, as they stumbled, the land was empty of men, and the prophets of bad weather alone walked in their neighbourhoods. Three tinkers appeared out of silence by the chapel wall. Capel Cader, said the panman. Parson is down on tinkers, said John Bucket. Cader Peak, said the scissor-man, and up they went. They passed the midwife close; she heard the scissors clacking, and the branch of a tree drum on the buckets. One, two, three, they were gone, invisibly shuffling as she hugged her skirts.

Mrs Price crossed herself for the second time that day, and touched the garlic at her throat. A vampire with a scissors was a Pembroke devil. And the black girl screamed like a pig.

Sister, raise your right hand. The seventh girl raised her right hand. Now say, said the doctor's daughter, Rise up out of the bearded barley. Rise out of the green grass asleep in Mr Griffith's dingle. Big man, black man, all eye, one tooth, rise up out of Cader marshes. Say the devil kisses me. The devil kisses me, said the girl cold in the centre of the kitchen. Kiss me out of the bearded barley. Kiss me out of the bearded barley. The girls giggled in a circle. Swive me out of the green grass. Swive me out of the green grass. Can I put on my clothes now? said the young witch, after encountering the invisible evil.

Throughout the hours of the early night, in the smoke of the seven candles, the doctor's daughter spoke of the sacrament of darkness. In her familiar's eyes she read the news of a great and an unholy coming; divining the future in the green and sleepy eyes, she saw, as clearly as the tinkers saw the spire, the towering coming of a beast in stag's skin, the antlered animal whose name read backwards, and the black, black, black wanderer climbing a hill for the seven wise girls of Cader. She woke the cat. Poor Bell, she said, smoothing his fur the wrong way. And, Ding dong, Bell, she said, and swung the spitting cat.

Sister, raise your left hand. The first girl raised her left hand. Now with your right hand put a needle in your left hand. Where is a needle? Here, said the doctor's daughter, is a needle, here in your hair. She made a gesture over the black hair, and drew a needle out from the coil at her ear. Say I cross you. I cross you, said the girl, and, with the needle in her hand, struck at the black cat racked on the daughter's lap.

For love takes many shapes, cat, dog, pig, or goat; there was a lover, spellbound in the time of mass, now formed and featured in the image of the darting cat; his belly bleeding, he sped past the seven girls, past parlour and dispensary, into the night, on to the hill; the wind got at his wound, and swiftly he darted down the rocks, in the direction of the cooling streams.

He passed the three tinkers like lightning. Black cat is luck, said the panman. Bloody cat is bad luck, said John Bucket. The scissor-man said nothing. They appeared out of silence by the wall of the Peak house, and heard a hellish music through the open door. They peered through the stained-glass window, and the seven girls danced before them. They have beaks, said the panman. Web feet, said John Bucket. The tinkers walked in.

At midnight the black girl bore her baby, a black beast with the eyes of a kitten and a stain at the corner of its mouth. The midwife, remembering birthmarks, whispered to the doctor of the gooseberry on his daughter's arm. Is it ripe yet? said Mrs Price. The doctor's hand trembled and his lancet cut the baby under the chin. Scream you, said Mrs Price, who loved all babies.

The wind howled over Cader, waking the sleepy rooks who cawed from the trees and, louder than owls, disturbed the midwife's meditations. It was wrong for the rooks, those sleepy birds over the zinc roofs, to caw at night. Who put a spell on the rooks? The sun might rise at ten past one in the morning.

Scream you, said Mrs Price, the baby in her arms. This is a wicked world. The wicked world, with a voice out of the wind, spoke to the baby half smothering under the folds of the midwife's overcoat. Mrs Price wore a man's cap, and her great breasts heaved under the black blouse. Scream you, said the wicked world, I am an old man blinding you, a wicked little woman tickling you, a dry death parching you. The baby screamed, as though a flea were on its tongue.

The tinkers were lost in the house, and could not find the inner room where the girls still danced with the beaks of birds upon them and their web feet bare on the cobblestones. The panman opened the dispensary door, but the bottles and the tray of knives alarmed him. The passages were too dark for John Bucket, and the scissor-man surprised him at a corner. Christ defend me, he cried. The girls stopped dancing, for the name of Christ rang in the outer halls. Enter, and, Enter, cried the doctor's daughter to the welcome devil. It was the scissor-man who found the door and turned the handle, walking into candlelight. He stood before Gladwys on the threshold, a giant black as ink with a three days' beard. She lifted her face to his, and her sackcloth fell away.

Up the hill, the midwife, cooing as she came, held the newborn baby in her arms, and the doctor toiled behind her with his black bag rattling. The birds of the night flew by them, but the night was empty, and these restless wings and voices, hindering emptiness forever, were the feathers of shadows and the accents of an invisible flying. What purpose there was in the shape of Cader Peak, in the bouldered breast of the hill and the craters poxing the green-black flesh, was no more than the wind's purpose that willy nilly blew from all corners the odd turfs and stones of an unmoulded world. The grassy rags and bones of the steep hill were, so the doctor pondered as he climbed behind the baby rocking into memory on a strange breast, whirled together out of the bins of chaos by a winter wind. But the doctor's conceits came to nothing, for the black child let out a scream so high and loud that Mr Griffiths heard it in his temple in the dingle. The worshipper of vegetables, standing beneath his holy marrow nailed in four places to the wall, heard the cry come down from the heights. A mandrake cried on Cader. Mr Griffiths hastened in the direction of the stars.

John Bucket and the panman stepped into candlelight, seeing a strange company. Now in the centre circle of the room surrounded by the unsteady lights, stood the scissor-man and a naked girl; she smiled at him, he smiled at her, his hands groped for her body, she stiffened and slackened, he drew her close smiling, she stiffened again, and he licked his lips.

John Bucket had not seen him as a power for evil baring the breasts and the immaculate thighs of the gentlewoman, a magnetic blackman with the doom of women in his smile, forcing open the gates of love. He remembered a black companion on the roads, sharpening the village scissors, and, in the shadows, when the tinkers took the night, a coal-black shadow, silent as the travelling hedges.

Was this tall man, the panman murmured, who takes the doctor's daughter with no how-d'you-do, was he Tom the scissor-man? I remember him on the highways in the heat of the sun, a black, three-coated tinker.

And, like a god, the scissor-man bent over Gladwys, he healed her wound, she stood his ointment and his fire, she burned at the tower altar, and the black sacrifice was done. Stepping out of his arms, her offering cut and broken, the gut of a lamb, she smiled and cried manfully: Dance, dance, my seven. And the seven danced, their antlers shaking, in the confusion of the unholy room. A coven, a coven, cried the seven as they danced. They beckoned the panman from the door. He edged towards them, and they caught his hands. Dance, dance, my strange man, the seven cried. John Bucket joined them, his buckets drumming, and swiftly they dragged him into the rising fury of the dance. The scissor-man in the circle danced like a tower. They sped round and round, none crying louder than the two tinkers in the heart of the swirling company, and lightly the doctor's daughter was among them. She drove them to a faster turn of foot; giddy as weathercocks in a hundred changing winds, they were revolving figures in the winds of their dresses and to the music of the scissors and the metal pans; giddily she spun between the dancing hoops, the wheels of cloth and hair, and the bloody ninepins spinning; the candles grew pale and lean in the wind of the dance; she whirled by the tinker's side, by the scissor-man's side, by his dark, damp side, smelling his skin, smelling the seven furies.

It was then that the doctor, the midwife, and the baby entered through the open door as quietly as could be. Sleep well, Pembroke, for your devils have left you. And woe on Cader Peak that the black man dances in my house. There had been nothing for that savage evening but an end of evil. The grave had yawned, and the black breath risen up.

Here danced the metamorphoses of the dusts of Cathmarw. Lie level, the ashes of man, for the phoenix flies from you, woe unto Cader, into my nice, square house. Mrs Price fingered her garlic, and the doctor stood grieving.

The seven saw them. A coven, a coven, they cried. One, dancing past them, snatched at the doctor's hand; another, dancing caught him around the waist; and, all bewildered by the white flesh of their arms, the doctor danced. Woe, woe on Cader, he cried as he swirled among maidens, and his steps gathered speed. He heard his voice rising; his feet skimmed over the silver cobbles. A coven, a coven, cried the dancing doctor, and bowed in his measures.

Suddenly Mrs Price, hugging the black baby, was surrounded at the entrance of the room. Twelve dancers hemmed her in, and the hands of strangers pulled at the baby on her breast. See, see, said the doctor's daughter, The cross on the black throat. There was blood beneath the baby's chin where a sharp knife had slipped and cut. The cat, cried the seven, The cat, the black cat. They had unloosed the spellbound devil that dwelt in the cat's shape, the human skeleton, the flesh and heart out of the gehenna of the valley roots and the image of the creature calming his wound in the far-off streams. Their magic was done; they set the baby down on the stones, and the dance continued. Pembroke, sleep well, whispered the dancing midwife, Lie still, you empty county.

And it was thus that the last visitor that night found the thirteen dancers in the inner rooms of Cader House: a black man and a blushing girl, two shabby tinkers, a doctor, a midwife, and seven country girls, swirling hand in hand under the charts that marked the rise and fall of the satanic seasons, among the symbols of the darker crafts, giddily turning, raising their voices to the roofs as they bowed to the cross reversed above the inner entrance.

Mr Griffiths, half blinded by the staring of the moon, peeped in and saw them. He saw the newborn baby on the cold stones. Unseen in the shadow by the door, he crept towards the baby and lifted it to its feet. The baby fell. Patiently Mr Griffiths lifted the baby to its feet. But the little mandrake would not walk that night.

THE SABBATH

by Charles Williams

CHARLES WILLIAMS *(1886–1945)* has been *described by his life-long friend, T. S. Eliot as a 'mystic' and a man with a profound knowledge of the occult and the supernatural. Among general readers he is not as well-known as he deserves, yet his books have been reviewed as 'works surpassing even those of the recognised masters of horror'. Born in 1886 of Welsh parents, he had little formal schooling, yet educated himself to the point of being allowed to lecture at Oxford and attaining the award of an honorary M.A. Much of his life he worked as an editor in a London publishing house, but he also produced some outstanding poetry, drama and criticism apart from a series of superb novels all primarily concerned with the battle between good and evil. The aura of the supernatural in Wales was a considerable influence on his writing and is to be seen in novels such as* War in Heaven *(1930),* Shadows of Ecstasy *(1933) and* Descent into Hell *(1937). He was a firm believer in the continuing existence of the supernatural in modern civilisation and some of his best work is concerned with the practise of white and black magic in urban settings. This facet of his talent is vividly shown in the next story which takes us to the very heart of that most secret of occult rituals,* The Witches' Sabbath . . .

'I met Mr Persimmons in the village today,' Mr Batesby said to the Archdeacon. 'He asked after you very pleasantly.'

'Yes,' the Archdeacon said.

'We had quite a long chat,' the other went on. 'He isn't exactly a Christian, unfortunately, but he has a great admiration for the

Church. He thinks it's doing a wonderful work—especially in education. He takes a great interest in education; he calls it the star of the future. He thinks morals are more important than dogma, and of course I agree with him.'

'Did you say "of course I agree" or "of course I agreed"?' the Archdeacon asked. 'Or both?'

'I mean I thought the same thing,' Mr Batesby explained. He had noticed a certain denseness in the Archdeacon on other occasions. 'Conduct is much the biggest thing in life, I feel. "He can't be wrong whose life is for the best; we needs must love the higher when we see Him." And he gave me five pounds towards the Sunday School Fund.'

'There isn't,' the Archdeacon said, slightly roused, 'a Sunday School Fund at Fardles.'

'Oh, well!' Mr Batesby considered. 'I daresay he'd be willing for it to go to almost anything *active*. He was very keen, and I agr—thought just the same, on getting things *done*. He thinks that the Church ought to be a means of progress. He quoted something about not going to sleep till we found a pleasant Jerusalem in the green land of England. I was greatly struck. An idealist, that's what I should call him. England needs idealists today.'

'I think we had better return the money,' the Archdeacon said. 'If he isn't a Christian—'

'Oh, but he is,' Mr Batesby protested. 'In effect, that is. He thinks Christ was the second greatest man the earth has produced.'

'Who was the first?' the Archdeacon asked.

Mr Batesby paused again for a moment. 'Do you know, I forgot to ask?' he said. 'But it shows a sympathetic spirit, doesn't it? After all, the second greatest—! That goes a long way. Little children, love one another—if five pounds helps us to teach them that in the schools. I'm sure mine want a complete new set of Bible pictures.'

There was a pause. The two priests were sitting after dinner in the garden of the Rectory. The Archdeacon, with inner thoughts for meditation, was devoting a superficial mind to Mr Batesby, who on his side was devoting his energies to providing his host with cheerful conversation. The Archdeacon knew this, and knew too that his guest would rather have been talking about his own views on the ornaments rubric than about the parishioners. He wished he would. He was feeling rather tired, and it was an effort to pay attention to anything which he did not know by heart. Mr Batesby's ecclesiastical views he did—and thought them incredibly silly— but he thought his own were probably that too. One had views for convenience's sake, but how anyone could think they mattered. Except, of course, that even silly views . . .

A car went by on the road and a hand was waved from it. To Gregory Persimmons the sight of the two priests was infinitely pleasurable. He had met them both and summed them up. He could, he felt, knock the Archdeacon on the head whenever he chose, and the other hadn't got a head to be knocked. It was all very pleasant and satisfactory. There had been a moment, a few days ago, in that little shop when he couldn't get out, and there seemed suddenly no reason why he should get out, as if he had been utterly and finally betrayed into being there for ever—he had felt almost in a panic. He had known that feeling once or twice before, at odd times; but there was no need to recall it now. Tonight, tonight, something else was to happen. Tonight he would know what it all was of which he had read in his books, and heard —heard from people who had funnily come into his life and then disappeared. Long ago, as a boy, he remembered reading about the Sabbath, but he had been told that it wasn't true. His father had been a Victorian Rationalist. The Archdeacon, he thought, was exceedingly Victorian too. His heart beating in an exalted anticipation, he drove on to Cully.

Mr Batesby was asleep that night, and the Archdeacon was, in a Victorian way, engaged in his prayers, when Gregory Persimmons stood up alone in his room. It was a little after midnight, and, as he glanced out of the window, he saw a clear sky with a few stars and the full moon contemplating him. Slowly, very slowly, he undressed, looking forward to he knew not what, and then—being entirely naked—he took from a table the small greasy box of ointment and opened it. It was a pinkish ointment, very much the colour of the skin, and at first he thought it had no smell. But in a few minutes, as it lay exposed to the air, there arose from it a faint odour which grew stronger, and presently filled the whole room, not overpoweringly, but with a convenient and irresistible assurance. He paused for a moment, inhaling it, and finding in it the promise of some complete decay. It brought to him an assurance of his own temporal achievement of his power to enter into those lives which he touched and twist them out of their security into a sliding destruction. Five pounds here, a clever jeer there—it was all easy. Everyone had some security, and he had only to be patient to find and destroy it. His father, when he had grown old and had had a good deal of trouble, had been inclined to wonder whether there was anything in religion. And they had talked of it; he remembered those talks. He had—it had been his first real experiment—he had suggested very carefully and delicately, to that senile and uneasy mind, that there probably was a God, but a God of terrible jealousy; God had driven Judas, who betrayed him, to hang himself; and driven the Jews who denied him to exile in all lands. And Peter, his father had said, Peter was forgiven. He had stood thinking of that, and then had hesitated that, yes, no doubt Peter was forgiven, unless God had taken a terrible revenge and used Peter to set up all that mystery of evil which was Antichrist and Torquemada and Smithfield and the Roman See. Before the carefully sketched picture of an infinite, absorbing, and mocking vengeance, his father had shivered and grown silent. And had thereafter died, trying not to believe in God lest he should know himself damned.

Gregory smiled, and touched the ointment with his fingers. It seemed almost to suck itself upward round them as he did so. He disengaged his fingers and began the anointing. From the feet upwards in prolonged and rhythmic movements his hands moved backward and forward over his skin, he bowed and rose again, and again. The inclinations gradually ceased as the anointing hands grew higher—around the knees, the hips, the breast. Against his body the pink smears showed brightly for a moment, and then were mingled with and lost in the natural colour of the flesh. All the while his voice kept up a slow crooning, to the sound of which he moved, pronouncing as in an incantation of rounded and liquid syllables what seemed hierarchic titles. He touched his temples and his forehead with both hands, and so for a moment stayed.

His voice grew deeper and charged with more intensity, though the sound was not noticeably quicker, as he began the second anointing. But now it was only the chosen parts that he touched— the soles of the feet, the palms of the hands, the inner side of the fingers, the ears and eyelids, the environs of nose and mouth, the secret organs. Over all these again and again he moved his hands, and again ceased and paused, and the intensity died from his voice.

For the third anointing was purely ritual. He marked various figures upon his body—a cross upon either sole, a cross inverted from brow to foot, and over all his form the pentagon reversed of magic. While he did so his voice rose in a solemn chant which entered with a strange power through those anointed ears, and flowed through his body as did the new faint light that seemed to shine through his closed eyelids. Light and sound were married in premonitions of approaching experience; his voice quivered upon the air and stopped. Then with an effort he moved uncertainly towards his bed, and stretched himself on it, his face towards the closed window and the enlarging moon. Silent and grotesque he lay, and the secret processes of the night began.

If it had been possible for any stranger to enter that locked room in the middle of his journeying they would have found his body lying there still. By no broomstick flight over the lanes of England did Gregory Persimmons attend the Witches' Sabbath, nor did he dance with other sorcerers upon some blasted heath before a goat-headed manifestation of the Accursed. But scattered far over the face of the earth, though not so far in the swiftness of interior passage, those abandoned spirits answered one another that night; and That beyond them (which some have held to be but the precipitation and tendency of their own natures, and others for the equal and perpetual co-inheritor of power and immortality with God)—That beyond them felt them and shook and replied, sustained and nourished and controlled.

After Gregory had laid himself upon the bed he made the usual attempt at excluding from the attention all his surroundings.

But tonight the powerful ointment worked so swiftly upon him, stealing through all his flesh with a delicious venom and writhing itself into his blood and heart, that he had scarcely come to rest before the world was shut out. He was being made one with something beyond his consciousness; he accepted the union in a deep sigh of pleasure.

When it had approached a climax it ceased suddenly. There passed through him a sense of lightness and airy motion; his body seemed to float upwards, so unconscious had it become of the bed on which it rested. He knew now that he must begin to exercise his own intention, and in a depth beyond thought he did so. He commanded and directed himself towards the central power which awaited him. Images floated past him; for his mind, rising as it were out of the faintness which had overcome it, now began to change his experiences into such sounds and shapes as it knew; so that he at once experienced and expressed experience to himself intellectually, and could not generally separate the two. At this beginning, for example, as he lay given up to that sensation of swift and easy motion towards some still hidden moment of exquisite and destructive delight, it seemed to him that at a great distance he heard faint and lovely voices, speaking to him or to each other, and that out of him in turn went a single note of answering glee.

And now he was descending; lower and lower, into a darker and more heavy atmosphere. His intention checked his flight, and it declined almost into stillness; night was about him, and more than night, a heaviness which was like that felt in a crowd, a pressure and intent expectation of relief. As to the mind of a man in prayer might come sudden reminders of great sanctities in other places and other periods, so now to him came the consciousness, not in detail, but as achievements, of far-off masteries of things, multitudinous dedications consummating themselves in That which was already on its way. But that his body was held in a trance by the effect of the ointment, the smell of which had long since become part of his apprehension, he would have turned his head one way or the other to see or speak to those unseen companions.

Suddenly, as in an excited crowd a man may one minute be

speaking and shouting to those near him, and the next, part of the general movement directed and controlled by that to which he contributes, there rose within him the sense of a vast and rapid flow, of which he was part, rushing and palpitating with desire. He desired—the heat about his heart grew stronger— to give himself out, to be one with something that should submit to him and from which he should yet draw nourishment; but something beyond imagination stupendous. He was hungry—but not for food; he was thirsty—but not for drink; he was filled with passion—but not for flesh. He expanded in the rush of an ancient desire; he longed to be married to the whole universe for a bride. His father appeared before him, senile and shivering; his wife, bewildered and broken; his son, harassed and distressed. These were his marriages, these his bridals. The bridal dance was beginning; they and he and innumerable others were moving to the wild rhythm of that aboriginal longing. Beneath all the little cares and whims of mankind the tides of that ocean swung, and those who had harnessed them and those who had been destroyed by them were mingled in one victorious catastrophe. His spirit was dancing with his peers, and yet still something in his being held back and was not melted.

There was something—from his depths he cried to his mortal mind to recall it and pass on the message—some final thing that was needed still; some offering by which he might pierce beyond this black drunkenness and achieve a higher reward. What was the sacrifice, what the oblation that was greater than the wandering and unhappy souls whose ruin he had achieved? Heat as from an immense pyre beat upon him, beat upon him with a demand for something more; he absorbed it, and yet, his ignorance striking him with fear, shrunk from its ardent passions. It was not heat only, it was sound also, a rising tumult, acclamation of shrieking voices, thunder of the terrible approach. It came, it came, ecstasy of perfect mastery, marriage in hell, he who was Satan wedded to that beside which was Satan. And yet one little thing was needed and he had it not—he was an outcast for want of that one thing. He forced his interior mind to stillness for a moment only, and in that moment recollection came.

From the shadowy and forgotten world the memory of the child Adrian floated into him, and he knew that this was what was needed. All gods had their missionaries, and this god also who was himself and not himself demanded neophytes. Deeply into himself he drew that memory; he gathered up its freshness and offered it to the secret and infernal powers. Adrian was the desirable sacrifice, an unknowing initiate, a fated candidate. To this purpose the man lying still and silent on the bed, or caught up before some vast interior throne where the masters and husbands and possessors of the universe danced and saw immortal life decay before their subtle power, dedicated himself. The wraith of the child drifted into the midst of the dance, and at the moment when Adrian far away in London stirred in his sleep with a moan a like moan broke out in another chamber. For the last experience was upon the accepted devotee; there passed through him a wave of intense cold, and in every chosen spot where the ointment had been twice applied the cold concentrated and increased. Nailed, as it were, through feet and hands and head and genitals, he passed utterly into a pang that was an ecstasy beyond his dreams. He was divorced now from the universe; he was one with a rejection of all courteous and lovely things; by the oblation of the child he was made one with that which is beyond childhood and age and time— the reflection and negation of the eternity of God. He existed supernaturally, and in Hell . . .

When the dissolution of this union and the return began, he knew it as an overwhelming storm. Heat and cold, the interior and exterior world, images and wraiths, sounds and odours, warred together within him. Chaos broke upon him; he felt himself whirled away into an infinite desolation of anarchy. He strove to concentrate, now on that which was within, now on some detail of the room which was already spectrally apparent to him; but fast as he did so it was gone. Panic seized him; he would have screamed, but to scream would be to be lost. And then again the image of Adrian floated before him, and he knew that much was yet to be done. With that image in his heart, he rose slowly and through many mists to the surface of consciousness, and as it faded gradu-

ally to a name and a thought he knew that the Sabbath was over
and the return accomplished.

'Adrian's very restless,' Barbara said to her husband Lionel. 'I
wonder if the scone upset him. There, darling, there!'

'He's probably dreaming of going away,' Lionel answered softly.
'I hope he won't take a dislike to the place or Persimmons or
anything.'

'Hush, sweetheart,' Barbara murmured. 'All's well. All's well.'

WEEK-END AT CWM TATWS

by Robert Graves

ROBERT RANKE GRAVES (*1895–*), *the poet and Master of Mythology, spent much of his childhood and youth at Harlech in North Wales. Despite long years away since living in Majorca he has retained a strong affection for the country. The son of Alfred Perceval Graves, the Irish poet and leader of the Celtic revival, Robert Graves himself came to public note while serving in the Royal Welsh Fusiliers in the First World War. The poetry he wrote in the trenches rapidly established him as a major literary figure, and at the end of hostilities he decided to further his education by becoming an undergraduate at Oxford. To support himself and his family he ran a small shop until his graduation and thereafter was appointed Professor of English at Cairo University. Eventually he turned to his poetry and writing full-time and settled on Majorca. Graves' major works include the mythological novel,* The White Goddess, I, Claudius, *which won both the James Tait Black and Hawthornden prizes in 1934, and its sequel,* Claudius the God. *He has also written some varied and accomplished short stories, several of which—like the example I have selected here—show his remembrance of Wales and its customs. In recent years, despite living so far away, Graves has proved himself a champion in the fight against indiscriminate development and copper mining proposals in mid-Wales. His campaigning has earned him headlines throughout the country and he has hinted darkly that 'the Gods of the Welsh valleys will exact revenge if they are disturbed'.*

I shouldn't bring the story up—there's nothing in it really, except the sequel—if it wasn't already current in a garbled form. What happens to me I prefer told my own way, or not at all. Point is: I fell for that girl at first sight. So much more than sympathetic, as well as being in the beauty queen class, that . . .

In spite of my looking such a fool, too.

And probably if she'd had a wooden leg, a boss eye and only one tooth . . . Not that I was particularly interested in teeth at the moment, or in any position to utter more than a faint ugh, or even to smile a welcome. But how considerate of her to attend to me before taking any steps to deal with the heavy object on my lap! Most girls would have gone off into hysteria. But *she* happened to be practical; didn't even pause to dial 999. Saw with half an eye that . . . Put first things first. Besides looking such a fool, I was a fool: to get toothache on a Saturday afternoon, in a place like Cwm Tatws. As I told myself continuously throughout that lost week-end.

The trouble was my being all alone: nobody to be anxious, nobody to send out a search party, nobody in the township who knew me from Adam. I had come to Cwm Tatws to fish, which is about the only reason why anyone ever comes there, unless he happens to be called Harry Parry or Owen Owens or Evan Evans or Reece Reece or . . . Which I'm not. Tooth had already stirred faintly on the Friday just after I registered at the Dolwreiddiog Arms; but I decided to diagnose neuralgia and kill it with aspirin. Saturday, I got up early to flog the lake, where two- and three-pounders had allegedly been rising in fair numbers, and brought along my bottle of aspirins and a villainous cold lunch.

No, to fish doesn't necessarily mean being a Hemingway fan; after all, there was Izaak Walton, whom I haven't read either.

By mid-afternoon Tooth woke up suddenly and began to jump about like . . . I hooked a couple of sizeables, though nothing as big as advertised; both broke away. My error was waiting for the lucky third. That, and forgetting that it was Saturday afternoon. It was only when I got back to Cwm Tatws, which has five pubs (some bad, some worse), a police station, a post office, a branch bank and so forth—largish place for that district—that I decided to seek out the town tooth-drawer, Mr Griffith Griffiths, whose brass plate I had noticed next to 'Capel Beulah 1861'.

Not what you thought. Mr Griffith Griffiths was at home all right, most cordial, and worked Saturday afternoons and evenings because that was the day when everyone . . . But he had recently slipped on a wet rock in his haste to gaff a big one and chipped a corner off his left elbow. Gross bad luck: he was left-handed.

'Let's look at it,' he said. And he did. 'No hope in the world of saving that poor fellow. I must yank him out at once. Pity on him, now, that he's a hind molar, indeed!'

What should X do next? Mr Griffith-heard-you-the-first-time will be out of action for the next month. X could of course hire a motor-car and drive thirty miles over the hills to Denbigh, where maybe tomorrow . . .

I pressed and pleaded. 'Is there nobody in this five-pub town capable of . . . A blacksmith, for instance? Or a barber? Why not the vet? Under your direction?'

'Well now, indeed, considering the emergency, perhaps, as you say, Mr Rowland Rowlands the veterinarian might consent to practise on you that which he practises on the ewes.'

Unfortunately Mr Rowland-say-it-twice had driven off to Denbigh himself in the last 'bus-motorr' (as they call it in Cwm Tatws), to visit his whatever she was.

Mr Griffith Griffiths right-handedly stroked his stubby chin. He couldn't shave now and thought the barber saloon vulgar and low. Said: 'Well, well, now, I shouldn't wonder if dear old Mr Van der Pant might peradventure play the good Samaritan. He is English too, and was qualified dental surgeon in Cwm Tatws, not altogether fifteen years ago; for it was from Mr Van der Pant that I bought this practice. A nice old gentleman, though a confirmed recluse and cannot speak a single word of Welsh.'

Welshlessness being no particular disadvantage in the circumstances, I hurried off to Rhododendron Cottage, down a wet lane, and up an avenue of wetter rhododendrons. By this time my tooth was . . .

You are wrong again. I found Mr Van der Pant also at home, and he had not even broken an arm. But took ten minutes to answer the bell, and then came out only by accident, having been too deaf to hear it.

Let us cut short the dumb-show farce: eventually I made him understand and consent to . . .

The room was . . . Macabre, isn't it? 'Only Adults Admitted'. Had been locked up since whenever, by the look of it. Cobwebs like tropical creepers. Dental chair deep in dust. Shutters askew. No heating. Smell of mice. Presence of mice. Rusty expectoration bowl and instrument rack. Plaster fallen in heaps from the ceiling. Wallpaper peeled off. Fascinating, in a way.

I helped him screw in an electric light bulb, and said: 'No, please don't bother to light a fire!'

'Yes, it must come out,' he wheezed. 'Pity that it's a posterior molar. Even more of a pity that I am out of anaesthetics.'

Fortunately he discovered that the forceps had been put away with a thin coating of oil, easily wiped off with . . . He eyed it lovingly. Might still be used.

Was used.

By this time the posterior molar . . . Or do I repeat myself? It could hardly have been more unfortunate, he complained. That forceps was not at all the instrument he should have chosen. Mr Griffith Griffiths had bought his better pair along with the practice. Still, he'd do his best. Would I mind if he introduced a little appliance to fix my jaws apart, so that he could work more cosily? He was getting on in years, he said, and a little rusty.

And please would I keep still? Yes, yes, most unfortunate. He had cut the corner of my mouth, he was well aware, but that was because I had jerked.

Three minutes best unrecorded. Not even adults admitted.

Mr Van der Pant then feared that we were getting nowhere. That forceps!

Tooth was rotten and he had nipped off the crown. Now we must go deeper, into the gum. It might hurt a little, And, please, would I keep still this time? I should experience only a momentary pain, and then . . . Perhaps if I permitted him to lash me to the chair? His heart was none too good, and my struggles . . .

Poor blighter! 'You can truss me up like an Aylesbury duckling, if you care, as long as you dig this . . . tooth out,' I said. He couldn't hear, of course, but guessed, and went out to fetch yards and yards of electric light flex

Trussed me up good and proper: sailor fashion. 'Had he ever been dentist in a man-of-war?' I asked. But he smiled deafly. It was now about six-thirty on Saturday evening, and curiously enough he had begun telling me of the famous murderer—one Crippen, before my time—who had been his fellow dental-student when . . . His last words were: 'And I also had the privilege once of attending his wife and victim, Miss Belle Ellmore, an actress, you will remember. She had split an incisor while biting on an . . .'

I wish people would finish their sentences

So, as I say, *she* turned up, providentially, at about eleven-fifteen Monday, Mr Van der Pant's grand-niece, on a surprise visit. Lovely girl, straight out of Bond Street, or a band-box.

And there I sat in that dank room, on that dusty dental chair, with a dead dentist across my knees; my jaws held apart by a little appliance, a chill, a ripening abscess, my arms and legs and trunk bound tightly with yards of flex; not to mention, of course . . .

Yes, I like to tell it my own way, though there's not much in it. Might have happened to any other damned fool.

But the sequel! Now that really was . . .

JORDAN

by Glyn Jones

GLYN JONES *(1905–   ) is one of the leading contemporary Welsh literary figures and in his book* The Dragon Has Two Tongues *(1968) has provided an essential reference book for all those interested in the country's literature and language. Born in Merthyr Tydfil, and educated at Cheltenham, Glyn Jones was for a time a schoolmaster in Cardiff. His writings include several impressive novels including* The Valley, The City, The Village *(1956) and* The Island of Apples *(1965), and some fine modern short stories brought together in* The Blue Bed *(1937) and* The Water Music *(1944). The critic Edward Garnett has commented on the 'strange, imaginative quality' of these tales and the particularly effective use Jones makes of the supernatural. His fantasy stories are steeped in the lore of the Welsh and his ability subtly and terrifyingly to generate an atmosphere of horror is of the highest order. Few stories in recent years have so impressed me as that which follows, for not only has 'Jordan' got the chill of the grave about it, it also captures the Welsh ambience perfectly.*

I am worried. Today when I cut my chin with my white-handled razor I didn't bleed. That was the way Danny's shaving went. Danny was my friend. Together we had a spell working the fairs and markets out there in that country where there are nothing but farms and chapels. It was a sort of uncivilised place. I had invented a good line, a special cube guaranteed to keep the flies off the meat, and Danny had his little round boxes of toothpaste. This toothpaste he scraped off a big lump of wet batter, a few pounds of it, greenish in colour and with a bad smell, it stood on a tin plate and sometimes Danny would sell it as corn cure. So as to gather a crowd around his trestle he used to strip down to his black tights and walk about with a fifty-six pound solid iron weight hanging by a short strap from his teeth. This was to show what wonderful teeth you would have if you used Danny's toothpaste. It was only when he was doing this that you ever saw any colour in Danny's face. The colour came because he did the walking about upside down, he was on his hands doing it with his black stockings in the air.

Danny was thin and undersized. If I made a joke about his skinny legs he would lower his lids offended and say, 'Don't be so personal.' He was very touchy. His tights were coms dyed black and they looked half empty, as though large slices had been cut off from inside them. He had a fine, half-starved face, very thin and leathery, like a sad cow. There was only one thing wrong with his face and that was the ears. Danny's ears were big and yellow, and they stood out at right angles to his head. From the front they looked as though they had been screwed into his skull, and one had been screwed in a lot further than the other. His straight carrot hair was very long and thick and brushed back over his head. When he scuffled about on his bandy arms with that half hundredweight dangling from his teeth, his mop opened downwards off his scalp as though it was on a hinge, and bumped along the cobble-stones. He was very proud of his teeth. He thought so much of them he never showed them to anyone. Nobody ever saw Danny grinning.

My own line was that special cube I had invented to keep the flies off the meat. I used to soften down a few candles and shape the grease into dices with my fingers. Then I put one or two of these white dices on a cut of meat on my trestle in the middle of the market crowds. There were always plenty of fat flies and blue-bottles about in those markets, what with the boiled sweet stalls and the horse-droppings, but you never saw one perching on my meat with the white cubes on it. This wasn't because the flies didn't like candle-grease but because under the meat-plate I had a saucer of paraffin oil.

One night Danny and I were sitting on the bed in our lodging house. The place was filthy and lousy and we were catching bugs on our needles off the walls and roasting them to death one by one in the candle flame. Danny was bitter. The fair had finished but the farmers had kept their hands on their ha'pennies. And the weather was bad, very wet and gusty and cold all the time. Danny said we were pioneers. He said these farmers were savages, they didn't care about having filthy teeth, or eating their food fly-blown. He was very down-hearted. He hadn't had much to eat for a few days and between the noisy bursting of the bugs his empty belly crowed. I was down-hearted too. We had to get money from somewhere to pay for our lodgings and a seat in the horsebrake drawing out of town the next morning. I asked Danny to come out into the town to see what we could pick up but he wouldn't. At first he said it was too cold. Then he said he had got to darn his tights and his stockings. In the end I went by myself.

The town had been newly wetted with another downpour and Danny was right about the cold. As I walked up the dark empty main street I could feel the wind blowing into the holes in my boots. Everywhere was closed up and silent and deserted. I looked in at the Bell and the Feathers and the Glyndwr, but they were all empty. Then from the swing door of the Black Horse I saw inside a big broad-shouldered man sitting down by himself in the bar. Apart from him the bar was deserted. He was by the fire and his back was towards me. I knew bumming a drink out of him would be as easy as putting one hand in the other. I knew this because he had a red wig on coming down over the collar of his coat, and a man who wears a wig is lonely.

On the table in front of the man I could see a glass of whisky and in his hand was a little black book. He was singing a hymn out of it in Welsh. It was sad, a funeral hymn, but very determined. I stood by the door of the empty bar and listened. The Horse was small and gloomy inside. I wondered if I would go in. The man seemed huge in the neck and across the shoulders, and every time he moved all the flesh on him seemed to begin to tremble. If he kept dead still he stopped trembling. I went in past him and stood the other side of the table by the fire.

When I got round to the front of this man something snapped like a carrot inside me. His face was hideous. The flesh of it looked as though it had been torn apart into ribbons and shoved together again anyhow back on to the bones. Long white scars ran glistening through the purple skin like ridges of gristle. Only his nose had escaped. This was huge and dark and full of holes, it curved out like a big lump of wood with the worm in it. He was swarthy, as though he was sitting in a bar of shadow, and I looked up to see if perhaps a roof-beam had come between him and the hanging oil-lamp lighting the bar. There wasn't a hair on him, no moustache or eyebrows, but his wig was like the bright feathers of a red hen. It started a long way back, half way up his scalp, and the gristly scars streamed down over his forehead and cheekbones from under it. He had a tidy black suit on and a good thick-soled boot with grease rubbed in. The other leg was what looked like a massive iron pipe blocked up at the end with a solid wooden plug. It came out on to the hearth from the turn-up of his trousers.

It is best to tell the tale when you haven't got any cash to put on the counter. When I began to talk to him by the fire I tucked my feet under the settle and said I was a salesman. Although Danny and I could put all our belongings in a tobacco-box, I soon had a fine range of second-hand goods for sale. The man closed his little book to listen. He told me he was Jordan, man-servant to the old doctor of the town. I took a polished piece of rabbit's backbone out of my waistcoat pocket and passed it over to him. It looked like a small cow's skull, complete with horns. He examined it slowly, trembling all the time. He had huge soft hands and his finger-nails were as green as grass. I told him he could keep it. He called for whisky for both of us.

As I drank my whisky I enjoyed thinking what I had for sale. I had a little harmonium, portable, very good for Welsh hymns, perfect except for a rip in the bellows; a new invention that would get a cork out of a bottle—like that!; a nice line in leather purses, a free gift presented with each one—a brass watch-key, number eight, or a row of glass-headed pins; a pair of solid leather knee-boots, just the thing for him because they were both for the same leg. The man's eyes were small, they looked half closed up, and he watched me hard without moving them all the time. In the heat of the fire a strong smell came off him. It was a damp clinging smell, clammy, like the mildewed corner of some old church, up there behind the organ where they keep the bier. At last he bent forward and held his smashed face close to mine. I stopped talking. He trembled and said softly, 'I am interested in buying only one thing.'

Somehow I felt mesmerised, I couldn't say anything. I am not often like that. I lifted my eyebrows.

Jordan didn't answer. His little eyes slid round the empty bar. Then he moved his lips into a word that staggered me. I stared at him. For a minute by the blazing bar fire I went cold as clay. He nodded his head and made the same mouthing of his smashed face as before. The word he shaped out was, 'Corpses'.

There was a dead silence between us. The clock in the bar echoed loudly, like a long-legged horse trotting down an empty street. But I let my face go into a twist and I squeezed a tear into the end of my eye. I crossed myself and offered the serving man the body of my brother. I had buried him, I remembered, a week ago come tomorrow.

Jordan took his hat and stick out of the corner. The stick was heavy, with a lot of rope wound round it, and the black hat had a wide brim. When he stood up he was like a giant rising above me. He was much bigger even than I thought. He looked down hard at the little bone I had given him and then threw it on the back of the fire. We went out into the street. As we walked along, his iron leg bumped on the pavement and made a click-clicking noise like a carried bucket. He would show me where to bring the corpse and I was to come between midnight and daybreak.

We walked together out of the town into the country. It was pitch dark and soon the way was through wet fields. It was still cold but I didn't feel it any more. Jordan had his peg leg but he was big, and I sweated keeping up with him. He trembled all the time as he walked but his shaking didn't make you think he was weak. He was like a powerful machine going full force and making the whole throbbing engine-house tremble to the foundations with its power. I trotted behind him breathless. He was so busy singing the Welsh burial hymn that he didn't drop a word to me all the way.

At last we came to a gate across the lane we were following. There was a farm-house beyond it, all in darkness. Jordan stopped singing and shouted, twice. There was no reply. He started singing again. He poised himself on his iron leg and his walking stick and gave the gate a great kick with his good foot. It fell flat. We found ourselves going at full speed across a farmyard. A heavy sheep-dog ran out of the shadows barking and showing a fringe of teeth. He looked huge and fierce enough to tear us in pieces. Jordan didn't pause and I kept close behind him. The dog changed his gallop into a stiff-legged prowl, and he filled his throat with a terrible snarl. Then suddenly he sprang straight at Jordan's throat. As he rose in the air Jordan hit him a ringing crack on the head with his stick. He used both hands to bring it down. The dog dropped to the pebbles of the yard passing a contented sigh. He didn't move again. Jordan put his good foot on him and brought the stick down on his head again and again. He went on doing this, his sad hymn getting louder and louder, until the dog's brains came out. I went cold in my sweat to hear him. At last he wiped the handle of the stick in the grass of the hedge and went down the lane, singing.

We came in sight of the lights of a big house. 'That's the place,' he said. 'Bring it round to the back door. Good night.'

He went off into the darkness like a giant in his broad-brimmed hat. I wiped the sweat off my head. After he had disappeared I could hear his hymn and his leg clicking for a long time. His hymn was slow and sad, but it didn't make me unhappy at all. It frightened the life out of me.

On the way back to the town I kicked the dead dog into the ditch.

Danny never let his job slide off his back. As I climbed up the stairs of our lodging house I came face to face with two eyes watching me through the upright bars of the top landing banister. It was Danny dawdling about on his hands, practising. I had a lot of trouble persuading him to be a corpse. All he had to do was pretend to be dead and to let me and the blackman on the landing below carry him out to the doctor's house. Then when we were paid and everybody in the house was asleep he could get out of one of the downstairs windows. We would be waiting for him. We could leave the town by the first brake in the morning. It was safe as houses. Nothing could go wrong. At last Danny agreed.

At midnight the three of us set out for Jordan's house. We were me, Danny and Marky. Marky was a half-caste cheapjack, a long thin shiny man the colour of gunmetal, selling fire-damaged remnants and bankrupt stock and that. He used to dribble and paw you at close quarters but he would do anything you asked him for tuppence or thruppence. We walked through the fields carrying a rolled up sack and my trestle until we came in sight of the house Jordan had shown me. Danny stripped to his coms under a tree and hid his clothes. He put on an old cream-flannel nightgown Marky had brought out of stock. Then we sewed him in the sack and put him on the planks of my trestle. It was pitch dark and cold, with the small rain drizzling down again as fine as pepper.

The doctor's house was all in darkness. We went round to the little pointed wooden door at the back of the garden. I whispered to Danny to ask if he was all right. There were two answers, Danny's teeth chattering and the uproar of dogs howling and barking inside the garden. I had never thought about dogs. What were we going to do?

At once I heard the click of the leg the other side of the wall and Jordan's voice speaking. 'Down, Farw. Down, Angau,' he growled. The narrow pointed door was thrown open, and suddenly we saw Jordan. He was stripped naked to the half and he had left off his wig. He looked so huge, so powerful and ugly in the doorway, with his swelling nose and his fleshy body all slashed, I almost let go of our load with fright. And behind him the hounds, three of them, black and shaggy and big as ponies, yelped and bayed and struggled to get past him to attack us. Jordan spoke sharply to them and at last we were able to carry Danny into the garden. He was as light on the boards as a bag of hay. Jordan spoke only to the dogs. He made a sign and led us hobbling along the pebble path across the yard towards some dark out-houses. The three hounds paced whining beside us, sniffing all the time at the sack and spilling their dribble.

The room we went into smelt like a stable. It was dim and empty but there was an oil lamp hanging from a nail in a low beam. We laid Danny across some feed-boxes under this lamp. Jordan stood back by the stable door with the whimpering dogs while we were doing it, watching us all the time. I could feel his eyes burning into my back. His skin was very dark and his chest bulged up into big paps resting above his powerful folded arms. But all his body was torn with terrible wounds like his face. Long shining scars like the glistening veins you see running through the rocks of a cliff-face spread in all directions over his flesh. His bald head had a large dome on it and that was covered with scars too. His whole body gleamed down to his waist, the drizzle had given him a high shine like the gloss of varnish.

We left Danny lying on the boards across the feed-boxes and came back up to the door to ask for our money. Jordan didn't reply. Instead he took a large clasp-knife out of the pocket in the front of his trousers and opened it. Then, ordering the dogs to stay, he went past us and bumped over to where Danny was lying in his sack. He seemed to take a long time to get there. There was dead silence. As he went from us we could see a black hole in his back you could put your fist into. My skin prickled. Marky's eyes rolled with the dogs sniffing him and he began to paw the air. I looked round and saw a hay-fork with a stumpy leg in the corner. Jordan turned round under the lamp and looked back at us. The blade of the open knife trembled in his hand. He turned again and cut open the sewing in the sack above Danny's face. I could hardly breathe. Danny was so white under the hanging lamp I thought he was really dead. My hair stirred. Danny's teeth showed shining in his open mouth, and in the lamplight falling right down upon them the whites of his half-opened eyes glistened. He was pale and stiff, as if he had already begun to rot. Jordan bent over, gazing down at him with the knife in his hand, the lamp spreading a shine over the skin of his wet back. I was frightened, but if Danny's teeth chattered or his belly crowed I was willing to use that pitchfork to get us out. At last Jordan turned. He spoke for the first time.

'He is a good corpse,' he said.

'He is my brother,' I told him.

'Where did you get him from?'

'I dug him up.'

He nodded. He left the knife open on the feed-box and came over to us. Putting his hand again into his front pocket he brought out a large lump of wadding. This he opened and in the middle lay three gold sovereigns. He passed the coins over to me with his huge trembling hands and motioned us out roughly. He went back and blew out the oil-lamp and we left Danny alone there in the darkness. Jordan locked the stable door and the hounds trotted round us growling as we left the garden through the little door.

'Good night,' said Jordan.

'Good night, brother,' I said.

We walked about in the fields, trying to keep warm, waiting for the time to go back to get Danny out. Marky had gone icy cold. I was worried, especially about those dogs. I wished I had a drop of drink inside me. When we thought everything would be quiet again we went back to see if it was safe to give Danny the whistle. I threw my coat over the bottle-glass stuck on top of the garden wall and climbed up. I could see a candle lit in a downstairs window of the doctor's house and by its light Jordan moved about inside the room in his nightshirt and nightcap. Presently his light disappeared and all was in darkness.

An owl in a tree close by started screeching. Marky was frightened and climbed up on to the garden wall near me. There was no sign of Jordan's dogs in the garden. It was bitterly cold up there on top of the wall without our coats on. The wind was lazy, it went right through us instead of going round. It had stopped raining again. There was a moon now but it was small and a long way off, very high up in the sky, and sunken enough to go into your cap.

We waited a long time shivering and afraid to talk. Marky's eyes were like glass marbles. At last I saw something moving in the shadows by the stables. My heart shot up into my throat. Marky caught hold of me trembling like a leaf. A figure in white began to creep along the wall. It was Danny. He must have got out through one of the stable windows. I whistled softly to him and at that there was uproar. The three hounds came bounding across the yard from nowhere, making straight for Danny, baying and snarling like mad. I didn't know what to do for the moment with fright. The dogs were almost on top of him. Danny sprang on to his hands and began trotting towards them. His black legs waved in the air and his night-shirt fell forward and hung down to the ground over his head. The dogs stopped dead when they saw him. Then they turned together and galloped away into the shadows howling with fright. When Danny reached the wall we grabbed him firmly by the ankles and pulled him up out of the garden at one pluck. We were not long getting back to our lodging-house. The next morning we paid our landlord and the brake driver with one of the sovereigns we had had off Jordan.

I didn't have any luck. All the rest of the summer it was still wet and there were hardly any flies. I tried selling elephant charms, very lucky, guaranteed, but the harvest failed and in the end I couldn't even give them away. Danny got thinner and thinner and more quiet. He was like a rush. He had nothing to say. There never was much in his head except the roots of his hair. Having been a corpse was on his mind. And he was like a real corpse to sleep with, as cold as ice and all bones. He lost interest even in standing on his hands.

We visited a lot of the towns that held fairs but without much luck. One market day we were sitting in a coffee tavern. It was a ramshackle place built of wooden planks put up for the market day in a field behind the main street. The floor was only grass and the tables and benches stood on it. You could get a plate of peas and a cup of tea there cheap. Danny didn't care about food now even when we had it. Because it was market day this coffee tavern was crowded. It was very close inside, enough to make you faint, and the wasps were buzzing everywhere. All the people around us were jabbering Welsh and eating food out of newspapers.

Presently, above the noise, I heard a bumping and clicking sound in the passage. I felt as though a bath-full of icy water had shot

over me inside my clothes. I looked round but there was no way
of escape. Then I heard the funeral hymn. In a minute Jordan was
standing in the entrance of the coffee tavern. He was huge, bigger
than ever, a doorful. In one hand was his roped-up stick and in
the other his black hymn-book. His broad-brimmed hat was on
his head, but instead of his wig he had a yellow silk handkerchief
under it with the corners knotted. He stopped singing and stood
in the doorway looking round for an empty seat. A man from our
table just then finished his peas and went out. Jordan saw the
empty place and hobbled in. We couldn't escape him. He came
clicking through the eating crowd like an earthquake and sat
down at our table opposite us.

At first I didn't know what to do. Danny had never seen Jordan
and was staring down at the grease floating on his tea. I tried to
go on leading the peas up to my mouth on my spoon but I could
hardly do it. Jordan was opposite, watching me. He could see I
was shaking. I pretended to fight the wasps. I could feel his bright
bunged-up eyes on me all the time. He put his arms in a ring on
the table and leaned over towards me. I was spilling the peas in
my fright. I couldn't go on any longer. I lowered my spoon and
looked at him. He was so hideous at close quarters I almost threw
up. The big black block of his nose reached out at me, full of
worm-holes, and the rest of his face looked as though it had been
dragged open with hooks. But he was smiling.

'Jordan,' I said, although my tongue was like a lump of cork.
'Mr Jordan.'

He nodded. 'You've come back,' he said. 'Where have you been
keeping?'

The whole coffee tavern seemed to be trembling with his movements. I felt as though I was in the stifling loft of some huge pipe-
organ, with the din coming out full blast and all the hot woodwork
in a shudder. His question had me stammering. I told him I had
been busy. My business kept me moving, I travelled about a lot.
The wooden building around me felt suffocating, airless as a glass-
house. I glanced at Danny. He looked as though he had been tapped
and all his blood run off. Even his yellow ears had turned chalkey.

Jordan nodded again, grinning his terrible grin. 'The chick born in hell returns to the burning,' he said. All the time he watched me from under the front knot of his yellow handkerchief. He ignored Danny altogether. His eyes were small, but they looked as though each one had had a good polish before being put into his head.

'Our bargain was a good one,' he went on, still smiling. 'Very good. It turned out well.'

I was afraid he would hear my swallow at work, it sounded loud even above the jabbering. 'I am glad,' I said, 'I did my best. I always do my best.'

'My master was pleased,' he said. He leaned further forward and beckoned me towards him. I bent my head to listen and his wooden nose was up touching my ear. 'A splendid corpse,' he whispered. 'Inside, a mass of corruption. Tumours and malignant growths. Exactly what my master needed. Cut up beautifully, it did.'

There was a loud sigh from Danny. When I turned to look at him he wasn't there. He had gone down off his bench in a heap on the grass. People all round got up from their tables and crowded round. Some of them waved their arms and shouted. 'Give him air,' they said, 'he's fainted. Give him air.' For a minute I forgot all about Jordan. I told the people Danny was my friend. They carried him out of the coffee tavern and laid him on the grass at the side of the road. 'Loosen his neck,' somebody said, and his rubber breast and collar were snatched off showing his black coms underneath. The crowd came on like flies round jam. At last Danny opened his eyes. Someone brought him a glass of water out of the coffee tavern. He sat up, bowed his shoulders and put his hands over his face as though he was crying. I spotted something then I had never noticed before. There was a big bald hole in his red hair at the top of his head. He looked sickly. But before long he could stand again. I pushed his breast and collar into my pocket and took him back to our lodging house. I looked round but I couldn't see Jordan at all in the crowd. Danny was in bed for a week. He was never the same again. For one thing if he cut himself shaving he didn't bleed. The only thing that came out of the cut was a kind of yellow water.

Before the year was out I had buried Danny. It was wild weather and he caught a cold standing about half-naked in his tights in the fairs and markets. He took to his bed in our lodgings. Soon he was light-headed and then unconscious. Every night I sat by him in our bedroom under the roof with the candle lit listening to his breathing.

One night I dropped off to sleep in the chair and he woke me up screaming. He dreamt Jordan was trying to chop his hands off to make him walk on the stumps. I was terrified at the noise he made. The candle went out and the roar of the wind sawing at the roof of the house was deafening. My heart was thumping like a drum as I tried to relight the candle. I couldn't stop Danny screaming. A few minutes later he died with a yell. Poor Danny. Being a corpse was too much for him. He never struggled out from under the paws of his memories.

The next night the man from the parish came. He asked me if I wasn't ashamed to bury my friend like that. He meant that Danny hadn't had a shave for a week. In the candle-light he had a bright copper beard and he wasn't quite so much like a cow. When the man had gone I started to shave the corpse. It was hard doing it by candle-light. High up on the cheek-bone I must have done something wrong, I must have cut him, because he opened one of his eyes and looked at me with it. I was more careful after that. I didn't want to open that vein they say is full of lice.

The morning of the funeral I borrowed a black tie off our land-lord. I bummed a wreath on strap. It was very pretty. It was a lot of white flowers on wires made into the shape of a little arm-chair. In the bars of the back was a card with the word 'Rest' on it done in forget-me-nots. Danny always liked something religious like that.

There was nobody in the funeral except the parson and me and two gravediggers. It was a bad day in autumn and very stormy. The long grass in the graveyard was lying down smooth under the flow of the wind. There were some willow trees around the wall

all blown bare except for a few leaves sticking to the thin twigs like hair-nits. The parson in his robes was a thin man but he looked fat in the wind. As he gabbled the service the big dried-up leaves blown along the path scratched at the gravel with webbed fingers, like cut-off hands. I wanted to run away. When Danny was in the earth the gravediggers left. The parson and I sang a funeral hymn. The wind was roaring. As we were singing I heard another voice joining in in the distance. It was faint. I had been waiting for it. I didn't need to look round. I knew the sound of the voice and the clicking leg. They came closer and closer. Soon the voice was deafening, the sad hymn roaring like a waterfall beside me. Jordan came right up and stood between me and the parson, touching me. For shaking he was like a giant tree hurling off the storm. His little black book was in his hand. Even in the wind I could smell the strong mouldiness that came off him, clammy as grave-clay. He was bigger than ever. The brim of his black hat was spread out like a roof over my head. As he stood beside me he seemed to be absorbing me. He put his arm with the night-stick in his hand around my shoulders. I felt as though I was gradually disappearing inside his huge body. The ground all around me melted, the path began to flow faster and faster past my feet like a rushing river. I tried to shout out in my terror. I fainted.

When I came round the parson was beside me. We were sitting on the heap of earth beside Danny's open grave. I was as wet as the bed of the river with fright. When I spoke to the parson about Jordan he humoured me. That was a fortnight ago. Yesterday when I cut myself shaving I didn't bleed. All that came out of the cut was a drop or two of yellow water. I won't be long now. I am finished. I wouldn't advise anybody to try crossing Jordan.

THE DARK ISLE

by Robert Bloch

ROBERT BLOCH *(1917–   ) is the last of the non-Welsh contributors to this volume, and, as arguably one of the best modern writers of horror stories, is a welcome inclusion. Although living and working in California, he is a devoted Anglophile and has utilised material collected on visits to Britain for several of his stories. Few writers have worked harder for their success than Robert Bloch, who began as a teenager contributing to fan magazines, graduated through the pages of the numerous American 'pulp' magazines of the twenties and thirties (including the legendary* Weird Tales*) and then found lasting fame when Alfred Hitchcock filmed his remarkable and terrifying novel* Psycho *in 1960. A prolific writer of short horror tales, all characterised by 'shock' endings, he is also a script writer and contributor to several television programmes and films. With the current widespread interest in the specific type of fantasy fiction dubbed 'Swords and Sorcery', it is interesting to find that Robert Bloch has found inspiration for such a tale in the legends of the Welsh druids and their ancient struggles with the Romans. Though 'The Dark Isle' takes liberties with some of the facts—as do many stories in this category—it is full of colourful drama, and shows the magic Welsh history has worked on yet one more foreign writer.*

I

The Celts knew it as Mona; the Britons called it Anglesey; but the Welsh spoke truly when they named the shunned spot 'Ynys Dywyll'—the Dark Isle.

But all the peoples of Britain feared it for its dwellers. Here were the oaken temples of the Druids, the caves and caverns of the forest people, and the strange altars reared to dread gods. In these times the Clan of Mabon ruled, and heavy was its hold upon the lands. Erin knew the furtive, bearded priests that stalked through the forests seeking stealthy counsel with voices that moaned in the night. The Britons paid their tribute, turning over the criminally condemned for unspeakable sacrifice before the menhirs of the Druids in groves of oak. The Welsh feared these silent wizards and wonder-workers who appeared at clan gatherings to dispense law and justice throughout the land. They feared what they knew of these men, but greater still was the fear of what they *suspected*.

It was said that the Druids first came from Greece, and before that, from lost Atlantis; that they ruled in Gaul and crossed the seas in boats of stone. It was whispered that they were gifted with curious magics, that they could control the winds and waves and elemental fires. Certainly they were a sect of priests and sorcerers possessing powers before which the savage, blue-painted Britons quailed; black wisdom to quell the wild clans of Erin. They made the laws of the land, and they prophesied before the tribal kings. And ever they took their toll of prisoners for altar rites, their tribute of maidens and young men rich in blooded life.

There were certain dark groves in isolated forests where the boldest huntsmen did not venture, and there were great domed hills bearing curious stones and dolmens where voices cried in the night—voices good folk did not care to hear. In glades of oak the priestcraft dwelt, and what they did there was not a thing to be rashly spoken of.

For this was an age of demons and monsters, when dragons slumbered in the seas, and coiling creatures slithered through burrows beneath the hills; the time of Little Folk, and swamp kelpies, of sirens and enchanters. All these the Druids controlled, and it was not good to stir their wrath. They kept their peace, and their island stronghold of Anglesey was inviolate to other men.

But Rome knew no master. Caesar came, and the legions thundered into bloody battle with the stout kings of Britain.

Emperor Claudius followed later, and the Eagle Standards were planted ever farther in the land. Then crafty Nero held the throne afar, and he sent Seutonius Paulinus to ravage Wales. And so it was that one black night, Vincius looked on Anglesey—the Dark Isle of the Druids.

II

Vincius the Reaper gazed on Anglesey with bold black eyes; wise, unblinking eyes that had seen much that was beautiful, and strange, and dreadful. These eyes had seen Imperial Rome, they had beheld the Sphinx, they had visioned the dark forests of the Rhine, the templed columns of ancient Greece.

They had witnessed blood and battle; fierce fighting, scenes of pain, anguish, barbaric torture.

Yet now they stared in a manner previously unknown; behind the dark pupils crept an unfamiliar tinge of fear. For the great dark island rising out of the sea was reputed a dreadful place. During the long sea-voyage to Britain, the fleet had buzzed with wild tales of the Druids; tales of their dire magic and hideous blood-thirst in the presence of enemies.

Vincius' friends—grizzled veterans of the legions—had known comrades serving against the Druids in Gaul. Some of these comrades had returned with horrific stories of almost unbelievable sorceries they had seen; of voices that cried out in the night, and of sentries found with mangled throats in the morning. They had whispered, these comrades, of how the beasts of the forest fought side by side with the blue barbarians; how packs of wolves and boars were summoned by wizard priests who piped. And these returning comrades of Vincius had been haggard, their laughter hushed, as though dark memories precluded all thoughts of gaiety again. Then too, many of Vincius' comrades had not returned at all. The tales of their dying were singularly unnerving—Druid killing and torture and sacrifice employed ghastly magics.

All through the voyage, rumours and hintings spread from vessel to vessel. For once the invincible might of the Roman standard was questioned; arms were not invulnerable to wizardry. And everyone knew that the fleet sailed to Anglesey—the great sullen island stronghold of the chief Druid clans. It had been a disturbing passage, through the dismal green seas of the North.

Now, anchored offshore, the fleet awaited morning to land and attack.

And Vincius, sleelpess, took the deck and stared out across the brooding waters towards the black bulk of the island.

His lean, lantern-jawed face, browned by Syrian sun in the last campaign, was set in a scowl of puzzled bewilderment. Vincius was a veteran, and there were many things about this night which past experiences warned him of.

For one thing, the great island was too dark, too silent. Usually on the eve of battle the barbarian peoples gathered for war-dances about great fires. They would shriek and prance to the thunder of drums, give frenzied sacrifice to the gods for victory. But here all was dark and still; and the darkness and the stillness hinted of secret thoughts and plottings.

Again, Vincius' trained senses told him that the fleet was being watched. Although they had anchored under the cover of a foggy dusk, he felt that their movements had been observed; nay, expected. And now eyes peered across the silent waters.

The old soldier scowled, and stroked an ancient scar which whitely slashed the bronze of his forehead. A restless uneasiness kept him from sleep; some inner intuition told him to wait out the night and the silence.

The silence—it was too silent! The sullen lapping of waters against the sides of the vessel had seemingly ceased. Instinctively, the Reaper's eyes turned towards the helm, where a sentry stood peering and still. In the murky torchlight Vincius saw that his eyes were open, but glazed. He had turned, so that his back was to the rail.

And now, in the soundless hush, Vincius stared at the rail—stared at the two blue talons that slowly crept above it and clutched for support.

Two *blue* talons!

And two blue arms—long, emaciated arms, leprous and phosphorescent in the night—writhed above the rail. A great shaggy head appeared over the side of the ship, a terrible head, haloed by a tumbling mass of matted white hair. It framed a face shaped in Hell; a gaunt, thin face with cadaverous cheeks, hollowed eye-sockets, and a snarling mouth opened to reveal animal fangs. Two burning yellow eyes blazed under corpse-lids.

The face was blue.

Vincius the Reaper stared transfixed, and gaped as the bony body slithered over the rail, dropped noiselessly to the deck and stood erect; a figure clad in animal skins; a figure whose moist and dripping skin was deep, unearthly blue—a burning blue no dye could produce.

The withered old man crept slowly towards the glassy-eyed sentry. His hands stretched out, and taloned claws sought a wind-pipe. Then Vincius moved.

A flash of reason bade him still the cry which instinctively rose to his lips. The enormity of this: a naked barbarian boarding a ship of the fleet and killing a sentry at will—it would be shocking and shameful were this fact revealed to the legions on the eve of battle. Better to keep silent; better to draw one's sword, leap silently across the deck, press the blade into the neck of the ancient horror.

Vincius did so. The old man dropped the sentry's body without a sound. As the lean claws released their hold, a muffled burbling came from the dying throat of the strangled soldier. Then the strange blue creature turned and stared.

Vincius held him, pinioning his arms with one hand and holding his sword with the other. His flesh crawled at the feel of the slimy wet flesh that seemed unnaturally cold, and dreadfully soft.

Still, his grip never relaxed as with his free arm he drew the naked sword-blade in an arc under the throat of the ancient horror that gazed at him unblinking and impassive. Looking deep into the empty yellow eyes, the Reaper shuddered. On the wrinkled forehead he now discerned the almost imperceptible outline of a coiled serpent set in raised weals against the terrible bluish flesh.

'A Druid priest!' The exclamation escaped him in a whisper. At the sound of the words his captive smiled.

'Aye.' A croaking voice wheezed out, as though the effort of speech were painful and the Latin tongue difficult.

'Aye,' said the blue man. 'Druid am I. Mark ye, Roman—I came to slay, but ye thwarted me in that; else there would be a dozen sentries dead, and as many ships at the mercy of my peoples.

'I came to slay, but I remain to warn. Tell this to your commander, oh blasphemer! On the morrow ye come to attack the shrines of our people; this we know. And we are ready. Aye! It will be a warm welcome—by Primal Nodens, know that we of the Druids can conjure magics for your confoundment. Tell your commander to turn back lest he and all his cursed hordes perish dreadfully before the Children of Mabon. Tell him, fool.'

The old man croaked out his words slowly, in deep gutturals which unnerved Vincius more than he durst admit even to himself. Impulse prompted him to drive his sword home and destroy this creature whose weird blue skin was somehow utterly unnatural.

Still, reason told him to wait. This old priest evidently knew the plans of the enemy. Threats might force him to talk, or else torture might be employed as a last resort.

Accordingly, the Reaper whispered.

'Speak of these plans, dog, or my sword will prompt your tongue.' The blade bit into the neck.

And the old man lifted his blue and ghastly face in a horrid smile. Retching mirth burst in cackles from his corded throat.

'Eeeeeeeh! The fool—the heathen fool threatens me with death. The jest is rich. Eeeeeeeh!'

Mad laughter, though Vincius shook the withered body in rage. Then the terrible eyes slitted, and the fretted mouth gaped again.

'Look at me,' hissed the ancient Druid. 'Did ye not mark the blue pallor of my flesh? Think ye the Druids are fools to send a common priest on a desperate errand such as this? No!'

Vincius guessed, with a thrill of horror, the next words.

'Look at me,' droned the croaking voice. 'No paint, no dye empurples the flesh to my hue. Yet ye think to threaten me with death! Know then, fool, that I *am* dead—dead and drowned these three years past!'

With a sort of madness, Vincius lunged his blade out at the laughing corpse-head, slashed at the bony yellow eyes set in flabby, bluing skin. The sword sheared the grinning face, and laughter ceased. The body fell, and like a pricked bladder, collapsed. No blood flowed forth, yet the form dwindled and shrank upon the deck. There was an instant of terrible coagulation as the flesh fused, and then the planks were drenched with a wave of gelatinous ichor. Where the twice-dead body had crumpled there was now only a greenish-black pool of slime that flowed bubbling over the deck towards the rail.

Vincius the Reaper turned and ran cursing from the spot.

III

Trumpets sounded the dawn. The boats set out, laden with cargoes of living steel. Armoured, and corseletted men glared shoreward through the mists. Sword, lance, spear, bow, shield, helmet, breast-plate—these were thousandfold duplicated jewels to glitter against the rising sun. These were thousandfold instruments to clash in marital symphony. These were thousandfold symbols of the might that was Mother Rome. The boats rode shoreward.

Vincius stared again at Anglesey as it loomed near. He had not spoken of the night to anyone. The ichor had vanished almost instantly from the deck when he returned after arousing another sentry to stand watch.

Wisdom had kept him from going to Paulinus, the commander, with any fantastic tale of a dead Druid who came to slay and warn. Not only was such a story difficult to credit, but even belief meant only disaster—for such a fearful warning might dishearten the leaders. As it was, Vincius noticed that there had been no report on the auguries taken this morning; no word that favourable omens had been observed before battle. It was a bad sign when the gods did not prophesy victory for the arms of Rome. The soldier's smile was grimly echoed by his comrades.

Now the boats were beached. The phalanx formed along the sandy shore as the leaders gathered under the Eagles. Britons and scouts delegated by the Army of Occupation were scurrying off into the deep woods offshore. They sought the Druid hordes in the woods.

Formations stood in silence; then signals flashed in sword-points against the sun. Bugles blared, and kettle-drums set up a martial clangour. The long lines swept on. If the Druids chose to keep silent and lurk in the woods, they would be hunted out—beaten from cover.

Armoured ranks swept across the rocky beach towards the still green depths. Clank of weapons set against the utter silence from beyond.

And then, soundlessly, a thousand serpents flew straight against the sun. A thousand barbed, feathered serpents, rigid and unswerving, dipped towards the legion rows.

Arrows!

From the seemingly deserted woods they poured, and found their marks. Men dropped.

Another cloud followed very swiftly. Screaming and cursing, the phalanx formations burst into a charge. More arrows met their advance, and hundreds fell. Each dart, wherever it struck, produced a hideous result. Within a moment after the wound was inflicted, the unfortunate victim was writhing on the ground, froth bubbling from shrieking lips. A moment later and the man was dead—dead and decaying!

Indeed, the Druids employed strange magic. Invisible, they poured poisoned arrows into the finest men of Rome.

The broken front ranks entered the outskirts of the woods. Arrows hummed about them as they sought foemen behind tree-trunk and buried boulder. They found only death—swift, writhing death.

Officers swore, bugles bleated vain commands, men shouted in confusion, fear, sudden agony. The dark woods closed about the legions—the bold legions that planned to swoop in unbroken lines straight across the barbarian island.

And still, no foes appeared.

Men cursed and died there in the green dark, as swarming arrows struck again and again—yet never a face of the enemy.

Vincius was in the van. Perhaps a hundred had managed to

penetrate the wood to any extent; behind them came the confused murmur which bore the shameful tale of an army in flight. The legion was retreating back down the beach!

Vincius' companions turned to follow, arrows pursuing. And then there were shrill whistlings and pipings all about them, and from beyond further trees robed figures appeared—blue faced, bearded men screaming in wild triumph as they closed in on the fleeing band. Now stone clubs whizzed about helmeted heads. To the commands conveyed by the pipings, little groups were creeping around to head off the escaping men. Stones catapulted into the running bodies. Arrows found screaming targets.

Vincius and two companions made for a thicket. The Reaper took the lead, beckoning for the others to follow. He knew that an instant's delay would be fatal, for the forest men had virtually cut off all avenues of escape.

He entered the brush—and five skin-clad savages rose to confront him. Roman swords and stone war-clubs met in blow, thrust, parry. A legion man went down, his face crushed to red pulp. A short dagger tore a bearded throat. The Reaper's sword whirled about in a pendulum-course of death. The blue-skinned men crept under the guard as the second Roman fell, pinned to the ground by a shivered spear. The Reaper fought alone, lopping at arms that brandished bludgeons and crude maces. He fought until a crouching figure sidled to his rear, half turned to meet the blow of his enemy; then sank to the ground as red fire drowned his senses.

IV

Vincius opened his eyes. He lay where he had fallen, in the shadow of a large rock.

He stirred tentatively, then sat up and rubbed his aching head where the glancing blow of the stone club had left its painful bruise. Satisfied that he had suffered no permanent or seriously incapacitating injury, the Roman glanced about.

The glade was very still, and there were no noises audible from the beach. Far out on the water, the galleys still rolled at anchor. But from them rose no martial clangour, no trumpeting of victory.

The pennons of triumph did not flutter forth amidst the billowed sails. The Reaper was puzzled—could it be that the attack had failed?

In the glade about him he found the answer with his eyes; the mute answer of arrow-riddled bodies, heaped in gory profusion. The men of the legions lay where they had fallen, and in death they were hideous to see. Some few had fallen by the sword or by the blow of club and axe, and these had made a peaceful passing compared to the greater number that lay slain by Druid arrows. For the latter were lying in twisted and contorted attitudes of agony. Their hands clutched at the sod in torture, their faces bore the mark of delirium. And their bodies—their writhing, convulsed bodies—were blue! Swollen, puffed, bloated with evil poison from the wounds, they had died in an instant; an instant that brought them madness. It was an awesome spectacle, and one which caused the soldier to shudder. Never before had he seen Romans in a death like this. It hinted of sorcery, of the dark magic prophesied by the Druid priest.

Vincius the Reaper rose to his feet slowly, his thoughts a confused jumble of pity for his companions, awe at their defeat, and furtive fear at the manner of their passing. But in a moment a much more personal note of concern obtruded.

For even as he rose, a hand fell upon his shoulder. Cat-like the Roman wheeled and faced—a Druid warrior!

Short, squat, his moon-face painted blue in ghastly simulation of the dead, the Druid confronted him. Vincius raised his sword.

The Druid held up his hand hastily and spoke; spoke in Latin —not as the old priest had spoken, hesitantly—but as though it were his native tongue.

'Wait, soldier,' the short man gasped. 'I'm Roman, not a savage.'

Half expectant of some treachery, though he now saw that the fellow was unarmed, Vincius lowered his blade.

'Who are you?' he growled. 'And if you're a Roman, what means this heathen garb?'

'I can explain,' babbled the little man, hastily. 'Lupus, my nickname is. I served on the triremes—at the oars, you know. Galley slave for bad debts. The ship foundered off this cursed coast three months ago, and I swam ashore. They captured me, the priests did, and gave me my choice: service or death. Well, I'd no mind to die; so since then I've lived with these blasted barbarians.'

'What do you seek now?' asked the Reaper, suspiciously.

The little man's face was pale beneath the woad-stains. He peered up at the tall soldier earnestly.

'Believe me in this,' he murmured. 'When I heard of the attack today I sought the shore hoping to escape; even the galleys are better than life among such godless swine. But more than that, I had hoped to find someone whom I could warn. The attack failed; I could not pass through the fray and make myself known in time. I've been skulking about in the bushes ever since, hoping to find some survivor to give my message to.'

'Well, speak up, man,' grunted the Reaper.

Lupus nodded gravely before continuing.

'My message is this,' he said. 'I've heard in their black council last night that these heathens mean to sink the fleet tomorrow.'

'Sink the fleet?' echoed the Roman, incredulously. 'Why, that's impossible! They've no boats, and besides they fight on land behind the trees like the cowards they are.'

'So?' said Lupus. His voice was mocking, but his manner gravely earnest. 'Did not the attack fail? Look around you and tell me what you see.' With a wave of his hand he indicated the blue and swollen bodies of the dead.

'I tell you that they spoke truly. If they vowed to sink the fleet they'll do it. Not with boats, or men, but with their cursed magics. It was magic that defeated us today, and it will be magic that brings doom on the morrow. I know. I've seen their devilish ways before. They control land, air, fire, water—and *things that dwell in them*. What demons they mean to conjure up for the deed I cannot say, but be warned. We must get news to the ships.'

The Reaper scowled.

'How are we to do this?' he questioned. 'We're marooned, practically prisoners here. There are no boats available, and the shore is probably guarded well.'

'I have a plan,' said Lupus, slowly. 'We can't get through to the beach without being observed. If we move inland we are equally liable to capture. But tonight there will be a big ceremony and sacrifice in the biggest temple grove.'

'I understand,' nodded the Reaper. 'We shall wait until then, and make for the beach.'

'Not so fast, friend,' returned the other, with a sad smile. 'It isn't as simple as that, by any means. The Druids are cunning. They keep guard everywhere along the shore, by night as well as by day. Only on the sea-wall is there no sentinel. And it is a thousand-foot drop of sheer rock.'

'Then what do you propose?' countered the Reaper.

'This.' Lupus lowered his voice to a confidential whisper. 'In my days here I have had occasion to observe many things. I watched, and I learned. There is one altar in the big glade that has a hollow base. Beneath it is a tunnel of some sort that runs under the island to an opening on the base of the sea-wall. This the priests have spoken of, and with my own eyes I have seen certain of them go and come by means of this tunnel below the altar. Methinks I can find that altar and learn the secret of its pivot.'

'But what is the purpose of this passage?' asked the soldier, a trifle incredulously. Lupus looked grave.

'That I do not know,' he answered. 'What the priests do down there I cannot say. Perhaps they commune with their black heathen gods. They are strange men. We may encounter peril below, but it is better than certain death above, say I.'

'Your plan?' persisted the Roman.

'Simply this. In the evening they will gather by the oak glade and perform some damnable rite or other. That I know. Then the woods between there and the beach-sentries will be free, and we can approach the spot. After their ceremonies will come some revel or feast. At any rate, the grove will be deserted for the rest of the night. We can enter then, find the altar-stone and the passage beneath it, and take our chances on making the shore by morning. From there we shall swim out to the ship, the gods willing.'

'Umm.' The Roman grunted. Then he placed his hand on the little man's shoulder. 'A pact it is, friend,' he said.

Until twilight they remained crouching in the concealment of the boulders. Lupus kept up a steady stream of conversation in a soft voice, narrating his story of captivity among the oak-men. He told the soldier of the Druid ways, and the strange faith of the nature-gods these people worshipped. He spoke of their black powers, and how their magic had driven back even the Roman might this afternoon.

Night fell, and as the moon crept across the sky, the two ventured forth from their place of concealment. The Roman was hungry. Down the path lay a body—that of a huge German mercenary, in full regalia. The Reaper, spying the provision pouch at the dead man's belt, stooped down and tugged it free. His eyes grew wide with loathing at the sight of that blue, contorted face, those blackened, swollen limbs that bore mute testimony to the strange power of Druid poison. With an oath, he tossed the pouch aside and followed his companion down the path that led into the woods.

They walked slowly, in wary silence. The trees about them rustled in the stillness, and Lupus started nervously upon several occasions.

How far they proceeded it was difficult to judge, but the moon rode high in the heavens when first the sound of voices was audible from somewhere ahead.

Soon faint flickers of light filtered through the twisting trees. Lupus leading, they warily circled the path and crept close through the untracked woodland. In a short time they were nearing the open space in the forest from which the light and sound proceeded.

The Reaper scowled at the spectacle before him. A throng of triumphant Druids moved about the grove, clustering before stone altars on which reposed the limp bodies of sheep and cattle. Blood bubbled redly on the slabs in the light of the torches flaring at the sides of the clearing; blood stained the robes and limbs of the celebrants.

Gongs clashed, horns blared, men and women moved and gestured, but the whole gathering maintained an attitude of expectancy.

Lupus gestured the Reaper to come forward, and together they took their station behind a thick cluster of underbrush.

Vincius saw the priests foregather about the central altar and heard the throbbing drums boom out in a subtle, augmented rhythm that steadily mounted to a delirious crescendo. Something was about to happen!

Drums beating, and the shadows on the trees. . . . For the first time the two men noticed that tree-bordered background and discerned what stood against it.

It seemed as though there were great, shadowy shapes weaving and hovering over the heads of the multitude; great shapes moving in rhythm with the surging drums; nightmare shamblers, tall as the tree-tops. The drums boomed madly. More torches flared.

'Look!' cried Lupus. His fingers dug into the Reaper's wrist as with his free hand he gestured excitedly towards the clearing ahead.

The Reaper gazed, and for all his stoicism he could not repress an involuntary shudder. For in the torchlight he discerned the out-lines of the great, shadowy figures; saw that they were green and moving; saw that these giants were like trees in the shape of men. And they were forty feet tall!

V

Crouching in the bushes, Vincius the Reaper stared in fascinated horror at the cyclopean shapes looming before him. Gigantic human trees? That was not possible. What then?

Lupus placed his mouth against the Reaper's ear as he whispered an explanation.

'It's the sacrifice,' he murmured. 'The Druids are disposing of the prisoners. I've heard tales of this: Caesar's men spoke of it in Rome. The devils build great wicker frames and place branches around them; these they shape into a series of cages until they construct the figure of a man. Then they fill these cages with prisoners and condemned and burn the tree-idol in honour of their heathen gods.'

The Reaper looked again and saw that his companion spoke truly. For ringed in a semi-circle stood six great green figures made in a horrid mockery of human form. Their lower limbs were trees, their arms vast pruned branches formed from whole trunks, stripped white in ghastly semblance of flesh.

Evil, painted faces were surmounted by leafy hair, so that each giant stood like a green ogre in the forest—a green ogre whose monstrous wicker belly was filled with living men!

Sweat beaded the Reaper's brow as he gazed at the gargantuan paunches that bulged forth in a wicker framework from those huge and dreadful simulacra. Through lattice and leafy interstice, through knotted rope and wicker vine he saw that each idol's body was in reality a vast cage, a cage packed with the huddled bodies of Roman soldiers and mercenaries. Stifled, half suffocated by the density of their crowding together, they clawed vainly at the bars of their prison, or stared down in white-faced horror at the dancing throng below.

Vincius caught the flash of armour through the green trellises, heard the moaning wails of frightened men as they huddled together awaiting an undreamt-of fate.

Nor was that fate long in coming. For even now the bearded priests had stepped forth from the throng, and, torches in hand, they approached the white columns of the giant feet. The torches flared, then quickly kindled the dry wood. The limbs of the moving monster-shapes burst into livid flame.

Others had climbed to adjoining trees, the Reaper noticed. Now, leaning out on the branches, they flung their brands into the bushy green hair of the gigantic images so that each painted brow now wore a flaming crown.

A scream of animal ecstasy rose exultant from the crowd below. It was echoed by a shriek of horror from the imprisoned men, as they strained at the iron bellies of the monsters that held them.

Vincius stifled an oath, and his hand leaped instinctively to his scabbard. But Lupus pulled him back into the concealment of the shrubbery.

'Don't be a fool, man!' he growled. 'One man can't help them. An army couldn't, now.'

It was true. The flames were eating into oaken arms and rising to girdle the wooden waists. Suddenly, with a grotesqueness utterly terrifying in its sheer unexpected horror, the six painted faces of the burning monsters were contorted as if with hideous pain. Great eyes rolled in anguish-torn sockets, and red lips writhed back to reveal clenched white teeth. Deep, droning bellows rose from the burning wooden throats.

The Reaper trembled. The voices of the tortured gods! Then common sense told him that the faces were hinged so that they could be manipulated with ropes by the priests below. Horns and bladders of air in the hollow necks produced the terrifying sounds. But the reality was dreadful, for the fiery images moved flaming arms as if in torment, and crumbling legs twisted in agony. The howling worshippers danced and bowed in adoration, their faces ever turned upward, for now the flames were reaching the bound bellies from both ends of the tree-monsters' burning bodies. The flames were licking at the wicker prisons, and the captives were wheezing and choking in the swirling smoke.

Tongues of fire licked between the oil-soaked bars. A man cried out terribly in a scream that rose even above the roar of the fire as he was consumed by the blast. Others within the prison beat at their flaming hair. The fire spread, until all six of the colossal shapes were merely great pillars of glowing flame; flame that glowed more redly as it sucked fresh nourishment from the burning bellies.

Then, one after another, the giants pitched forward, still burning. Showers of sparks singed the bodies of the fleeing crowd; the images fell with thunderous crashings and disintegrated into ashy embers or smoking dust. The fire still ate away at the skeleton bellies and a few awful shapes still writhed and twisted in the red furnaces.

But the priests and devotees had gone, back into the forest groves. From far away came the thudding thunder of their drums.

'It's over,' Lupus whispered. 'No one will disturb this spot till morning now. You see, the whole rite is connected with the religion; it is symbolic. The tree-images are those of Mabon and their other devil-gods. The prisoners are placed in the bellies to signify that the gods have devoured their enemies. The fire is a purification of the gods after their contamination by enemies. Now that the rite is accomplished the gods sleep appeased, and the Druids—curse their black entrails!—may celebrate their triumph unndisturbed by wrathful eyes. They will not return here to wake the divine spirits.'

Vincius grunted. The sonorous speech of his companion annoyed him. A man of action, he wanted only to escape. Consequently it was he who led the way into the clearing. Lupus followed, stepping gingerly to avoid the rosy ashes and still smoking embers that littered their path.

Soon they reached a spot untouched by the flames, for the bare, hard-packed earth did not allow the fire to spread. Then Lupus resumed his place as leader, and guided the soldier to a shadowy corner of the grotto. Here loomed an altar, grey against the darkness.

'This is the one,' the little man whispered. 'Give me your sword.'

Vincius complied; then, frowning, he watched his guide thrust the tempered blade amidst the small rocks at the altar's base.

'I'll find the pivot,' grunted Lupus, as he poked away. 'Damnably clever, these barbarians.'

The metal rang. Lupus tugged at the hilt of the weapon as he twisted it into some invisible niche. With a little click the stone tilted forward.

'Wrath of Jupiter!' the Reaper swore. Leaning forward, he stared down into a black chasm slanting deep into the earth beneath the altar-base. A series of stone steps was dimly discernible in the darkness.

'I was right, as I told you,' said Lupus, calmly, as he relinquished the sword to his companion. The soldier shoved it back into its scabbard with a sigh of satisfaction. But he knitted black brows as he gazed again at the cryptically yawning mouth of that mysterious pit.

'I don't like the looks of this,' he declared. 'Such crawling about in the dark is not to my liking. And if there be such things below as you hint of—'

The other held up his hand in a gesture of despair that served to silence the Roman.

'It's our only chance,' he whispered. 'We can't skulk about in those heathen-infested woods, and when the morning comes we'll be taken surely. I do not like the passages myself, but I like still less the usage accorded those in the wicker cages.' With a wry grimace, Lupus indicated the smudging remains of the fire-giants.

'What we may encounter there below I dare not say, but I would rather risk my skin with a chance of reaching the beach and escaping than stay behind. They'll kill you, but I shall assuredly be tortured.' Lupus subsided, awaiting a reply.

The Reaper smiled dourly. 'Come on, then,' he said, pushing his companion before him. 'We'll chance the caverns. But I'm not blundering through darkness.'

So saying he stooped and picked up a burning branch from one of the tree images. It made an admirable torch.

Steps led down. Torchlight flickered on stone stairs, low rock walls of a narrow passage. The Reaper turned, and drew the altar-base down over their heads. His muscles tautened with effort, and his face contorted.

Lupus's countenance was likewise contorted, but it expressed fear rather than exertion.

'There's no turning back now,' he whispered, eyeing the now immovable stone barrier above their heads. We'll have to risk whatever lies ahead, and I've little stomach for Druid magic this night.'

The Reaper smiled grimly.

'It's your decision,' he declared, 'and we must abide by it. Let's be off.'

Torch in hand, he padded down the stairs, Lupus following with obvious reluctance as he stared at the carved-out walls of the tunnel. The stairs turned, then abruptly gave way to a slanting stretch of stone that wound off into deep darkness. It was a hot, unhealthy darkness; as they walked, the rocky floor became damp. Moisture dripped from the walls and the low ceiling. Moss and lichens were green-coiled on wet walls beaded with a diamond sweat in the firelight. They walked on in silence, into still blacker abysses ahead.

Now the footing became precarious, as they toiled through the rocky under-earth. Occasionally side-passages pitted the walls, sometimes singly and sometimes in pairs like the eyeless sockets of some strange stone monsters.. The silence and damp heat were more oppressive as time went on. Stolidly, the Reaper plodded ahead; Lupus glanced about with increasing nervousness.

The little man grasped Vincius by the sword-arm, halting his stolid stride. He whispered shrilly in the soldier's ear.

'I've a feeling we're being observed. Quick—your torch'

Grasping the beacon, he flashed it suddenly towards the nearest opening in the wall just ahead. Was it fancy, or did the light indeed glint upon two staring eyes in the darkness? Neither man could say, for in a moment the half-fancied flash of reflection had disappeared. The flame disclosed only the silent blackness welling from the orifice mouth.

'Hurry,' mumbled Lupus.

Their feet quickened as they half ran along the rocky floor of the burrow. The Reaper was almost flung against the wall when with a sudden sharp turning the tunnel twisted still deeper into the earth.

Now the damp silence exuded tangible menace. As they gazed down the long corridor ahead, their pace slackened to a halt. They stared into the gloomy shaft, its sides so ominously slitted with grinning cavern mouths.

And then from afar rose the sound of a strange piping—a faint, eerie cascade of sweetness. Its import was unmistakable; only a combination of reed and lips could produce that high stabbing wail that held within its weird beauty a hint of summoning and dark command.

It came from one of the side-burrows ahead, and welled forth to echo through the stillness of the caves. The unseen piper played, and Lupus half turned as if to flee.

'We can't go back, you fool,' the Reaper muttered. 'The altar-stone is replaced.'

'Druid magic,' whimpered the other. 'We—'

'Come on.' Vincius half dragged his cowering companion along the path. 'There's a man playing that pipe, and I've something here to change the scoundrel's tune.'

His sword flashed silver as he thrust the torch into Lupus's trembling hands.

They advanced down the corridor, and still that high-pitched music swelled, luring and calling.

Abruptly another sound was superimposed upon the shrillness; a deep whispering, a rustling noise that gathered rhythmic volume. It came from the pit mouths, and slithered forth as though answering the music's summons.

The Reaper's eyes scanned each pitted opening in turn, seeking the source of the shrilling pipes. Then the strange rustling crawled, and the Reaper, glancing downward, saw coiled horror.

The path before him was filled with serpents. Weaving, writhing, hissing in dreadful rhythm to the sound of the far-off flute, they swayed and undulated forth from each pit until the floor of the shaft ahead was a wriggling mass of moving emerald menace. Snakes of every size and shape glided across the gelid stones.

For a moment Vincius recoiled. Lupus crouched behind him in sudden terror. His mumbled prayers were faint against the eery wailing, the rustle and hissing. The great living wave advanced.

Steeling himself, the Reaper met the attack. His sword rose, descended to shear the heads of a dozen wriggling foes. And still the serpentine sea moved forward, choking the narrow passage and rising knee-deep in living, writhing dread. The Roman slashed again, and again. Hissing in pain, a score twisted severed coils, but those behind swept on, commanded by the wild whistling of the unseen pipes.

The great mass bore down upon the two, a twisting torrent studded with opal eyes that flamed malignantly in the dusk. The Reaper scanned the choked path before him, then turned hastily to his cringing companion.

'Get ready to follow me,' he whispered. Lupus nodded, lips working in his white face.

Vincius stepped forward, both hands gripping the hilt of his weapon as he brought it down in a sweeping arc. Again and again it rose and fell, slashing, slicing, shearing at the shapes that now pressed his very legs. He felt the slimy wetness of cold bodies, smelt the sickening reek of their foulness. He hacked a pathway through, only to see it obliterated by fresh hordes from further pits. And the piping mocked from afar.

The writhing blob swept him back. The green strands of

Medusa's locks were coiling about his waist and thighs, dragging him down to fanged kisses and choking caresses.

'Follow,' he yelled, glancing at Lupus over his shoulder.

Wheeling he dashed back a few paces along the corridor, with Lupus at his heels. Then he turned and again confronted the reptile army. He ran forward, swinging his blade. To Lupus's startled eyes it looked as though he were running directly into the mass that crawled before him.

But as he reached the spot he leaped. His jump carried him over the heads of the foremost serpents. Lupus closed his eyes and followed suit. His feet left the ground, he sailed into space. His feet landed on a treacherous wriggling heap. He leaped again, seeing the Reaper ahead of him. The Roman was alternately leaping and landing. So sudden were his movements that the reptiles had no time to prepare themselves for striking, and each time he came down the sword swooped.

Within a few breathless minutes the two stood clear of the blocked corridor.

Vincius forced a wry smile.

'Much more of that,' he observed, 'and we'll never live to deliver our little message of warning before daybreak.'

It was quite evident from his frightened face that the little man agreed only too well with this statement. When the soldier started forward once more, Lupus restrained him.

'Don't go on,' he begged. 'They know we're here. The priests—the high priests—must be down here tonight. And I've a feeling that they are summoning up their Powers for the morrow.'

'What's this?' the Roman queried.

'This must be the Place of Mysteries they speak of,' Lupus went on. 'The place where the Arch-Druids and the inner circle come to seek aid of their gods for magic. Tonight they have to do with the wrecking of the fleet. We'd best turn back. Those devils would never let us through alive, and if we were to encounter what they may have summoned to aid them—'

'We must go on,' pronounced the Reaper, shortly. 'You know there's no turning back. And hurry.'

'It's death.'

'Death for the fleet if we don't get through,' Vincius reminded. 'We'll have to try.'

Turning, he hurried down the gloomy incline. Lupus dogged his heels, turning his head quickly from side to side and eyeing each burrow he passed as though expecting the worst.

Winding, twisting, writhing into darkness, deeper and deeper into the tunnelled maze they plunged. A hundred turnings, each with a thousand branch burrows, were passed at almost running speed. There were no further evidences of hostility, but both men still felt that peculiar sensation of being under scrutiny of alien eyes—wise, evil eyes that waited.

Then they took that final turning that led into the cyclopean chamber where the red torches flared interminably from rocky niches in the vaulted walls. They saw the piper waiting before them—a tall, white-robed Druid, with the shaven head of a Vate, and a bearded face alight with gloating expectancy. In one slim hand he bore the slender reed of his piping, and in the other he held a coiling viper that fawned up at him even as it hissed. And from out of the chamber's stone sides stepped other Druids, armed and ready for combat.

They were silent, and the Reaper did not speak as he reached again for his sword. But he was speechless not at the sight of them, but at the vision of what lay behind them. For he saw that which they guarded.

There was a pool in the centre of the cavern—a great murky pool of gelid water that rose subterraneously from some hidden spring below. It was black, unmoving. Beside its ringed orbit stood a flat stone and on it lay something huge and red and swollen— something that bled horribly, yet wobbled as though still pulsing with life. It was monstrous, gigantic, yet unmistakable—a swollen, severed *tongue*.

Vincius could not tear his eyes away from the tremendous ruby organ that lolled palpitant upon the stones. Imagination quailed before the thought of a beast so enormous as to possess a tongue of this incredible size. Lupus cowered behind him.

Then the slender, shaven-headed piper raised his head so that his gaze challenged and commanded attention. The other Druids grouped behind him in the red torchlight, standing upon the brink of the black chasm of water at their back.

The mocking Vate smiled, stepped forward.

'Who interrupts the Council of the Crescent?' he purred. 'You stupid Roman intruders have troubled our deliberations.'

Vincius scowled, but stood silent. His grimness cloaked a fear only too fully manifested by the quaking Lupus at his side. Why did this priest speak? Why not strike? His sneer of mockery seemed to veil a horror greater than anything yet revealed to the Reaper—and the Roman almost wanted to cast himself forward on the swords of the foe, to die in a red blaze that might drown the uneasy presence of dread which now oppressed him.

Yet the priest continued, sibilantly. 'Ye have dared the secret temple of our people, and for that ye shall die. But a few hours and all your kind shall perish. We Druids will never bow before the spawn of Rome. Even as today the Dragon's tongue venom laid your comrades low, so tomorrow the Dragon shall destroy the cursed ships which brought ye.'

Dragon's tongue? Vincius glanced again at the monstrous red thing lying on the stone—glanced at the oozing greenish fluid which dripped on to the floor—and knew the secret of the day's battle. This organ held poison; reptile venom, which, placed on the Druid arrows, had brought swift and dreadful death.

Dragon's tongue? Dragons—those were the terrible creatures of old British legend; great sea-serpents, reptilian monsters supposed to inhabit the subterrene sea-depths. But they were only legends, like the Tritons, and Dagon, and Greek monsters.

Or were they? This great red tongue was real, and the Druids could summon and control all beasts and creatures of the deep. Tomorrow they planned to wreck the fleet, and a Dragon could pull ships down into the sea. Was it possible?

Vincius mused for only a second. Then he realised that the cunning priest had revealed these words to him for that reason alone—so that in a moment's contemplation he would be lost.

Now the other priests had crept up behind, and Lupus screamed. The Reaper wheeled, to see three priests stab at the short man's unprotected throat. Roaring, Vincius slashed out. A head rolled to the floor, to stare up Medusa-like from a pool of serpentinely rilling blood.

Again the sword leaped and fell, parrying a stabbing thrust and coming down on the arm of the second priest. He dropped, howling as he clutched a jerking stump of shoulder.

And then a half-dozen priests were at his back. Vincius leaped, dodged, smote. They pressed forward, while the slim bearded leader urged them on.

'Into the pool!' shouted the Vate. 'Food for the Primal One! Take him—by the Three and Thirty Tests, I command ye!'

They fought grimly, though two fell. The Reaper's arm was tiring under the weight of the heavy blade. He all but slipped in a sticky red pool, and was forced to give ground again. Now he was being forced back to the brink of the terrible black chasm where inky water lapped. The Druid swords were everywhere. Vincius tried to round the stone on which the gigantic tongue rested. They pressed him back against it—one blade shot out under the Reaper's waist. His quick duck brought the Druid against him, and they grappled. Locked in deadly embrace, they reeled against the stone.

Then Vincius knew. His sword-arm jerked free. He plunged his weapon to the hilt in the great spongy red mass upon the altar-stone. It gave and something green and wet spurted on to the blade. Vincius tore the sword free and sought the enemy's back. At the first thrust the Druid stiffened and fell.

And Vincius swung. One swordsman after another felt the terrible point, felt the poisoned tip of the steel bite into his veins; fell in writhing death. The Vate piped wildly.

The last man he beheaded completely, then re-thrust his weapon into the envenomed organ. He raced after the fleeing Vate, who ran frantically back towards the tunnel entrance. The Reaper was swift. His blade was swifter. With a scream of anguish the last Druid priest went down in final agony.

Vincius turned. The black pool loomed. Beyond it was a dark slit in the rock—and poor dead Lupus had said that it led to the sea.

He must still warn the fleet, Dragon or no Dragon. Into the gelid waters, then.

Murky, clinging, slimy depths enfolded him as he leaped, sword tucked into his belt. The dark waves were sticky and warm, as though befouled. Vincius swam quickly, making for the orifice beyond, where he fancied he could detect a faint glimmering of starlight. A few strokes now . . .

Then horror came. From directly ahead the water spouted and inky jets spurted upward. A boiling froth arose, and great waves bubbled from the depths.

Suddenly a head appeared—a gigantic head, born only in a nightmare delirium and the realms of insane myth. Great, green, scaly head, red eyes glaring from behind huge, dripping jaws—and then a thrashing body; reticulated jade, gilled, slitted, winged, with a tremendous lashing tail.

The mad head rose and undulated above the waves on a long barrel-neck; then the great scarlet jaws drew back to disclose simitar fangs—and a great empty cavern that was red, bleeding, and *tongueless*!

It was the Dragon of Druid lore.

Vincius saw it tower above him in the slimy black water; heard the brazen bellow, and felt the carrion wind that was its breath.

Its tail was curving towards him, its clawing appendages reached out, its neck swooped down so that the cruel, tremendous maw yawned to engulf him.

It was true then. This was the Beast of Myth which the ancient, evil priests had summoned to destroy the fleet upon the morrow. By some magic power they had lured it here, prisoned it in the pool, and ripped out its tongue for venom to use in their archery warfare. Vincius thought this, but felt fear. The enormous horror had seen him. It thrashed towards his puny, swimming form, loomed larger than any ship. From depths of dread it had come, and on the next day it would drag down the armies of Rome to those drowned realms of dread.

Now the mouth rushed on, churning and bubbling as it cut the waves and reached to swallow the struggling man. No use to fight. Or—

Vincius remembered. His sword—the venom upon it! He groped, drew, raised the blade.

The gigantic teeth ground in his face, then raised. Another swoop and he would be drawn between those fangs. He raised up out of the water, threw himself forward.

As the throat opened, he jammed the blade into the bleeding, tongueless maw of the monster. A shrill scream blasted his eardrums as the beast reared back, sword jerking like a silver sliver in the open jaws. Titanic thrashing sent waves surging across the pool. The Dragon roared with pain; a great green body reared out of the black waters, then fell back to squirm in mad, thunderous pulsations of pain.

With a single moan of gigantic, convulsive agony, the hideous head sank beneath the waves, red eyes glazed in death. The nightmare's own poison had destroyed it.

Vincius trod water until the bubbling from below subsided, then stroked for the slit in the stone without glancing back into the chamber of fear. He entered the narrow opening, swimming on.

Ahead he saw starlight, paling into dawn. A few moments brought him out into open water. He swam slowly out towards the nearest vessel; nor did he even turn to gaze at the dark cliff-wall which shielded this side of Anglesey.

His mission was done. Now, with morning, the Romans might land freely; leaderless, the Druids would give way before the legions. They and their cursed barbarian sorceries would be blotted out for ever.

Vincius smiled as he neared the ship's side. Then he frowned at the final memory of the dying dragon, going down with the Reaper's blade wedged in its throat.

'I'll need a new sword for the morning,' he growled.

THE DARK WORLD

by Rhys Davies

RHYS DAVIES (1903–   ) most appropriately
brings this collection of Welsh fantasy and horror stories to a
close—for he is without doubt the best Welsh writer of
macabre fiction at work today. The Sunday Times has called
him glowingly, 'A Welsh Chekov' while across the Atlantic he
has been accorded the highest honour open to a writer in his
genre, The Mystery Writers of America Award. Rhys Davies
was born and brought up in the Rhondda Valley and saw little
outside this area until he served in the British War Office during the Second World War. His involvement with Welsh life
has been clearly reflected in much of his work and his uncom-
promising views on prejudice and morality have caused him to
be regarded as the successor to Caradoc Evans in this quarter.
He is certainly the most prolific of the modern Anglo-Welsh
writers, particularly in the area of short stories, and among
his best works can be numbered The Red Hills (1932), The
Painted King (1954) and his studies, My Wales (1937) and
The Story of Wales (1943). His contributions to literature
won him the Welsh Arts Council Prize in 1971 and he has
also been made an O.B.E. Those who enjoy his work have
commented on his unique ability to engross the reader in the
'matter' of the story right from the first sentence, particularly
in short stories. Selecting a tale by Rhys Davies has been
perhaps the most difficult task of all, so good are most of
them and so suitable. Yet in the end I have picked 'The Dark
World' because of its brooding Welsh atmosphere and the
feeling it gives that little has ever—or indeed will ever—

change in those dark and magic valleys through which we have
tramped in the pages of this book...

'Where can we go tonight?' Jim asked. Once again it was raining.
The rows of houses in the valley bed were huddled in cold grey
mist. Beyond them the mountains prowled unseen. The iron street-
lamps spurted feeble jets of light. There were three weeks to go
before Christmas. They stood in a chapel doorway and idly talked,
their feet splashed by the rain.

Thomas said: 'There's someone dead up in Calfaria Terrace.'

'Shall we go to see him?' Jim suggested immediately.

They had not seen any corpses for some weeks. One evening
they had seen five, and so for a while the visits had lost their
interest. When on these expeditions, they would search through
the endless rows of houses for windows covered with white sheets,
the sign that death was within, and when a house was found thus,
they would knock at the door and respectfully ask if they might see
the dead. Only once they were denied, and this had been at a villa,
not a common house. Everywhere else they had been taken to the
parlour or bedroom where the corpse lay, sometimes in a coffin,
and allowed a few seconds' stare. Sometimes the woman of the
house, or maybe a daughter, would whisper: 'You knew him, did
you?' Or, if the deceased was a child: 'You were at the same
school?' They would nod gravely. Often they had walked three or
four miles through the valley searching out these dramatic houses.
It was Jim who always knocked at the door and said, his cap in his
hand: 'We've come to pay our respects, mum.'

At the house in Calfaria Terrace they were two in a crowd. The
dead had been dead only a day and neighbours were also paying
their respects, as was the custom: there was quite a procession to
the upstairs room. The corpse was only a very old man, and his
family seemed quite cheerful about it. Thomas heard the woman
of the house whisper busily on the landing to a neighbour in a
shawl: 'The black blouse you had on the line, Jinny, it'll be a
help. The 'surance won't cover the fun'ral, and you know Emlyn
lost four days in the pit last week. Still, gone he is now, and there'll
be room for a lodger.' And, entreatingly: 'You'll breadcrumb the

ham for me, Jinny? . . . I 'on't forget you when you're in trouble of your own.' The dead old man lay under a patchwork quilt. His face was set in an expression of mild surprise. Thomas noticed dried soapsuds in his ear. Four more people came into the bedroom and the two boys were almost hustled out. No one had taken any particular notice of them. Downstairs they asked a skinny, cruel-looking young woman for a glass of water and to their pleased astonishment she gave them each a glass of small beer.

'It didn't seem as though he was dead at all,' Jim said, as if cheated. 'Let's look for more. In November there's lot of them. They get bronchitis and consumption.'

'It was like a wedding,' Thomas said. Again they stood in a doorway and looked with vacant boredom through the black curtains of rain sweeping the valley.

'My mother had a new baby last night,' Jim suddenly blurted out, frowning. But when Thomas asked what kind it was, Jim said he didn't know yet. But he knew that there were nine of them now, beside his father and mother and two lodgers. He did not complain. But of late he had been expressing an ambition to go to sea when he left school, instead of going to the colliery.

Jim, in the evenings, was often pushed out of home by his mother, a bitter black-browed woman who was never without a noisy baby. Jim's father was Irish, a collier of drunken reputation in the place, and the whole family was common as a clump of dock. Thomas's mother sometimes made one or two surprised remarks at his association with Jim. They shared a double desk in school. Occasionally Thomas expressed disgust at Jim's unwashed condition.

Again they set out down the streets, keeping a sharp look-out for white sheets in the windows. After a while they found a house so arrayed, yellow blobs of candle-light like sunflowers shining through the white of the window. Jim knocked and respectfully made his request to a big creaking woman in black. But she said gently: 'Too late you are. The coffin was screwed down after tea today. Funeral is tomorrow. The wreaths you would like to see?'

Jim hesitated, looking back enquiringly over his shoulder at Thomas. Without speaking, both rejected the invitation, and with mumbled thanks they backed away. 'No luck tonight,' Jim muttered.

'There was the small beer,' Thomas reminded him. A wind had jumped down from the mountains and as they scurried on it unhooked a faulty door of a street-lamp and blew out the wispy light. When they had reached the bottom of the vale the night was black and rough and moaning, the rain stinging hot on cheeks and hands like whips. Here was a jumbled mass of swarthy and bedraggled dwellings. A spaniel, dragging her swollen belly, whined out to them from under a bony bush. She sounded lost and confused and exhausted with the burden that weighed her to earth. In the dark alley-ways they found a white sheet. A winter silence was here, the black houses were glossy in the rain. No one was about.

'Let's go back,' whispered Thomas. 'It's wet and late.'

'There's one here,' Jim protested. 'After coming all this way!' And he tapped at the door, which had no knocker.

The door was opened and in a shaft of lamplight stood a man's shape, behind him a warm fire-coloured interior, for the door opened on to the living-room. Jim made his polite request, and the man silently stood aside. They walked into the glow.

But the taste of death was in the house, true and raw. A very bent old woman in a black cardigan, clasped at her stringy throat with a geranium brooch, sat nodding before the fire. Thomas was staring at the man, who had cried out: 'It's Thomas!' He sat down heavily on a chair. 'Oh, Thomas!' he said in a wounded voice. His stricken face was as though he were struggling to repudiate a new pain. A tall, handsome man, known to Thomas as Elias, his face had the grey, tough pallor of the underground worker.

The boy stood silent in the shock of the recognition and the suspicion prowling about his mind. He could not speak, he dare not ask. Then fearfully the man said:

'You've come to see Gwen, have you? All this way. Only yesterday I was wondering if your mother had heard. You've come to see her?'

'Yes,' Thomas muttered, his head bent. Jim stood waiting, shifting his feet. The old woman kept on nodding her head. Her son said to her loudly, his voice sounding out in suffering, not having conquered this new reminder of the past years: 'Mam, this is Thomas, Mrs Morgan's boy. You remember? That Gwen was so fond of.'

The old woman dreadfully began to weep. Her face, crumpled and brown, winced and shook out slow, difficult tears. 'Me it ought to have been,' she said with a thin obsession. 'No sense in it, no sense at all.'

Thomas glanced secretly at Elias, to see if his emotion had abated. Three years ago he used to carry notes from Elias to Gwen, who had been the servant at home. It seemed to him that Elias and Gwen were always quarrelling. Elias used to stand for hours on the street corner until he came past, hurry up to him and say hoarsely: 'Thomas, please will you take this to Gwen.' In the kitchen at home, Gwen would toss her head on the receipt of a note, and sometimes she indignantly threw them on the fire without reading them ... But Gwen used to be nice. She always kept back for him, after her evening out, some of Elias's chocolates. Once or twice she had obtained permission to take him to the music-hall and gloriously he had sat between her and Eilas, watching the marvellous conjurors and the women in tights who heaved their bejewelled bosoms as they sang funny songs. But Elias, he had felt, had not welcomed those intrusions. After a long time, Gwen had married him. But before she left to do this, she had wept every day for a week, her strong, kind face wet and gloomy. His mother had given her a handsome parlour clock, and Gwen had tearfully said she would never wind it as it would last longer if unused. Then gradually she had disappeared, gone into her new married life down the other end of the valley.

Elias looked older, older and thinner. Thomas kept his gaze away from him as much as possible. He felt shy at being drawn into the intimacy of all this grief. The old woman kept on quavering. At last Elias said, quietly now: 'You will come upstairs to see her, Thomas. And your friend.' He opened a door at the staircase and, tall and gaunt, waited for them to pass. Thomas walked past him unwillingly, his stomach gone cold. He did not want to go upstairs. But he thought that Elias would take a refusal hardly. Jim, silent and impassive, followed with politely quiet steps.

In a small, small bedroom with a low ceiling two candles were burning. A bunch of snowy chrysanthemums stood on a table beside a pink-covered bed. Elias had preceded them and now he lifted a starched white square of cloth from off the head and shoulders of the dead.

She was lying tucked in the bed as if quietly asleep. The bedroom was so small there was nowhere else to look. Thomas looked, and started with a terrified surprise. The sheets were folded back, low under Gwen's chest, and cradled in her arm was a pale waxen doll swathed in white. A doll! His amazement passed into terror. He could not move, and the scalp of his head contracted as though an icy wind passed over it. Surely that wasn't a baby, that pale stiff thing Gwen was nursing against her quiet breast? Elias was speaking in a hoarse whisper, and while he spoke he stroked a fold of the bed-clothes with a grey hand.

'Very hard it was, Thomas, Gwen going like this. The two of them. I was in the pit, and they sent for me. But she had gone before I was here, though old Watkins let me come in his car . . . I didn't see her, Thomas, and she asked for me—' His voice broke, and Thomas, in his bout of terror, saw him drop beside the bed and bury his face in the bed.

It was too much. Thomas wanted to get away; he wanted to run, away from the close narrow room, from the man beside the bed, from the figure in the bed that had been the warm Gwen, from the strange creature in her arm that looked as though it had never been warm. The terror became a nightmare menace coming nearer . . . Unconsciously he jerked his way out to the landing. Jim followed; he looked oppressed.

'Let's clear off,' he whispered nervously.

They were downstairs. The old woman was brewing tea, and in the labour seemed to forget her grief. 'You will have a cup,' she enquired, 'and a piece of nice cake?'

At this Jim was not unwilling to stay, but Thomas plucked his sleeve. Elias's heavy step could be heard on the stairs. Then he came in, quiet and remote-looking. He laid his hand on Thomas's shoulder for a second.

'Do you remember when we used to go to the Empire, Thomas?

You and Gwen used to like that Chinaman that made a white
pigeon come out of an empty box.'

But Thomas saw that he was not the same Elias who, though
he would wait hours for the indifferent Gwen like a faithful dog,
had been a strutting young man with a determined eye. He was
changed now, his shoulders were slackened. She had defeated him
after all. Thomas sipped half a cup of tea, but did not touch the
cake. He scarcely spoke. Elias kept on reminding him of various
happy incidents in the past. That picnic in the mountains when
Elias had scaled the face of a quarry to fetch a blue flower Gwen
had fancied. 'Didn't she dare me to get it!' he added, with a
strange chuckle in his throat. 'And then she gave it to you!' He
sat brooding for a while, his face turned away. Then, to Thomas's
renewed terror, he began to weep again, quietly.

The mother, hobbling across to her son, whispered to the two
boys. Perhaps they would go now. It was only yesterday her
daughter-in-law had died, and the blow was still heavy on her
son. She had stiffened herself out of her own abandonment to grief.
The boys went to the door in silence. Jim looked reserved and
uncommenting.

Outside, in the dark alley, he said: 'I wonder how she came to
chuck the bucket! The baby was it?' Receiving no reply, he added
with something like pride now: 'My mother's always having them,
but she's only abed for three days, she don't die nor nothing near it.'
Thomas still stumbling silently by his side, he went on: 'Perhaps
he'll marry again; he's only a young bloke. . . . I never seen a man
cry before,' he added in a voice of contempt.

But for Thomas all the night was weeping. The dark alley was
an avenue of the dead, the close-shuttered houses were tombs. He
heard the wind howling, he could feel the cold ghostly prowling
of the clouds. Drops of icy rain stung his cheeks. He was shivering.
Gwen's face, bound in its white stillness, moved before him like a
lost, dead moon. It frightened him, he wanted to have no connection
with it; he felt his inside sicken.

'Shall we look for more?' Jim said. A roused, unappeased appe-
tite was in his voice.

Thomas leaned against the wet wall of a house. Something

broke in him. He put up his arm, buried his head in it, and cried. He cried in terror, in fear and in grief. There was something horrible in the dark world. A soft, howling whine came out of his throat. Jim, ashamed, passed from wonder into contempt.

'What's up with you!' he jeered. 'You seen plenty of 'em before, haven't you? . . . Shut up,' he hissed angrily. 'There's someone coming,' And he gave Thomas a push.

Thomas hit out. All the world was threatening and hostile. The back of his hand caught Jim sharply on the cheekbone. Immediately there was a scuffle. But it was short-lived. They had rolled into a pool of mud, and both were surprised and frightened by the mess they were in.

'Jesus,' exclaimed Jim, 'I'll cop it for this.'

Thomas lurched away. He stalked into the rough night. All about him was a new kingdom. Desperately he tried to think of something else. Of holidays by the sea, of Christmas, of the nut-trees in a vale over the mountains, where, too, thrushes' nests could be found in the spring, marvellously coloured eggs in them. Jim, who had seen him weep, he thought of with anger and dislike.

At the top of the hill leading to his home he paused in fear. The bare high place was open to the hostile heavens, a lump of earth open like a helpless face to the blows of the wind and the rain. He heard derision in the howls of the wind, he felt anger in the stings of the rain.